THE HORROR
OF LOVE

THE HORROR OF LOVE

Lisa Hilton

PEGASUS BOOKS
NEW YORK LONDON

THE HORROR OF LOVE

Pegasus Books LLC
80 Broad Street, 5th Floor
New York, NY 10004

ISBN: 978-1-60598-392-9

10 9 8 7 6 5 4 3 2 1

Printed in the United States of America
Distributed by W. W. Norton & Company, Inc.
www.pegasusbooks.us

To Caroline Dalmeny

CONTENTS

Contents

ACKNOWLEDGEMENTS

This book could not have been attempted without the generosity and kindness of Charlotte Mosley, who gave me a great deal of time, access to both Nancy Mitford's unpublished letters to Gaston Palewski and her own then-unpublished research and a magical winter walk in Eaton Square.

I am most grateful to the Dowager Duchess of Devonshire for permitting me a telephone interview. Anthony Beevor was extremely helpful, particularly in giving me the benefit of his great expertise on the complexities of Free French politics, as were those who shared their memories of Gaston Palewski with me in interviews: Lord Thomas, Lord Weidenfeld, Paul Johnson and Viscount Norwich provided invaluable insights into their personal relationships with Nancy and Gaston.

The assistance of Marcella, Lady Dashwood and Sir Alistair Horne at West Wycombe is much appreciated, as is that of Professor John Rogister and Lady Antonia Fraser, Anne-Sophie Sabouret, the Comtesse Caumont de la Force and the Marquis de Segure. For an evening in the sixième such as Nancy might have known, I thank Alexandre Pradere, the Princesse de Beauvau-Craon and Anne de Lacretelle. Anka Muhlstein and Philip Ziegler both shared their own impressions of Gaston's character.

David Valence, the director of the Fondation Charles de Gaulle in Paris, was most kind in giving me access to the archive. Charlotte Javelot was very helpful with correspondence. I particularly wish to thank Tom Staley, director of the Harry Ransom archive at the University of Austin, Texas, where I was lucky enough to speak to Lady Selina Hastings, whose own work has proved an essential resource. Sir Peter Westmacott, the British ambassador to France, and Lady Westmacott were the most gracious and patient of hosts for a weekend at the Hotel Charost and its gardens. I would also like to acknowledge the efficiency and dedication of the staffs of the Archives Nationales de France, the French Embassy in Rome, the British Library and the London Library, and the generosity of Andrew Neil and Fraser Nelson in allowing me to work in the *Spectator* archive.

Michael Alcock helped me to develop the idea for this book, and my agent, Georgina Capel, made it happen. Many thanks, too, to Alan Samson and Susan Lamb at Weidenfeld. My editor, Caroline North, agreed to work with me once again, with invaluable brilliance and efficiency.

Much of the work on this book was done at Rosebery House, where thanks are due to Craig and Sheryl Wilkinson for their interest and assistance. I am immensely grateful to Lord and Lady Dalmeny, who gave me the gift of peace and space to write in their beautiful home, not to mention the key to their wine cellar.

LIST OF ILLUSTRATIONS

Waiting for love (National Portrait Gallery, London)
Nancy and Peter Rodd (Getty Images)
Gaston, 'the Colonel' (Topfoto)
The Connaught Hotel (Getty Images)
Piccadilly and Leicester Square in the Blitz (Getty Images)
Rue Bonaparte (Private Collection / Archives Charmet / The
    Bridgeman Art Library)
General De Gaulle on the BBC (Getty Images)
Nancy at Rue Monsieur (Rex Features)
Dior's atelier (Sueddeutsche Zeitung Photo / Lebrecht Music &
    Arts)
Churchill and De Gaulle (Photography by IWM, Camera Press,
    London)
Gaston in action (Press Association)
Gaston's achievements (Wikimedia Commons / Mu (Own work)
    [CC-BY-SA-3.0])
The Pont Royal (Getty Images)
The Zattere in Venice (Getty Images)
Palazzo Farnese (Fratelli Alinari Museum Collections – Mal-
    andrini Collection, Florence)
Boucher's 'Autumn Pastoral' (By kind permission of the Trustees
    of the Wallace Collection)
Louise de Vilmorin (Getty Images)
Susan Mary Alsop (Topfoto)
The park at Versailles (Photograph by Dorothea Schmid / Laif,
    Camera Press, London)
L'Escalier Daru (Giraudon / The Bridgeman Art Library)
Nancy at Versailles (Getty Images)

AUTHOR'S NOTE

Of her correspondence with the scholar Theodore Bestermann when she was working on her biography *Voltaire in Love*, Nancy Mitford wrote: 'If you want to bore your reader, tell them everything.' This book is, or aims to be, the biography of a love affair. It is not a 'Mitford' book, nor a history of Général de Gaulle's role in the Second World War, though inevitably it is coloured by aspects of both narratives. It attempts to reconfigure the role of Gaston Palewski in Nancy Mitford's life, and to present Gaston to English-speaking readers, who might know him best as Fabrice de Sauveterre, as the significant politician he was. For a fuller account of Nancy's life, readers might wish to consult the excellent biographies by Selina Hastings and Laura Thompson, while for the Mitford sisters, Mary S. Lovell's account is the most comprehensive. For the progress of the Free French, Jean Lacouture and Jonathan Fenby give more thorough histories than are presented here.

'A well born man knows in advance all the procedures he should follow and encounter in the various phases of gallant love; it often displays more refinement than true love since nothing about it calls for passion or spontaneity, and it is always very witty.'

Stendhal, *On Love*

PROLOGUE

In the summer of 1941, two Englishmen, a Welsh Guards officer named Peter Rodd and his brother Francis, met a Frenchman in Addis Ababa to talk about a railway. Colonel Palewski, the commander of the Free French forces in East Africa, needed to ascertain the British position with regard to the French concession in the Addis–Djibouti railway line. A year later, Colonel Palewski arranged a meeting on a bright evening in the garden of the Allies Club on Park Lane with Rodd's wife, who he thought would be glad to hear news of her husband. In her most famous novel, *The Pursuit of Love*, Nancy Mitford described the effect of this 'short, stocky, very dark' Frenchman: 'Linda was feeling, what she had never so far felt for any man, an overwhelming physical attraction. It made her quite giddy, it terrified her. She could see that Fabrice was perfectly certain of the outcome, so was she perfectly certain, and that was what frightened her . . .'

Some days later, Nancy invited Gaston Palewski to dinner at her home in Blomfield Road. She waited for him in the dining room of her small, elegant house with its swagged pink moiré wallpaper, until she heard that sound, 'a sound more intimately connected with the urban love affair than any except the telephone bell, that of a stopping taxicab. Sun, silence and happiness' (*The Pursuit of Love*).

Gaston Palewski was no one's dream of an ideal French lover, yet in his alter ego Fabrice de Sauveterre Nancy established an ideal of the type which even the stuffy *Daily Telegraph* was obliged to concede dominated the English mind for twenty years. Gaston had acne-pitted skin, 'a face like an unpeeled King Edward',[1] receding hair and, according to some of his mystified

I

contemporaries, halitosis that could stop traffic. 'Oh, Gaston,' recalled Anka Muhlstein, a family friend, '*how* ugly he was.' But women adored him, perhaps because he so thoroughly adored them. Gaston's 'pretty ladies' were the despair and the scandal of Général de Gaulle's suite. Gaston operated on a principle of maximum returns, making passes at practically every woman he came across, enjoying an astonishing (and to his peers quite infuriating) degree of success.

At a meeting in the Café de Flore, Paris in 2009, a group of ladies of considerably more than a certain age agreed to be interviewed in strict anonymity about Gaston. All tiny dogs and Dior, it took no more than a *kir à la pêche* for these women to begin reminiscing, with much giggling, about the friends, sisters, cousins who had fallen for the Colonel.

'But did she give in, then?'

'No, that was the summer he dumped her at Cannes and went to Switzerland with her sister.'

'It can't be, because that was the year *I* was with him at Biarritz ...'

Perhaps, given their relative youth, these ladies were rather inclined to exaggerate their personal involvement with the legendary Beast of the Rue Bonaparte, but they agreed on two things. Gaston (giggles) was '*doué pour faire plaisir aux femmes*' (the best translation of this would be 'built for love') and the Englishmen of their youth were absolutely hopeless. By the third year of marriage, they claimed, Englishmen barely look at their wives at all. The stereotype of the Englishman as a diffident and incompetent lover is firmly entrenched in the psyches of both nations. Edith Cresson, the French prime minister, was attacked for her airy assertion that 'the Anglo-Saxons are not interested in women as women ... It is a problem of upbringing and I consider it a sort of disease,'[2] but no one really disagreed with her. Nancy Mitford was firmly in Mme Cresson's camp. In her 1951 novel *The Blessing*, the worldly Mme Rocher wonders at the mystery of English marriage: 'English husbands? They go to their clubs, their

Boat Race, their Royal Academy – they don't care for making love a bit.'

Nancy's portrait of Fabrice, Duc de Sauveterre in *The Pursuit of Love* seduced a generation of Englishwomen with its blissful depiction of *l'amour à la Française*. The real Fabrice, Gaston Palewski, was for thirty years one of France's most distinguished politicians and diplomats, a connoisseur and patron of the arts and a significant influence in the post-war project for European federalism, yet none of his contemporaries is in any doubt that it was Nancy who really made him famous. The reality of Nancy's twenty-nine-year relationship with her pompous, pockmarked colonel was far from the bliss she imagined for Linda Radlett and Fabrice, but the *coup de foudre* of that third summer of the war provided them both with the most significant personal and emotional attachment of their lives. Gaston's story has, in English at least, been told very much as an accessory to Nancy's life, which has been extensively documented as part of the myth of her beautiful, fanatical, compelling family. Yet that story, which encompasses one of the most passionately exciting periods of French history, illuminates not only the life of an extraordinary man, but the work of one of the most popular and influential writers of the twentieth century.

Nancy Mitford's popular reputation diminishes her in something of the same manner as does Jane Austen's. Bonnets and bosoms in Jane's case, diamonds and darlings in Nancy's. Film and television representations of their work have tended to focus on what Austen herself termed the 'light, bright and sparkling'. Nancy's name is also inevitably associated with the 'U and non-U' essay which she wrote simply as a joke to tease her friend Evelyn Waugh but which nevertheless has seen her branded ever after as a horrendous snob. Yet there is a toughness, a darkness even, to Nancy's writing which can be traced through her early novels to the late and celebrated biographies, a vision of love which could not be further removed from the chick-lit happy endings of Bridget Jones and Mr Darcy. Nancy poked fun at the romantic fantasies of dizzy debutantes, but, through both her own experiences and those of her family, no one could have been more bitterly exposed to the disastrous consequences of blindly romantic love than she.

Nancy's first two post-war bestsellers deal respectively with a serial adulteress who dies in childbirth and a sexually molested child who marries her abuser and destroys her family in the process. They might be read as the last of the attenuated tradition of the English Gothic novel. Her later novels, *The Blessing* and *Don't Tell Alfred*, take a more 'Enlightenment' approach, essays in Gallic didacticism whose pragmatism contrasts with the wilder, romantically violent loves which lurk beneath the glittering surface of *The Pursuit of Love* and *Love in a Cold Climate*. As her relationship with Gaston continued, Nancy's perspective on love became progressively more 'French', or perhaps rather more eighteenth century. The keystones of her romantic philosophy become civilization and adulthood. *The Blessing* provides an unsentimental education for its English heroine, Grace, who is gradually brought to accept, even to endorse, her French husband's infidelity; *Don't Tell Alfred* is an exploration of and a warning against the imported American worship of youth.

Nancy's correspondence also touches repeatedly on these themes throughout her life. Gaston was her great love, and he dominated her beliefs about art, politics, about the way life should be approached and lived. Nancy might have been madly in love with the colonel, but she was quite aware of his imperfections. She was always conscious that in person he was far less than the ideal she would have him embody, but that ideal eventually became her ideology, in her relationships and her books. To be a civilized adult seems a spare ambition, but for Nancy it was the end of art and of life.

Many writers have argued that Nancy's philosophy was achieved by default, that she was merely, in her own words, 'putting on a good shop-front', making a virtue of necessity. Several of her biographers have portrayed her as a victim of her hopeless passion for Gaston, her life with him as a wasted one of humiliation and denial. Her letters are often raw with the pain Gaston caused her, yet they also reveal the potential of an intimacy based upon ideas which contemporary women would find frankly appalling. Fidelity is not the point of marriage, though it may well be the end; adultery, if properly managed, may be a highly civilized pursuit (despite the tiresomeness of always having to go to bed in the afternoon), the one essential for happiness is not self-exposure or mutual dependency but great good manners. None of these points is necessarily revolutionary, but a glance around a bookshop or any women's magazine shows that we are still bewildered, enthralled and terrified by our failure to achieve what feminism has taught us we deserve. Nancy and Gaston were two middle-aged, not particularly attractive people. He was a selfish, career-obsessed philanderer; she was febrile, needy and given to 'shrieking', yet the discipline, tenderness and *gentillesse* of their relationship exposes the limitations of many modern sexual mores.

Nancy was constitutionally incapable of bathos. Sadness and loss she knew very well, and she handles them in her novels so dexterously that the lightness of her touch initially disguises her very real capacity to convey pain and hopeless longing. Yet her great funniness, remarked on by all who knew her, whether or not they cared for it, meant that she could never play the tragic heroine for long, even to herself, as this exchange with Gaston demonstrates: '"I've given up everything", I said, "My friends, my family, my country," and he simply roared with laughter and then of course so did I.'

PART ONE

1901–39

1

GASTON

All his life, Gaston Palewski's father, Moise, sought to recreate the elements of a family which, in his own words, had been 'brutally dispersed'.[1] The Palewskis were Polish Jews: on the paternal side they had their origins in Vilno, in Russian Poland, on the maternal they came from Galicie in southern Russia, near the Romanian border. The family were linked by trade and marital alliances to a large Jewish community in the Grodno area, with many relatives in the small cities of Antopol, Pinsk and Kobryn. Educated members of the lesser middle class, many of the men trained to be rabbis while accommodating the concessions demanded of a devout, insular community in its negotiations with the commercial world. In a memoir written after the First World War, Gaston's brother, Jean-Paul, observed a certain quiet humility in his relatives, an ability to combine remarkable intellectual talent with 'the legitimate contentment of duty done, a bottomless instinct of charity and an often mystical devotion to the nicest forms of ideas'. He also remarked on the laws of segregation which caused the 'unhappy Jewish nation in Russia'[2] to live in a tightly closed circle, never aspiring to worldly success beyond the most unassuming of trades. Gaston Palewski had an uneasy relationship with these origins all his life. No one could have been more eager than he to shake off the heavy garments of the *shtetl*, to recreate himself as the sophisticated *mondain* he so brilliantly became, yet the qualities identified by his brother – duty, kindness and the capacity for a certain mystic

9

idealism – shaped his life as surely as his more explicit rejection of his family's past.

Moise's father, Peisach Abramovich, was born in 1840 in Kobryn. A cultivated, emotional man with a fondness for poetry, he was employed as a manager for a Polish landowner and well respected in the city. He married Rachel Notkowa, a devout, intelligent woman five years his junior who spoke four languages and raised her six children with scrupulous respect for Jewish tradition. Moise was born in 1867, and as a small boy showed a rebellious streak. He recalled being reprimanded by his father for sneaking off to the theatre or displays of military exercises when he ought to have been at his studies. The family lived a quietly comfortable life until Peisach developed cancer of the mouth at the age of thirty-three. According to Jean-Paul's memoir, it was not the disease that killed him, but the poisonous concoctions of a local chemist. Whatever the case, Rachel found herself a widow at thirty. Without her husband's wages, her prospects looked extremely bleak. Her brother-in-law, a doctor named Michel Israel Rabbinowicz, offered to take the Palewski children with him to Paris, where he would oversee their education, and Rachel agreed to make the sacrifice, though she was unable to part with her youngest boy, two-year-old Paul. The others, Moise, Albert, Leon, Frieda and Judith, aged between twelve and four, set off with their uncle for France.

The Palewskis later liked to claim that one of their family had been active in the anti-Russian insurrection of 1863 which saw many liberally inclined Polish aristocrats looking to France in a diaspora known as the 'Grande Emigration'. Michel Rabbinowicz belonged to a less grand category of emigrants, a group of doctors, lawyers, artists and intellectuals, many of them Jewish, seeking refuge from Russian persecution. Michel lived in the unfashionable Faubourg-Poissonière district, in what is now the tenth arrondissement of Paris. His nephews attended the College Rollin and subsequently the Springer Institute, where Moise passed his *baccalauréat* in 1887. Although Michel had so conscientiously provided them with a home, there was little money, and Moise's experiences of Paris during the flowering of the Belle Epoque were far from gay. He remembered weary miles walked to save the price of an omnibus ticket, sandwiches carefully divided on chilly park benches, an upbringing which while not actually deprived was nevertheless shabby and pinched.

There remained also a disturbing current of anti-Semitism in French society, which created an atmosphere of danger, a sense of a precarious existence lived permanently on the brink of poverty and persecution. France was still recovering from the bitter divisions provoked by the Dreyfus Affair, in which a young Jewish army captain, Alfred Dreyfus, had been falsely accused of passing military secrets to the German Embassy in Paris. The inflammable conflict between Dreyfusards and anti-Dreyfusards had exposed anti-Jewish prejudice in the most exalted echelons of French society, creating an enduring legacy of hostility and suspicion. Moise was troubled by the visits of an elderly relative, a refugee of the pogroms, who was to die in penury in London, and he grew up with a sense of uncertainty which propelled him to seek a secure place in a threatening world.

Moise was a talented and driven student who won a place at the competitive Ecole Centrale des Arts et Manufactures, achieving his engineer's qualification in 1892. For the next few years he held a series of engineering jobs, none of them lucrative, but his ambition can be discerned in the metamorphosis that had taken place in the year of his marriage. By 1895, the Polish immigrant Moise had become the *ingénieur diplomé* Maurice. He did not, however, marry 'out'. His twenty-six-year-old bride, Rose Diamant-Berger, came from a similar Eastern-European Jewish background, with roots in Russia, Moldavia and Bucharest. Rose's father, Yvan-Joseph, had brought his family from Romania to Paris in 1882 and was granted French citizenship a decade later. He had some success in business, as evinced by the fact that in the declaration of means required for French civil marriages, his daughter was provided with a dowry of 25,000 francs, as compared with the groom's meagre savings of 1,000.

Rose might have been something of an heiress by the standards of the Faubourg-Poissonière, but the young couple were by no means well off. Their first home was an apartment at 51 Rue Rochechouart, a similarly unfashionable address, where their second boy, Gaston, was born on 20 March 1901. (The desire of the Palewskis to become thoroughly integrated is discernible in their choice of the Frenchest possible names for their sons.) Soon afterwards, the family moved to the nearby Square Petrelle in the ninth arrondissement, a quadrangle of severe post-Haussmann-style buildings around a small courtyard. The third-floor flat featured a salon with an orange velvet sofa and a dining room overlooking the court. Gaston later claimed (with perhaps something of the Mitford capacity to reinvent history along more charming lines) that he and his brother spent much of their time in a large cupboard opening off their shared bedroom.

The Palewskis lived a tranquil life of modest routines, but Maurice clearly tried to give his boys a more joyful upbringing than he had known. Gaston recalled rollerskating in the square downstairs, violin lessons, trips to the Coliseum cinema in the Rue Rochechouart and weekly visits to museums to hear tour guides explaining the exhibits. Gaston and Jean-Paul would wriggle beneath gilded tables to reach the front of the audience. Both boys shared a greedy delight in beautiful things and the histories behind them. Gaston recalled vividly the feeling of holding his father's hand as they walked through the immense salons of the Louvre and the Petit Palais, and at home the boys turned the drawing room into their own 'museum'. Jean-Paul, too, retained a vivid physical memory of traversing the city on huge exploratory walks, from the peaks of Montmartre to the château of St Germain-en-Laye. From the first, Paris belonged to Gaston as profoundly as did the Cotswold uplands of her own childhood to Nancy Mitford. It was in his blood and in his bones, and its poetry called to him all his life.

During the excursions with his father, Gaston was particularly struck by the nineteenth-century Escalier Daru, which houses the *Victory of Samothrace* in the department of antiquities at the

Louvre. The staircase is disarmingly plain, monumental in both the grandeur of its scale and the austerity of its lines, drawing the eye upwards to the perfect classical female torso of the sculpture. 'One day,' Gaston said, 'I'll live in a house with a staircase like that.'

French literature of the nineteenth century abounds with adventurous young men on the social make: Julien Sorel, Lucien de Rubempre, Eugene de Rastignac. Gaston was often compared by contemporaries to Rastignac, the charming, unscrupulous society mountaineer of Balzac's *Comédie Humaine*, whose talent, and particularly his attraction for women, propel him to the zenith of the Parisian world, the *gratin* of the old aristocracy who inhabit the Faubourg Saint-Germain. There could be no more apt correlative for the trajectory of Gaston's ambition than the Escalier Daru. He always knew where he wanted to be, there at the top with Paris at his feet and a beautiful woman in his arms. His arriviste tendencies were not among his most endearing qualities and his snobbery was often figured as risible, but his desire to move amid *les gens du monde* – society people – formed part of his concept of the best way of life. As Fabrice explains to Linda early in their relationship:

> *Les gens du monde* are the only possible ones for friends. You see, they have made a fine art of personal relationships, and of all that pertains to them – manners, clothes, beautiful houses, good food, everything that makes life agreeable. It would be silly not to take advantage of that. Friendship is something to be built up carefully, by people with leisure, it is an art ... You should never despise social life – *de la haute société* – I mean, it can be a very satisfying one, entirely artificial of course, but absorbing. Apart from the life of the intellect and the contemplative religious life, which few people are qualified to enjoy, what else is there to distinguish man from the animals except his social life? And who understands it so well and who can make it so smooth and so amusing as *les gens du monde*? (*The Pursuit of Love*)

This was entirely Nancy's view, and one that she spent much of her early years trying frustratedly to live out. Yet there was another aspect of Gaston's personality which, according to his nephew Dominique Palewski, informed his relationship with France on a more profound level. At the end of the war, Gaston presented Dominique with an illustrated book on the Hôtel des Invalides, in which he inscribed: 'To my nephew Dominique, that he also might be accorded the honour of bearing arms in the service of a great cause.'[3] Dominique believed that, as an immigrant family, the Palewskis were intent on becoming *enracinés* in France (in French, as well as meaning 'rooted' it has implications of national identity) and that their love and respect for their new country, which had allowed them to flourish, was manifest in a deeply emotional loyalty. This was one of the sources of the absolute commitment to the service of France, which, above all else, dominated Gaston's life.

The Palewskis were also typical immigrants in that they wanted the best possible education for their children. Both Jean-Paul and Gaston were to prove superlative students, though Gaston experienced more struggles than his older brother. Until 1911, Gaston attended the College Rollin, as his father had done, after which he entered the Lycée Michelet. At first he seemed a promising pupil, even brilliant, but in adolescence something went wrong. Maurice and Rose grew concerned that their lively, intelligent son was growing lazy and lumpen, complaining of headaches and seemingly incapable of applying himself to work. A doctor prescribed a change of air, and in 1915 the Palewskis decided to send Gaston for a year to England, where he would study the language at Brighton College. He mastered English perfectly and though he always spoke it with a comically thick accent, his fluency would prove to be one of his most defining accomplishments. When he returned to Paris, it was to the family's new home on the Left Bank at 162 Rue de Grenelle. It was hardly the Faubourg Saint-Germain, but the Faubourg-Poissonière lay safely on the other side of the Seine. The Palewskis were definitely on the up.

In 1901, Maurice had entered a partnership to set up a machine-tool company. At first the rewards were 'very mediocre', but by 1913 he and his partner Morin had premises of their own in the Rue Vivienne and Maurice was developing his interest in the exciting new business of aeronautics, in which he became a pioneer. The company was now directed to manufacturing protective coverings for planes, and the First World War made Maurice a wealthy man. Gaston was just too young to fight, but Jean-Paul enrolled at the military academy of St Cyr and spent two years at the front. Rose and Maurice were doubly blessed. Unlike so many, many parents, both of their sons survived. One writer has attributed Gaston's 'powerful taste for all forms of existence . . . gardens, books, paintings, pretty girls'[4] to this sense of having escaped, of having been spared conscription at the last moment. This does not mean that he was unaffected by what a recent French critic has called 'the unprecedented moral crisis'[5] of the war.

Young people of Nancy's and Gaston's era, the 'Bright Young Things' who danced their way through *les Années Folles*, were beset by both a feeling that they had been betrayed by the older generation and a powerful guilt that they had avoided sacrifice. 'It is a queer world which the old men have left them . . . they will not be a happy generation,' observed Evelyn Waugh in an essay for his school magazine. Rejection of everything the 'old men' stood for, contempt for the nineteenth-century faith in the infinite march of progress, produced a sense of futility that many attempted to subdue in frenetic hedonism. Every generation of teenagers believes itself to be unique, but the phenomenon of the Bright Young People contained a self-consciousness of their status as a 'lost generation', who, as Linda complains to Fanny in *The Pursuit of Love*, were doomed to be sandwiched together between two world wars, obliterated, forgotten.

Jean-Paul Palewski, who had served at the front, criticized his brother for what he saw as his 'girlish'[6] need for physical affection and reassurance. One of Nancy's complaints about her own mother was that she was physically undemonstrative; Rose

Palewski, by contrast, was warm and gentle, holding her youngest son for hours on her knee, kissing and caressing him whenever he was unhappy. Jean-Paul saw Gaston as 'soft', unable, as a student, to choose a path and stick to it. One of the notable features of the Twenties generation was their infantilism, their urge to recreate a happy childhood with nursery parties and nursery pranks, as though the world beyond the schoolroom was too terrifying to cope with. Dressing up as babies, albeit with gin in their bottles, was obviously a way of rejecting the 'adult' values that had almost destroyed Europe, but in a culture which had sent teenage boys to die in their thousands in the trenches, why would any of them have wanted to grow up?

Brighton at least appeared to have cured Gaston of his academic lassitude. In July 1921 he graduated from the prestigious Sorbonne university with a diploma in foreign languages and literature, specializing in English, then for the academic years 1921–3 attended the 'grande école' of political science (affectionately known as Sciences Po and effectively the French equivalent of Oxbridge). He studied in the 'private finance' department, founded by Emile Boutmy in 1872, which had a reputation for innovative courses with a strong international slant. Simultaneously, Gaston developed his early taste for paint-ings and *objets d'art* by attending classes at the Ecole du Louvre, acquiring a rigorous background in art history. He joked later that in many ways he had had a 'young girl's education'. Perhaps the most significant part of his intellectual formation, though, came from the months he spent at Worcester College, Oxford during the Trinity term of 1922.

Gaston was accepted as a 'research student', which entitled him to wear the long scholar's gown in which he is depicted, complete with mortarboard and co-ordinating spats and gloves, in a contemporary photograph. He 'adored' his time at Wor-cester, which he described in his memoirs as 'one of the oldest colleges in the university, with its Gothic buildings surrounded by a famous garden, whose lawns stretched to a lake bordered by trees, a ravishing backdrop to the setting sun'. For Gaston, many of Nancy Mitford's friends who emerged from the university largely unencumbered by academic laurels, scholarly life was not the point. He began a thesis on Thackeray, but cheerfully admitted not having taken it very seriously. Nor did he show an interest in sport or in the then-influential politicking of the Union Society. What he did acquire was style, the ineffable Oxford manner that even today has the capacity to dominate and infuriate in equal measure. Maurice Druon remarked of the differences between the French and the English methods of instruction:

> The teaching in the French *supérieurs* produces an elite . . . inclined to bear constant witness to the profundity of their knowledge or the weight of their responsibilities, or at least to allow this to be guessed. The ancient English universities produce an elite of politicians, scholars and scientists who affect not to take what they do very seriously . . . one asks oneself when they work, they who bring to their labour the modesty in which others wrap their leisure.[7]

It took a war, Druon adds, to show the French that the English were quite capable of earnestness. There is an excellent word in Italian for this overlaying of effort with seeming diffidence: *sprezzatura*, the art of doing that which is difficult while appearing to do nothing at all, and it suited Gaston's temperament perfectly. Although this brilliant diffidence was to prove extremely effective in his understanding of English methods of conducting politics, it nevertheless provoked dislike and mistrust among his French (and later American) colleagues, who were bewildered by the 'false lightness of his comportment'. No one could be more French than Gaston, as was illustrated by his rather mournful recollection of the lack of girls at Oxford ('some misogynist dons arranged for them to read the most indecent authors of the Restoration, which caused them to flee'), but the ability to slip on the well-cut mantle of the English gentleman when required gave him great pleasure. Oxford also provided him with a network of acquaintances which formed another step on the staircase of ambition which climbed away from the Faubourg-Poissonière.

The conversation of dons and the mysterious rites of High Table gave a richer polish to Gaston's already impressive intellect, while the company of men like Ivor Spencer-Churchill, cousin to the future prime minister, who took him to visit the family house at Blenheim, introduced him as a guest to the world he was so determined to inhabit. No more paying for a ticket and wriggling under a table to get a good view: at Blenheim Gaston could stroll beneath the Thornhill ceilings or the oaks in Capability Brown's park as an invited equal. Gaston's memories of Blenheim make their way into *The Blessing*, where Charles-Edouard de Valhubert installs a bust of the Duke of Marlborough in Grace's bedroom and goes about humming, 'Marlbrou s'en va-t-en guerre.' (One of Gaston's most distinctive traits, remembered by everyone who knew him, was his habit of inserting snatches of song into his speech. The Duchess of Devonshire, Nancy's sister Deborah, was astonished that he even knew English nursery rhymes, and one critic of Nancy's novels found it a ridiculous exaggeration. It was, however, quite true.) In November 1944, when he organized a victory luncheon for Churchill in Paris, Gaston dug out a bust of the prime minister's ancestor, the scourge of Louis XIV, to display at the table. 'It's too much,' remarked Churchill, but he was rather touched.

A good deal has been made of Nancy Mitford's enduring romance with France, but Gaston had a similar *tendresse* for many aspects of Englishness. Picturing him wandering at Blenheim, it is irresistible not to see him as an (admittedly spottier) Charles Ryder, the artistic middle-class boy intoxicated by the splendours of the old aristocracy in Waugh's *Brideshead Revisited*. Perceptions of Oxford have been coloured for good or ill for half a century by Waugh's great elegy at the opening of the novel, and Gaston was not immune to the lure of the aquatint. 'I lodged in one of the ancient monastic buildings of the sixteenth century,' he recalled. 'How young we were, and how those times seem far away!' His brother Jean-Paul describes Gaston's experience in terms that echo his praise of their Polish ancestors: 'He took no vanity [from Oxford] except in so much as to clarify his vision of society and the world, which directed him to the pursuit of what there is of the most refined and the most elegant, the most distinguished and without doubt the best of our humanity, blending from this culture the type of a truly superior man.'[8]

At Oxford, Gaston discovered the cavalier poet Richard Lovelace, the adherent of Charles II who was wounded fighting under Grand Condé at Dunkirk and died in alluringly romantic poverty. He later wrote of his affection for a particular poem, 'To Lucasta, Going to the Wars', which perfectly summed up the relationships with Mars and Venus that coloured his life:

> *Tell me not, sweet, I am unkind*
> *That from the nunnery*
> *Of thy chaste breast and quiet mind*
> *To war and arms I fly.*
>
> *True, a new mistress now I chase,*
> *The first foe in the field,*
> *And with a stronger faith embrace*
> *A sword, a horse, a shield.*
>
> *Yet this inconstancy is such*
> *As you too shall adore;*
> *I could not love thee, dear, so much,*
> *Loved I not honour more.*

2

NANCY

In 1956, Nancy wrote to Gaston about a new edition of the peerage which 'makes everyone out to be utter *nouveaux-riches*'. Her own family origins had been downgraded from the tenth to the fourteenth century, but they were still a great deal grander than the Palewskis'. As Evelyn Waugh relished pointing out, the 'Honourable' prefix attached to Nancy's name was not appended until 1916, when she was twelve and her father succeeded as 2nd Baron Redesdale, but Nancy's perception of herself was entirely and unapologetically aristocratic. Not that the Mitfords were particularly rich by the standards of their class (one reason Nancy claimed she could never get on with Americans was that they seemed to believe class was in some way related to money), but everything about her upbringing reinforced the notion that she was a member of that tiny elite of the sensible and ample of means who were born to rule wherever the map was coloured red.

Nancy was only just Honourable, true, but her family connections were deeply entwined in the mesh of the British aristocracy. Her great-grandmother Henrietta was the daughter of the 2nd Baron Stanley of Alderley, and married David Ogilvy, 10th Earl of Airlie. Henrietta's eldest daughter, Blanche, 'Aunt Natty', was the mother of Clementine Hozier, who married Winston Churchill. Her second daughter, Clementine, was the wife of Algernon Bertram Mitford, the 1st Baron Redesdale. Through the Stanleys, Nancy was distantly connected to the Earls of Derby and Rosebery and the Duke of Manchester. There was also a connection with the Dillon family, which meant that, to Nancy's delight, she could claim kinship with Madame de la Tour du Pin, the celebrated memoirist of the French Revolution. Unlike Gaston, Nancy was possessed of an unshakeable confidence in her own roots, a sense of security derived from centuries of belonging.

As well as a sense of entitlement, writing ran in the family. Nancy's paternal grandfather, Bertram, known as Bertie (pronounced 'Barty' to confound the Non-U), the great-grandson of William Mitford, a distinguished though now-forgotten historian of Greece, drew on a long career in the Diplomatic Service to produce a translation of Japanese legends, *Tales of Old Japan*, as well as two volumes of memoirs considered to be among the most authoritative accounts of Japanese culture as it was first exposed to the West. He was inevitably credited, to the glee of his grandchildren, with having also produced two children by a 'geisha lady'. Lady Redesdale's origins were not quite so distinguished. On her mother's side, Nancy was descended from Thomas 'Tap' Bowles, the illegitimate son of a Mr Milner Gibson and, according to Cynthia Gladwyn, a cook or a midwife. Tap had covered the 1870 siege of Paris as correspondent to the *Morning Post* and founded the magazines *Vanity Fair* and *The Lady*. Both grandfathers became Conservative MPs in 1892, and in 1894 Bertie invited Tap to speak at a meeting near his home at Batsford in Gloucestershire. Here Tap's fourteen-year-old daughter Sydney met the seventeen-year-old David Freeman-Mitford. As the beauty of their children would attest, both David and Sydney were extremely good-looking. David, tall, blond and blue-eyed, was described by Nancy's friend James Lees-Milne as the best-looking man of his generation. The images conveyed by Edwardian photographs do not resonate with modern ideas of attractiveness, but Sydney, darker, also tall and with huge, dreamy eyes, was considered one of the most beautiful debutantes of her year.

Sydney's own upbringing was very unconventional. Tap was widowed with four children and though the boys, Geoffrey and

George, were sent away to school, their father preferred that Sydney and her sister Dorothy (Nancy's Aunt Weenie) remain with him. Dressed in stiff, ugly sailor suits specially tailored at Gieves, the girls spent much of their childhood on Tap's boats, the *Nereid* and the *Hoyden*, making a year-long trip to the Middle East and frequent voyages to France. When they returned to live in Lowndes Square, Sydney acted as housekeeper to her father, and though she developed an early dislike of drunken, disobedient male servants and hired only women for her own indoor staff, she became an impressive manager and hostess. She developed a distracted air which puzzled and frustrated her daughters, gliding through life with a seemingly imperturbable serenity that David Mitford, whose own life had been marred by uncontrollable fits of temper, clearly found very appealing. Unlike his favoured elder brother Clement, David had not been sent to Eton, but to Radley, lest his tantrums compromise Clement's career. He was not nearly so illiterate as his daughters liked to make out, but he was uninterested in much except country sports, so the hearty, games-oriented life of Radley was a torment to him. He did not go on to university, but spent four years as a tea-planter in Ceylon (where he picked up his favourite and most famous term of abuse), joining the Royal Northumberland Fusiliers when the Boer War broke out during his first home leave in 1898.

David was much happier in the army, serving as orderly to the commanding officer Lord Brabazon. He was wounded three times, the last a chest wound which put him in a field hospital for four days after which he was hauled back to camp in a bullock wagon. His children relished the description of this journey, particularly the detail of the writhing nest of maggots in his lung. While David was in hospital he dictated a love letter to Sydney to be given to her should he die, and two years after he was invalided home from Africa they were married at St Margaret's, Westminster. They honeymooned on the *Hoyden* and in Paris, which they both loved. David spoke French perfectly, as the Mitford boys did all their lessons in the language with a French tutor, while Sydney had known France all her life, and through her father had many French acquaintances, including the painter Paul-Cesar Helleu. Helleu painted Sydney several times, as he was to do with her even more beautiful daughter Diana. In 1964 Gaston Palewski gave Nancy a Helleu as a birthday gift.

Sydney and David's first home was 1 Graham Street, off Eaton Terrace in Belgravia. David had been given a job by his father-in-law as office manager of *The Lady*, and for ten years he went to the magazine's offices in Covent Garden every day. His boss was his brother-in-law George, general manager and co-owner. Although the work was not congenial, George, an ex-president of the Cambridge Union and editor of *Granta*, found him competent enough. By way of distraction, he hunted a mongoose through the rat-riddled eighteenth-century building. David and Sydney were never society types. David actively loathed company beyond the family and a very few friends and though Sydney was more gregarious, the birth of her first child, Nancy, nine months after her marriage and their relative lack of money (their income of £1,000 per year allowed them to employ five servants, but was not sufficient for serious entertaining), made her content to follow her husband's preferences.

Nancy was followed by Pamela in 1907, Tom in 1909 and Diana in 1910 before the family moved to 49 Victoria Road in Kensington. One of Nancy's first letters, dated 1912, is to her mother at the new house:

> Dear Muv,
>   It has been hot and sunny it is now cold and wet. Please tell Farve—
>   There was an old Farve of Victoria Road which was a
>   Very nice abode. Four children and a wife who lived a
>   Happy life such a jolly old Farve of Victoria Road.

Until 1914, Nancy's life was bounded by the orderly, predictable routine of the Edwardian nursery. The children were cared for by Laura Dicks, 'Nanny Blor', who stayed with the

Mitfords for thirty years. In her old-fashioned black bonnet and cloak, she walked them to Kensington Gardens and the museums on the Cromwell Road, washed and brushed them for tea in the drawing room and supervised occasional trips to the pantomime or a magic show. Contrary from the first, the Mitfords despised anything they recognized as patronizing sentimentality. When Peter Pan asked plaintively if all the children in the theatre believed in fairies, they delighted in roaring out 'No!'. Despite Nancy's protestations that she never went to school, she attended the Francis Holland school in Belgravia for a few years, and all the girls were well taught at home, first by Sydney (who expected them to be capable of reading the leader in *The Times* by the age of six, which is more than would be demanded of most modern children) and later by a series of more or less persecuted governesses who followed the PNEU system, an accredited method of home education. After lessons there was a small menagerie of 'creatures' to be cared for and played with: the mongoose, three dogs, birds, mice and a pony called Brownie that David had brought home in a cab. He lived in a first-floor boxroom until he could be taken down by train to the cottage Sydney had rented at High Wycombe. Ponies were not allowed to travel first class, so the family bundled into a third-class carriage, with Pamela stuffed in the luggage rack.

Like any sensible child, ten-year-old Nancy longed for war. As Sydney awaited the birth of her fifth baby at Victoria Road, the children were sent to stay at their grandfather's house overlooking Kensington High Street. Kensington Gardens became a camp, and from Grandfather Redesdale's balcony the children could watch the troops marching past, working at peculiar knitted garments meant for the War Effort. Nancy 'a miniature tricoteuse'[1] made an endless scarf in an unpleasant shade of puce. David Mitford talked the doctors into permitting him to rejoin his regiment and left for the front a month after Unity was born, in September 1914. His health was unable to withstand a winter in the field and he was again invalided home in January 1915. Seven-year-old Pamela remembered being astonished a few months later to see her father weeping. His brother Clement had been killed, leaving his wife three months pregnant with their second child.

David was passed fit to return to France in April. During the second battle of Ypres he served as a transport officer, riding once or twice every evening across the town with the battalion's ammunition supplies. He accompanied every delivery personally, and with his strategy of bringing the wagon horses up to a gallop and then storming flat out through the town through the Menin Gate, he never lost a man. In October he learned that Clement's widow had produced another daughter, Clementine, which left him heir to the title and the estates. Sydney let Victoria Road and the cottage and moved into a house on the Batsford estate to economize, but just a year later, Bertie Redesdale, too, was dead, crushed by the death of his beloved elder son. David was invalided home once more in 1917, to be stationed at Oxford, travelling once a week to visit the family in their new home at Batsford Park, where Sydney gave birth to their sixth child, Jessica.

Batsford was the Mitfords' first real experience of country life. While Deborah (born in 1920) always loved the countryside and Jessica always loathed it, the views of the other sisters were more equivocal. In her memoir *Hons and Rebels*, Jessica described how, during the 'interminable' time it took her to grow up, she became conscious of how monotonous country life was, how distant from 'anything exciting'. In her second novel, *Christmas Pudding*, Nancy's heroine Philadelphia Bobbin is cast into dreariness when her smart London friends depart: 'Philadelphia found herself once more without any occupations or interests ... assailed by the deadly boredom only known to those who live in the country but have no love for country pursuits ... And in the clutches of that boredom, too boring even to describe, she remained ...'

In her own memoirs, Diana recalled playing a game which made its way into *The Pursuit of Love*.

'What's the time, darling?'

'Guess.'
'A quarter to six?'
'Better than that.'
'Six!'
'Not quite so good.'
'Five to?'
'Yes.'

Yet all the sisters except Jessica were countrywomen at heart. One of Nancy's nephews remembered her showing him how to lead a pony, grasping the reins coolly in her Dior-gloved hands, and reminding him that she had, actually, grown up in the countryside. When she was dying, Nancy said that what she longed for was just one more day's hunting. Even when she became the 'French lady writer', she frequently wrote to her mother of her desire to live in the country. Eccentric rural touches, like the pretty white hen that was saved from becoming the colonel's dinner and lived ever after in Nancy's elegant Parisian flat, or the wild flower lawn (or seedy hayfield) of her last home at Versailles, which she refused to mow, were always part of her character. Her friends agreed that despite her beautiful French and impeccable couture wardrobe, Nancy remained English to her perfectly straight backbone. She was to write with intense lyricism about the English countryside. The rhythm of her love for its beauty sings through the exhausted jog trot of a pony on a high Cotswold road, in the shrill, jarring whine of a dying rabbit, in the often startling palette from which she conjures its landscape. Nancy was no Romantic: she was aware of the cruelty of nature and the poverty beneath the picturesque, yet it was those very *chiaroscuro* qualities which for her made the countryside so entrancing. She felt that people of her class had a unique, atavistic relationship with their land, and she mourned its passing even as she despised the boorish, philistine squires among whom she claimed, rather disingenuously, to have grown up.

The new Lord Redesdale had inherited a considerable fortune

but most of it was tied up in land in Gloucestershire, Oxfordshire and Northumberland, and it was considered impossible for the growing family to remain at the vast Victorian mansion with which Grandfather Redesdale had replaced his pretty Georgian house in 1880. Batsford was sold in 1919 and the family moved to Asthall, a beautiful sixteenth-century manor house near the village of Swinbrook, where the new Lord Redesdale intended to build a family house. Nancy was already a bookworm – she was reading Walter Scott at six – and she was saddened when David also sold off much of her grandfather's impressive library. Entering her teens and no longer so enchanted with 'creatures' or playing hide-and-seek in the endless, dust-sheeted rooms of Batsford, she had begun there the programme of serious reading she kept up all her life. David was famous in the family for only ever having read one book, *White Fang*, which he considered so fine he never bothered with another. Sydney tried reading *Tess of the D'Urbervilles* aloud, but when David, in floods of tears at the hanging scene, learned it was fiction, he was outraged. 'D'you mean the damn fella made it up?' Despite this trauma he built his children a new library at Asthall, converting a barn and adding a covered walkway they named the Cloisters.

The library was the children's territory. Tom played the piano when he was home from school and they all read and read. For a woman who always lamented her lack of a thorough education, Nancy was impressively versed in the English canon and was later more than able to hold her own among some of the most brilliant literary minds of her day. Country life was not quite so grim as Jessica later made it sound. The children were sometimes allowed to follow Lord Redesdale when he went shooting, fishing or coursing, they hunted when they were old enough – Nancy on a smart little mare called Rachel – there were expeditions to the skating rink in Oxford and shopping trips to Moreton-in-Marsh. Nancy founded a family journal, *The Boiler*, featuring stories by the editor under the pen name of W.R. Grue. Sydney encouraged her children to farm, 'renting' land from their father to keep goats, pigs, and chickens. She herself set an example with beehives and eggs, which were sent to London to be sold. With the profits, she paid the governess's salary. Only Pam was really passionate about her smallholding, insisting on her right to attend the tenants' dinner, but the others participated too, if only as a means to earn pocket money. Nancy boasted later that there was nothing she didn't know about chickens.

It was not *Debrett's* that was the source of the Mitfords' much-derided Society of Hons. The children developed several private languages, including Boudledidge, spoken by Jessica and Unity and understood by the others, and Honnish, the language of the society (members: Jessica and Deborah). In Honnish, 'hen' was pronounced 'hon', with an aspirated 'h', so the club was inspired by chickens, not honourables, as is still assumed by many journalists, although the mistake has been corrected by all of Nancy's biographers. Tom's nickname, Tuddemy, was the Boudledidge translation of his name, thought immensely funny as it rhymed, sort of, with 'adultery', a subject of intense fascination. It was bestowed on him after he once asked: 'Grandfather, you know *adultery...*'

It was not until she reached adulthood that Nancy could see the charm in any of this. Despite 'Farve's' explosive rages and 'Muv's' irritating vagueness, the Mitfords, so clever, so lucky, so beautiful, lived a life most children could only imagine. Once Nancy got the point and reproduced them as the Radletts in *The Pursuit of Love*, the world was fascinated, enchanted and disgusted in equal measure with the Mitford childhood, and remained so for fifty years, but to Nancy, 'longing to be grown-up and live with grown-up people',[2] it seemed terribly tedious. By her own account, she was quite horrid to her siblings. She informed Jessica, Unity and Deborah that the middle letters of their names spelled out 'sic', 'nit' and 'bore'. She dressed up as a tramp, going to highly convincing trouble, to frighten her sister Pamela with a demand for a kiss. She forced Pamela and Diana to become girl guides, which she hated as much as they did, just to have the chance to boss them around. She told Deborah that everybody cried when she was born, another unwanted girl. The weight given to Nancy's teasing has perhaps been exaggerated – anyone who has spent time with groups of siblings will note their capacity to be astonishingly foul to one another. What made it so memorable in Nancy's case was that she was so good at it. The reverse of her genius for spite was her funniness. When she and Lord Redesdale teased one another at table, Deborah remembered that it was better than a play, while Jessica recalled that the wildness of the Mitford imagination – the complicated jokes, the passionate rivalries, the insistence that, above all, it was one's duty to amuse and never to bore – 'sprang full-blown from Nancy'.

All the Mitford girls claimed to be jealous of Tom's education. School was tried for Unity, but it didn't last long ('not *expelled*', Lady Redesdale would insist, 'asked to leave'), and later for Deborah, who hated it so much it made her physically ill. The Redesdales conceded to Nancy's agitating in 1921, permitting her to attend Hatherop Castle for a year. Hatherop, run by a Mrs Cadogan, was more of a pension-cum-finishing school than a serious intellectual establishment – she took in a few 'nice' girls to educate along with her own daughters, with whom Nancy continued the French that, apart from a little piano and gracious deportment, Lord Redesdale considered the only real essential for girls, had her bottom pinched in her netball skirt by Commander Cadogan and worked on her sketching and dancing. Nancy enjoyed Hatherop as, at least, a change from home and was even more thrilled the next year when, with four other girls, she was sent on a cultural tour of Paris, Venice and Florence under the chaperonage of a Miss Spalding, the headmistress of a London girls' school.

'Louis XIV fell in love with Versailles and Louise de la Vallière at the same time; Versailles was the love of his life,' Nancy declared in *The Sun King*. Like her beloved Bourbon king, her first great love was for a place. In 1927, she wrote to her brother Tom from Paris: 'One can be more cheerful there than anywhere else in the world and I have often danced all the way down the Champs Elysées ... I think all day La Muette, Place de la

Concorde, Place de l'Etoile, Avenue Hoch, Avenue du Bois, Place des Vosges, Palais Royale, Rue de Rivoli.' From her first visit to the city until she achieved her dream of settling there over twenty years later, this was her mantra, Paris her promised land.

The beauty of Paris still catches at the heart of even the most sophisticated modern traveller. Hardly surprising, then, that to a sheltered schoolgirl who had spent much of her life, in the words of her friend Brian Howard, 'hidden amongst the cabbages of the Cotswolds',[3] it appeared so dazzling. Nancy's first view of the city was from the Grand Hôtel du Louvre, perfectly placed on the Right Bank of the Seine to offer vistas of four of its most eloquent scences: the Louvre itself, the Opéra Garnier, the Place du Palais Royale and the Comédie Française. Writing once more to Tom, the eighteen-year-old Nancy described an attack of Stendhal syndrome. The Avenue Henri Martin in the sixteenth arrondissement was 'more perfect and melancholy than any place you've ever seen. I don't know why but I waited for a bus there once and when the bus came I was in tears.'

Nancy was not yet 'out', her black-coffee hair still coiled at her neck, weighty as the Edwardian etiquette under which she had been raised, and her impression of the city on her first trip abroad was one of naïve and pure delight. In ecstatic letters home she describes 'a very scrumptious "croissant"', her pleasure in the pictures in the Louvre, the 'heavenly' shops and the beauty of the Place de la Concorde at night. It is a tourist's view, but also a sensualist's, inviting her mother, Lady Redesdale, to share in the soft slip of a perfect *omelette aux fines herbes*, the airy stickiness of a perfect *éclair*.

Meanwhile, across town, a young student at the Sorbonne was experiencing a very different side to the city. Paris in the 1920s, Gaston Palewski recalled, was illuminated by the last, dying light of the Belle Epoque. In defiance of the cataclysm of the Great War, the grand houses remained open, the salons still exercised their influence and aristocrats serenely wedded tradesmen's daughters to provide the funds necessary to maintaining the illusion that nothing much had happened since 1788.

Money carried the elite of the Faubourg St Honoré calmly over the waves of social upheaval; patronage of the arts and above all, the belief in *douceur de vivre* obtained unchallenged: '*Le gout du décor ancien, la science d'un certain art de vivre . . . on pouvait se réunir, se rencontrer, s'apprécier, s'aimer. Charmante epoque!*' Indeed, the great trial of the war had served to stimulate a fever of artistic and literary creation. This was the Paris of Diaghilev, Stravinsky, Cocteau, Picasso. Cole Porter was installed at 17 Rue Monsieur with sixteen dressing gowns and nine cigarette cases, Gertrude Stein with her unrivalled art collection and her moustachioed lover Alice B. Toklas in the Rue de Fleurus; the American colony – Dorothy Parker, ee cummings, John dos Passos, Fitzgerald, Hemingway – who took time off from carousing and creating to meet at Sylvia Beach's English bookshop, Shakespeare and Company, at the Odéon. A young man possessed of charm, brilliance and a decent suit might go anywhere. Palewski met the celebrated painter Armand Jan, who introduced him to Picasso, and in the studio of Jacques-Emile Blanche he first heard of an extraordinary debutant writer named Proust who, in one flourish of his unknown hand, 'stole the glory of which his entire generation dreamed'. Nancy Mitford and Gaston Palewski did not meet for more than twenty years after her first breathless glimpse of the city, but somehow she knew, instinctively, that it was in his Paris she belonged, that he would offer her the key to 'that low door in the wall, which others, I knew, had found before me, which opened on an enclosed and enchanted garden, which was somewhere, not overlooked by any window, in the heart of that grey city'.[4]

3

COMING OUT

Nancy Mitford attended her first 'grown-up' dance at Asthall in 1922, the same year that Lady Edwina Mountbatten's underclothes for her wedding journey were exhibited to the general public. For all that the 1923 debutante season was considered to be the most glittering and glamorous since the war, Lady Edwina's lace-edged frillies did not invoke a new spirit of liberation among the girls who lined up in their ostrich feathers to curtsey to Queen Mary. As far as the Redesdales and their peers were concerned, it might have been 1903: the aim of the Season was to get a girl respectably married as soon as possible. Then, and only then, might she contemplate any form of adult life. Lady Redesdale took her tiara out of the bank, rented a house in Gloucester Square and, as she was to do for all her daughters, resigned herself to the peculiar martyrdom of women of her class: chaperonage.

Nancy learned to kick out her white satin train, made her curtsey, attended girls' luncheons, dinners and dances nearly every evening, drank fruit cup and sat out to eat ices, did all that was expected of her as her mother nodded in the corner on a hired gold chair. Her first Season was a success: 'Yes, she was very pretty, she enjoyed it all,' commented Deborah. 'She was popular, everyone liked her.'[1] Deborah's own picture of a typical 'deb dance' is rather more telling:

> Rather a small square room to dance in and many too
> many people in the doorway and on the stairs ... My

conversation to the debs' young men goes like this:

The chinless horror 'I think this is our dance.'

Me 'Oh yes, I think it is.'

C.H. 'What a crowd in the doorway.'

Me 'Yes isn't it awful.'

The C.H. then clutches me round the waist and I almost fall over as I try to put my feet where his aren't.

Me 'Sorry.'

C.H. 'No, my fault.'

Me 'Oh, I think it must have been me.'

C.H. 'Oh, no, that wouldn't be possible.'

Then follows a long and dreary silence sometimes one of us saying 'sorry' and the other 'my fault'. After a bit we feel we can't bear it any longer so we decide to go and sit down.

The disillusion of the debutante's long-yearned-for coming of age in *The Pursuit of Love* bears out Deborah's description:

This then is a ball. This is life, what we have been waiting for all these years . . . How extraordinary it feels, such unreality, like a dream. But alas, so utterly different from what one had imagined . . . the women so frowsty . . . the men, either so old or so ugly. And when they ask one to dance it is not at all like floating away into a delicious cloud, pressed by a manly arm to a manly bosom, but stumble-kick, stumble-kick. They balance, like King Stork on one leg, while with the other they come down, like King Log, on one's toe. As for witty conversation . . . it is mostly 'Oh-sorry', 'Oh-my fault'.

One of the few truly eligible young men who attended Nancy's dance at Asthall was Henry Weymouth, heir to the Marquess of Bath, who introduced her to friends including Brian Howard, one of the models for Evelyn Waugh's fantastic aesthete Anthony Blanche in *Brideshead Revisited*. Howard was immediately charmed: 'A delicious creature, quite pyrotechnical my dear, and sometimes even profound.'[2] Mark Ogilvie-Grant appeared at a dance given by some local neighbours, the Masons, and soon became a close friend and confidant. Through Howard and Ogilvie-Grant Nancy began to meet the young men who formed her real social circle throughout the Twenties: Harold Acton, diplomat and writer; Robert Byron, the renowned Oxford aesthete and later distinguished travel writer; the film-maker John Sutro, Cecil Beaton, Evelyn Waugh, Oliver Messel, John Betjeman and Henry Yorke (whose novels were published under the name of Henry Green), Tom Driberg. Many of them were homosexual, or flirted with homosexuality; all were clever and witty and beneath their delight in shocking the older generation concealed surprisingly serious ideas about art, about what was valuable and what was not. They represented Nancy's first exposure to the sort of people with whom she wanted to spend her life, those who recognized the nascent intimation given to Fanny among the floating panels of disillusion at her first ball that 'the behaviour of civilized man really has nothing to do with nature, that all is artificiality and art more or less perfected'.

In 1926 the Mitford family moved to Swinbrook House, the hideous modern home Lord Redesdale had built for them and which he was greatly hurt to discover all of them except Deborah loathed (Nancy called it 'Swinebrook'). The friends she asked to stay became the 'Swinbrook Sewers', derived from Lord Redesdale's favourite insult, '*sua*' – 'pig' – picked up in Ceylon. Jessica recalled them 'sweeping down in merry hordes' with their smart jargon – how too, too divine, how sickmaking, darling, how shamemaking, how bogus. If the Redesdales didn't exactly approve, Nancy's friends were tolerated – indeed, Mark succeeded to the dubious honour of favourite. His rewards included the pleasure of eating sweetbreads at eight o'clock sharp with Lord Redesdale. 'Brains for breakfast!' became a maxim of their letters.

Much as she loved her new friends, Nancy could not really follow them to the darker side of the Bright Young scene. Although her life was now much less restricted, Edwardian standards still pertained. Leaving the house in London without a chaperone was virtually impossible and even then certain areas, such as the clubland of St James's, were off limits. The seedy nightclubs of Soho and Fitzrovia were banned, and even something as innocent as having tea in Oxford with Brian Howard was treated as a crime. When she was caught in the act, Lord Redesdale bellowed at his grown-up daughter that were she married this would give her husband grounds for divorce. At the age of twenty-two, Nancy dared to cut her long hair, to which Lady Redesdale responded that she would never get a husband now, and the minor transgressions of her generation – slacks, lipstick, the odd cigarette – were treated as major offences. So although Nancy was mixing with some of the most brilliant young men of her generation, there remained an innocent quality to her which she retained all her life (later, in Paris, she still seemed 'almost virginal',[3] capable of discussing the necessity of breaking with her family to become a painter with Brian Howard, but simultaneously enjoying fancy-dress parties and the shocking pleasure of an occasional cocktail.

The painting idea never came to much. Nancy, astonishingly, was permitted to attend the Slade, but realized very soon that she had absolutely no talent: 'What a *very* depressing drawing. I wonder how you manage to draw so foully,' was her teacher's comment. Even more astonishingly, the Redesdales allowed her, at the age of twenty-three, to move into a bedsit in South Kensington. Much to the dismay of Jessica, who was already saving up to run away, this lasted a mere month. The advancing heaps of underclothes on the floor just became too menacing ('No one to pick them up, you see.'). Nancy wanted freedom, but not the kind that came with a basin in the corner.

Writing began to look like a serious way out. If one were posh but poor, gossip-writing was a useful source of pocket money. Nancy had paid for a visit to her friend Nina Seafield at Cullen Castle in Scotland by photographing the party for the *Tatler*. She went on to produce occasional pieces for *Vogue* – the plight of the bridal confidante in 'The Secret History of a London

Wedding', tips for the lady guest in 'The Shooting Party' ('it is advisable to wear a little coat over your dinner dress ... there are few houses where it is considered good form to rise during dinner and beat the breast in order to stimulate circulation') – and then, through her family connection with the magazine, she secured a weekly column on *The Lady*, for which she attended the regular events of the Season, a Commem. Ball at Oxford, the Chelsea Flower Show, the Fourth of June. In the first three months of 1929, she had made a very respectable £22, and decided to try a novel.

As a debutante, she was well past her sell-by date, yet Nancy needed money for something other than the maintenance of her self-respect. In 1928, she had met Hamish St Clair Erskine, then in his first year at New College. The second son of the notorious roué the Earl of Rosslyn, Hamish, in James Lees-Milne's words, was possessed of 'the most enchanting looks, though not strictly handsome, mischievous eyes, slanting eyebrows. He was slight of build, gay as gay, always snobbish and terribly conscious of his nobility.'[4] The fact that Hamish was 'gay as gay' didn't put Nancy off falling in love with him, even though he had had a sexual relationship with her brother Tom at Eton. Hamish's one object in life was admiration, but along with his vanity he was endowed with huge charm and the ability to make his friends laugh until they wept, the best possible quality in Nancy's eyes. She convinced herself that his heavy drinking, his love of sleazy nightclubs, his selfishness and irresponsibility needed only a firm, loving hand, and after five increasingly frustrating years on the deb circuit she was sure she was the woman to reform him. Flattered by her unconditional devotion and the regard in which she was held by her brilliant homosexual circle of friends, Hamish went along with the idea that they were engaged, sentencing Nancy to five years of humiliation and wretchedness.

Hamish's sexuality was in some senses typical of the times. Many of Nancy's contemporaries, including Evelyn Waugh, Cyril Connolly and her brother Tom, had experienced intense emotional and sexual relationships with men at school and university before turning wholeheartedly to women. In his Eton memoir, Nancy's great friend Lord Berners conceded that 'a good deal of this sort of thing went on, but to speak of it as homosexuality would be unduly ponderous. It was merely the ebullience of puberty.'[5] Since homosexuality was never spoken of, there was no pressure to nail one's colours to the mast by 'coming out' and it was perhaps more acceptable for some young men to pass through this phase without defining their sexuality when they were still emotionally immature. Many others, however, were definitely 'so' and happy to remain that way, though beyond the safe nurseries of the public school and universities they had to contend with both crushing prejudice and fear of the law. One historian of Nancy's generation has commented on the fact that 'no English youth movement . . . has ever contained such a high proportion of homosexuals or – in an age when these activities were still illegal – been so tolerant of their behaviour'.[6] Jessica Mitford, recalling the homosexual culture of the all-male environments in which her peers spent their youth and early manhood, remarked that 'some stuck to it, some didn't, but nobody paid much attention either way'.

It was difficult for an inexperienced young woman to judge whether a wavering young man might not yet turn out to be good husband material, but Nancy was not entirely naïve. Evelyn Waugh gave her an embarrassed lecture at the Ritz about 'sexual shyness' in men after Hamish confessed that he didn't think he would ever be capable of sleeping with a woman, and one of James Lees-Milne's lovers agonized for months to prepare himself for the great event. The Duchess of Devonshire suggests Nancy was quite unaware that Hamish was thoroughly homosexual. 'Those days, you know, I don't think she knew he was queer . . . otherwise why would she have said she was engaged to him?'[7] Nancy was certainly sophisticated enough to make jokes about 'pansies' in her letters: to Mark Ogilvie-Grant she wrote that she had had tea with his mother 'and inadvertently gave her one of your letters to read in which a lift boy is described as a "Driberg's

delight"'. Mrs Ogilvie-Grant had no idea what this meant –
'Dear Mark has *such* an amusing gift for describing people' – but
clearly Nancy did. Or did she? She might have been able to find
her friends' pashes on boys amusing without really considering
or knowing what was involved. Certainly her relationship with
Hamish could not have been more asexual. She described an
evening staying with Nina at Cullen Castle, when she and
Hamish draped themselves in chiffon and put vine leaves and
roses in their hair. Nancy curled Hamish's locks with tongs
and 'he looked more than lovely'. Assuming Nancy wasn't simply
stupid, was she playing along with Hamish's tendencies in the
blind hope that he would grow out of them? Or was there
something about cavorting in fancy dress that appealed to her
own undeveloped and apprehensive sexuality?

Hamish was safe in a way that other suitors weren't. Nancy
had one serious admirer, Sir Hugh Smiley, who was everything
a debutante's anxious mother could wish for. Sir Hugh, of the
Grenadier Guards, proposed several times during 1932. Nancy
considered it, but couldn't talk herself into pretending to love
him. The prospect of his 'gingerbread mansion' was tempting –
'one could be so jolly well dressed and take lovers' – but behind
her attempts at sophistication, there was a real fear of the confinement marriage could bring. She had had relationships with
at least three other quite eligible young men, but she stuck with
Hamish, who made her miserable, giggling with him over poor
Sir Hugh's shoulder as he sat at a nearby table at the Café de
Paris. She had written to Tom: 'If only I had any real talent I
would so much rather remain single like Edith Sitwell.' Then,
immediately, she backed out: 'No, I think it would probably be
nicer to be married really or shall I become a celebrated demi
mondaine, one of the really snappy ones?' To Mark Ogilvie-
Grant she explained that she thought financial independence
was the greatest human happiness, and even at the lowest points
of her relationship with Hamish she kept working away at it,
grasping faintly but firmly at the prospect of another life, one
that could be lived on her own terms.

And Hamish did make her extremely miserable. The 'engagement' dragged on and on, opposed by both families. Nancy's letters to Mark Ogilvie-Grant alternate between protestations of Hamish's innate goodness, wince-inducing descriptions of his cleverness – 'Hamish was funny yesterday . . . he had five glasses of brandy and crème de menthe (on top of sherry etc.) and then began to analyze himself. He said "the best of me is that I can talk Homer to Maurice [Bowra, celebrated Warden of Wadham College] just as well as Noël Coward to you, in fact I am clever enough to amuse everybody"' – and lacerating despair. During one of the many severances of the engagement, she wrote that she had tried to commit suicide by gas. It came out as a joke: 'It is a lovely sensation just like taking anaesthetic so I shan't be sorry any more for schoolmistresses who are found dead in that way.' Nancy explained that she had been put off by the thought of the distress her corpse might cause to her pregnant hostess – suicide as bad manners – yet to have gone through the motions at all, and evidently needing somehow to talk about this, indicates a genuine agony, even if the exposed wound had to be immediately concealed beneath a cicatrice of laughter.

Nancy told Mark that Lord Rosslyn said she might have his son if she could make £1,000 per year and certainly her primary motivation in publishing her first novel, *Highland Fling*, was to make money. The circumstances of its composition could hardly have illustrated more clearly the ignominious position in which she found herself as an unmarried elder daughter: the book was finished in Paris, at 12 Rue de Poitiers, the flat of the Guinness family, into which Diana had recently made a brilliant marriage. Her wedding to Bryan Guinness, the clever, good-looking heir to the immense Guinness fortune, had taken place on 29 January 1929. At just nineteen, Diana was possessed of a fantastically wealthy husband who adored her, a London house and a position at the pinnacle of the fashionable intellectual London society to which both she and Nancy had so yearned to belong during the endless waiting out of their adolescence in the country. In November that year, the Guinnesses, Evelyn Waugh and Nancy went to Paris. Diana was halfway through her first pregnancy and would rest in bed in the mornings while her husband and friends worked respectively on *Singing Out of Tune*, *Labels* and *Highland Fling*. If Nancy was irked that her younger sister was now considered a suitable chaperone, she did not allow it to spoil the pleasure to be taken in her beloved city. When their work was over the group enjoyed visits to the theatre or galleries, including a significant exhibition of Surrealist art, with dinner and dancing in the evenings.

Evelyn's second novel, *Vile Bodies*, was published the following January, dedicated to Bryan and Diana. It was a huge success, though Nancy confessed herself disappointed in it. Much has been made by some critics of the influence of anxiety in Nancy's relationship with Evelyn, perhaps similar to that which many attribute to Edith Wharton in her relationship with Henry James. At this stage of her career, Nancy was certainly in awe of Evelyn's abilities, though later they developed something of a relationship of peers, if not equals, when it came to their writing. However, *Highland Fling* is interesting in that it sheds light on how Nancy's own work may have influenced Evelyn's. The book is an uneven comedy of manners, using the stock device of an ill-assorted house party assembled to shoot in the Scottish highlands, to pit Bright Young Things against the older generation with attitudes to art as one of their battlegrounds. At one point the pretentious Albert Gates insists on declaiming from T.S. Eliot's 1925 'The Hollow Men' – 'Shape without form, shade without colour\Paralysed force, gesture without motion' – in a scene that anticipates Anthony Blanche's recitation of *The Wasteland* to the Christchurch hearties in *Brideshead*.

Eliot's poem is complex and allusive, drawing on references as diverse as Dante, Joseph Conrad and Guy Fawkes, concerned with the difficulty of faith in a post-war world. Nancy's use of it sends up the Bright Young Things' pretensions as much as their elders' conservativism. The feckless Walter Monteath's own attempt at Modernist poetry, 'With angels rising from the Guinness foam', is a neat in-joke, yet the inclusion of the Eliot reference adumbrates Nancy's thoughtful, rather poignant position on the *querelle des generations*. To General Murgatroyd, aesthete Albert addresses a diatribe which might have come from the Bright Young Things' manual:

> It was your war, and I hope you enjoyed it … But let me tell you, even when you have succeeded, even when you have brought another war upon us, it won't be any good. None of my generation will go and fight. We don't care for wars, you see. We have other things to think about … people of your class notoriously enjoy wars and fighting … Your very recreations consist in killing things. But in future you will do well to avoid stirring up the great civilized nations against each other.

He is put in his place by the folklore bore Mr Buggins (whose wife languishes sinisterly offstage in a lunatic asylum), who observes that four years in the trenches have deprived his generation of their spirit and self-respect.

> Everybody knows – you are at no pains to conceal it – that the young people of today despise and dislike the men and women of my age. I suppose that never since the world began have two generations been so much at variance. You think us superficial, narrow-minded, tasteless and sterile, and you are right. But who knows what we might have become if things had been different?

Much of the novel is little more than a series of set pieces based on the more notorious antics of the younger set. A mock funeral refers to the sham wedding staged in January 1929 by Robert Byron, Elizabeth Ponsonby and Oliver Messel, while Albert's art exhibition recalls the Bruno Hat hoax got up by Diana, Bryan and their friends, in which Tom Mitford posed in a wheelchair and false moustache as a naïf artist with works hurriedly mocked up by Brian Howard in the style of Picasso and Braque. Some of Nancy's lighter themes are gestured at – the perennial dowdiness of Englishwomen, a prototype of the immortal Bolter in Mrs Fairfax, the discomfort of country-house life – yet there is also a nascent engagement here with those issues that develop subtly but persistently into her maturity as a novelist: the consequences of war, the meaning of civilization and the role of art and the intellect. In her first novel, true, they are slight, barely showing their whiskers amid the barrage of inconsistently successful jokes, but they are there nonetheless. There is also, early on, a rather harsh description of the heroine, Jane Dacre, which reads like Nancy brutally setting out her sense of her own inadequacies at the age of twenty-eight.

> Thought by some to be exceptionally stupid and by others brilliantly clever, she was in reality neither. She had certain talents which she was far too lazy to develop, and a sort of feminine astuteness which prevented her from saying silly things. Like many women she had taste without much intellect, her brain was like a mirror, reflecting the thoughts and ideas of her more intelligent friends and the books she read ... She had, however, a certain sense of humour and except for a certain bitterness with which, for no apparent reason, she regarded her father and mother, the temperament of an angel.

The book was published in the same period as Nancy's suicide attempt. It was well reviewed and sold respectably, but Nancy's letters to Mark Ogilvie-Grant at the time reflect little of the delight of the first-time author. There is a sense of futility, of 'gesture without motion', of a voice which knows it must take itself seriously if it is to progress, but which, trapped in circumstance, is unable quite to do so. There is nothing of the truly vicious despair of *Vile Bodies*, and Nancy's comedy is by no means as yet as dazzling as Waugh's, but perhaps it is fair to say that both books are the product of disaffected love, Waugh's for his wife Evelyn Gardner, whose marriage to him collapsed in the face of her adultery halfway through its composition, and Nancy's for Hamish, which dragged fruitlessly on until 1933.

Nancy's second novel, *Christmas Pudding*, is a much more confident book, its teases more self-mocking ('It's no good writing about the upper classes if you want to be taken seriously – Station masters!') and subtle, as when a greasy-flannelled young man at a Chelsea party waxes lyrical about the bucolic delights of the Russian timber camps (aka gulags). Some of the writing, particularly the mini-drama within the Victorian diary of Gloria, Lady Bobbin, is superlatively done. If Albert Gates owes much to Hamish, Bobby Bobbin, the teenage baronet in *Christmas Pudding*, is a portrait from life. Again, the action centres on a country house party in which the forces of art and true love are pitched against the old and the philistine. Love, though, is much more thoroughly considered here, and considerably less idealized. Tellingly, the newly married Jane and Albert Gates are spied at a party and described as 'wretched'.

The heroine, Amabelle Fortescue, is a development of the 'really snappy' *demi-mondaine* for whom Nancy had shown a certain fascination in her letters, the first original and impressive character her author creates: a ten-grand-a-night hooker with a diplomat's brain. Her worldliness is beautifully, though rather wishfully, drawn and her aperçus are the beginning of Nancy's philosophy of love: 'The trouble is that people seem to expect happiness in life. I can't imagine why, but they do. They are unhappy before they marry and they imagine to themselves that the reason for their unhappiness will be removed when they are married. When it isn't, they blame the other person, which is clearly absurd.'

Love, Amabelle declares, is a talent like any other, but unlike, say, a talent for tennis or playing the violin, no one is prepared to admit to not being possessed of it. Through Philadelphia Bobbin's infatuation with her brother's tutor and her eventual acceptance of a much more reasonable match in an eligible marquess, we see that love is to be approached with thought and consideration, distinguished from juvenile fantasy, and impossible to maintain without a solid compatibility of interest and outlook (we might compare Elizabeth Bennet's pash on Mr Wickham and her slow understanding of the real love she feels for Mr Darcy in *Pride and Prejudice*). That Nancy can recognize this in art, if not act upon it in life, is clear from the character of Bobby Bobbin. It is not gushingly positive; indeed, at times her analysis is painfully cold:

> Bobby has a peculiar character, I must say. I suppose he is the one complete egoist of his generation. It is very lucky for him because it means that he will never, in his whole life, know the meaning of the word boredom. He will always be quite happy as long as he is with other people because it is wildly interesting to him to watch the effect he is producing and their reactions to his personality . . . Leave him alone and he would collapse, of course.

Bobby's aesthetic pretensions are exposed as a sham – he keeps Proust on display while preferring the *Tatler*; he is profoundly conventional in his ideas about society and professes a secret love for hunting. Nancy evidently considers him an engaging fraud, despite being far more painfully engaged than the reader. She is also very aware of Bobby's predilections – his first appearance in the novel is 'writing a note to an older boy' – even if she still doesn't quite see how precisely they applied to Hamish and herself. A month before publication she was writing to him about a fancy-dress party Diana was giving at her country house at Biddesden: 'Your dress is lovely, really divine, I hope you'll think so too. I tried it on this morning . . .'

The ball at Biddesden was memorable for more than Hamish's outfit. Since early 1932, Diana Guinness had been conducting an affair with Sir Oswald Mosley, the dashing, maverick politician whose British Union of Fascists was officially inaugurated in October that year. At the party, he appeared all in black to Diana's white and silver and, to the anguish of his wife Cynthia (née Curzon), the demon king and the fairy princess disappeared immediately after dinner, remaining upstairs until it was time for the hostess to say goodbye to her guests. Mosley was a notorious philanderer, but Diana was not content for their relationship to remain merely a discreetly sanctioned liaison of the kind which was openly tolerated among her set so long as scandal was contained. A month later, she told her husband Bryan she intended to leave him. Mosley had made it clear that he had no intention of getting a divorce from his wife, but Diana was so utterly convinced that they were meant to be together that she was prepared to throw away her marriage and her fortune, jeopardize her children and submit to social opprobrium to become no more than his official mistress.

Diana remained implacable in the face of appalled opposition from her parents, her in-laws and much of London society. She took a house at the north end of Eaton Square, 'the Eatonry', where Nancy, still in the no-man's-land of the failed deb, was glad to be given a room, and devoted herself to the man she called the Leader whenever his political duties allowed.

In May 1932, a month before the Guinness divorce was to be heard Cynthia Mosley died of a sudden attack of peritonitis. Diana was greatly in need of her sisters' support, and the day before the hearing, 14 June, Pamela and Unity joined Nancy at the Eatonry. Mosley arrived before supper, presenting Unity with a Fascist badge, and during the evening Hamish telephoned and asked for Diana. Nancy took the call, to be told, untruthfully, that Hamish was engaged to another woman. Unity, Diana and Mosley (Pamela, who could not bear Mosley's company, had left earlier), tactfully removed themselves and Hamish appeared to face the inevitable scene.

The letter Nancy wrote afterwards is generous and humble, straining for a somewhat abject dignity: 'Please think of me with affection always and never blame me for what I may become without you. Don't think of me as a selfish and hysterical woman, even if I appeared so tonight.'

The end of the affair was as much of a farce as the 'engagement' had been as Hamish had no intention of marrying Kit Dunn, the woman for whom he claimed he had jilted Nancy. Yet Nancy had to believe that the relationship which had cost her five years of her life had been real, so her letter must be read on her terms, not as pathetic grovelling, but as an attempt to invest the whole charade with some semblance of genuine feeling. Perhaps Diana's daring example suggested that it was not enough for a woman to sit passively by and wait for her prince to come; perhaps the humiliation of Hamish's behaviour was intolerable unless it could be proved that another man desired her. Either way, a week later, Nancy was engaged to another man.

4

FAUX PAS

Gaston's sybaritic student habits were about to receive a rude jolt. He had been excused military service in France for two years to permit him to complete his studies, but in November 1923 he was obliged to take up his post as a member of the 67th Infantry Regiment and attend the military college of St Cyr close to Paris. After his sophisticated independent existence at Oxford, Gaston was appalled by what he saw as the boorishness of barracks life, and swiftly managed to contract 'nervous depression', in light of which he was permitted to return to his parents' home. He had hardly changed out of his uniform before he was off for a spot of *flânerie* on the boulevards, at which point a military doctor, summoned urgently to treat a dangerously depressed soldier who had 'seen the walls of his bedroom advancing to crush him',[1] arrived at Rue de Grenelle to find his patient not at home. Back to barracks. Gaston endured his obligatory six months, though he left St Cyr with the lowly rank of sergeant, and was then instructed to report for duty by 1 June 1924 to the 1st Regiment of Zouaves, about to embark for Casablanca. The Zouaves were a distinctly un-Faubourg corps, light infantry drawn mainly from conscripts in France's North African colonies. In the nineteenth century they had enjoyed a reputation as an elite volunteer force, but though their record was exemplary and their uniform one of the most cheerful in the military, they were definitely not smart.

Gaston's career in the air force later proved him to be an exceptionally competent and courageous military man, but at this point he was disinclined towards the more active duties of regimental life. His colonel, Pompée, noticed this and kindly suggested Sergeant Palewski undertake the task of writing a history of the unit. Sergeant Palewski was equally disinclined towards regimental memoirs and consigned the job to a private who claimed to have a literature degree. When the finished opus was delivered to the colonel, he was horrified. Treachery and rivers of blood from slit Zouave throats were the main themes. The private turned out not to have a degree, but managed to substitute sacrifice and glory for murder and bloodshed to an extent which satisfied the colonel; still, it was the end for Sergeant Palewski of the Zouaves.

Gaston was spared total disgrace by the intervention of his first cousin Marcel Diamant-Berger, the elder son of his mother's brother Mayer-Saul, a successful military doctor. Marcel was ten years older, but the two men were close and would become closer. Unlike his feckless cousin, Marcel had already achieved military distinction, serving at the age of eighteen in the First World War as a sub-lieutenant in the cavalry. Wounded near Ingolstadt, he was imprisoned by the Germans at Hirschberg, from where he had attempted a daring escape, accompanied by a certain Captain Charles de Gaulle, like Gaston a graduate of St Cyr. He declared that the experience had created a fraternal link between himself and De Gaulle which would endure all their lives. Marcel then moved to the 1st African Cavalry Regiment, where he became part of the personal escort of the resident general of the French colony of Morocco, Hubert Lyautey. After leaving the army in 1919 to take up a business career, Marcel remained in contact with Lyautey, who had been impressed by him. When Lyautey, now promoted to the highest French military rank of maréchal, let it be known that he was looking for a young man to work as an attaché in his office, Marcel proposed Gaston for the post. So Sergeant Palewski left for Rabat on the Moroccan coast, since 1912 the administrative capital of the colony.

It is true to say of the three most politically extreme of the

Mitford sisters, Diana, Unity and Jessica, that their passionate beliefs were symbiotically entwined with equally passionate loves. Diana and Oswald Mosley, Unity and Adolf Hitler, Jessica and Esmond Romilly – the cause could not be separated from the man who espoused it. Nancy's own political views were less terrifyingly ideological, yet her 'cause', her belief in a particular value system, also came to be conflated with the very person of the man with whom she would fall in love. Considerations of Gaston Palewski's political career neglect to take into account that he possessed a similar trait. Like the Mitford girls, he had need of idols, and in Lyautey he found his first. It was his admiration for Lyautey and his need to excel to please him that transformed the unwilling soldier and dilettante *boulevardier* into one of the most brilliant and committed French politicians of his generation.

The situation between the Moroccan population and their French 'protectors' was one of suspicion and unrest. When Gaston took up his post, the tribes of the Rif mountains, in a confederation led by Abdelkrim El Khattabi, had been fighting the French and Spanish armies for three years. El Khattabi was loyal to the Moroccan sultan, Moulay Youssef, who feared disturbing the concord he had achieved with the French occupiers, yet continued to rally the tribes with a view to a future revolution. France, which controlled the majority of the country, was lending aid to the Spanish who, after a disastrous defeat at Anoual, were confined to a few coastal outposts. Lyautey's policy was one of 'capitalist colonization' aimed at equipping the country for eventual independence, an approach that set him at odds with many members of the French government, who favoured exploitative assimilation as practised in Algeria. Lyautey's vice-regal lifestyle did little to endear him to a strongly republican Cabinet, and in 1925 Maréchal Pétain was sent to Rabat on what purported to be a visit of inspection. Lyautey dispatched Gaston to Paris to discuss with the secretary general of the Ministry of Foreign Affairs the impossibility of governing alongside Pétain, but in September that year the command was handed to Pétain and Theodore Steeg was named as resident general, a solution that pleased everybody except the Moroccans.

Gaston's position with Lyautey thus lasted just eight months, but he found it both inspiring and influential. Lyautey lived by a maxim whose spirit Gaston adopted as his own: 'The soul's joy lies in doing.'[2] The marshal was a member of the Académie Française, deeply read, always immaculately presented. The conversation in the dining room of the residence at Rabat, with its fountains and terrace of orange trees, was 'the gayest and most brilliant I have been lucky enough to hear'. Though Lyautey was a monarchist, many of his ideas chimed with what became known as Gaullism – respect for social hierarchy with an emphasis on religion as a cohesive force, belief in order, a dislike of revolutionary thinking, a paternalistic approach to social welfare. To Gaston, posing as an aesthete suddenly seemed rather embarrassing. Lyautey taught him that it was possible to be intensely devoted to a duty while retaining all the refinements of a cultivated existence. Dominique Palewski remembered Gaston's 'classical elegance',[3] his taste for beauty and the life of the spirit, which melded seamlessly with his integrity and commitment to political service – qualities Gaston himself attributed to the lessons of Lyautey.

On his return to Paris, though, Gaston was unsure what to do next. He had vague dreams of an attaché's posting to Peking, but they collapsed when he discovered the necessity of sitting a competitive examination. He was determined on success, but was still arrogant enough to demand it on his own terms.

5

THE FASCISTERS

When she met Gaston Palewski in 1942, Nancy had long since decided that her husband, Peter Rodd, was the most boring man in the world. She minded less about his fecklessness, drunkenness, laziness and dishonesty, but she had already acknowledged to herself that their marriage was a failure. In a matter of days she had rebounded straight from the unwilling arms of Hamish St Clair Erskine into an engagement with Peter, and now, twelve years on, she was no longer prepared to keep up her impeccable 'shop-front', even to herself.

In his favour, the Hon. Peter Rodd, known, inevitably, as Prod, was genuinely brilliant. He had been a Balliol man, in the days when that meant something, at least until he was sent down for entertaining women in his rooms. He was an extremely gifted linguist and appeared to be an expert on the most recondite subjects. He was also gloriously handsome, a tow-haired Adonis with an enthusiastically heterosexual reputation. Evelyn Waugh described his looks as reminiscent of the 'sulky arrogance' of the young Rimbaud, his features combining a classical hauteur and sensuality to give him a look of 'a chorister on his way to a brothel'.[1] And he was, in Diana's words, 'wild', which may have appealed to the reforming, maternal instinct Nancy had so embarrassingly wasted on Hamish. He was also very cosmopolitan, a result of his upbringing as one of the five children of a highly glamorous diplomatic couple, Lord and Lady Rennell. After serving in Egypt, Sweden, Norway, Abyssinia and Germany, Peter's father, Rennell Rodd, had been appointed ambassador to Rome in 1908, and Peter and his brothers grew up multilingual and rootless in an endless shift of different schools and countries.

After his ignominious departure from Balliol, Peter was sent down the traditional black sheep's route of a job abroad, in a Brazilian bank. He spent his time there drinking and polishing up his Russian and Portuguese before being arrested as a destitute and extracted by his elder brother Francis, who worked at the Foreign Office. Peter clearly had a promising future as a loser, and this was the first of many times when his family would be obliged to bail him out. Brazil was followed by a short spell in the City (sacked), a post with *The Times* in Germany (sacked), then a two-year trip with the patient Francis to the Sahara. When he became reacquainted with Nancy, whom he knew slightly from the debutante scene, he was employed by an American bank in Lombard Street, though within the first year of their marriage he had once again lost his job.

Perhaps, having tried most other things, Peter fancied having a go at wedlock. Or, to take a kindlier view, perhaps he was seeking ballast, something to pin down his waywardness and force him to grow up. Either way, he had proposed to numerous women – on one occasion, two in a single night – before Nancy accepted him at a party, and though he wrote to her suggesting squirmingly that the proposal had merely been a joke, Nancy for once refused to see it. Battered by Hamish's rejection and veering dangerously close to the fearsome age of thirty, she too had found a life raft and she was determined to cling to it. Nancy had certainly become engaged to Peter with painful alacrity, but she was no longer the immature girl who had made eyes at Hamish while her serious suitor proposed. Peter represented pretty much her last chance, and she knew it. In the volume of family letters she edited, *The Stanleys of Alderley*, Nancy is quite hard on the 'old, pathetic, ugly' spinster daughters, Rianette and Louisa. Jessica goes into more detail about the terrible fate of the Maiden Aunt, a gentle, wispy type who lived alone in a small London flat with one maid. The status of the Maiden Aunt had remained generally unchanged since Victorian days. She subsisted on an allowance carefully designed to provide minimum necessaries, a sum considered sufficient but not excessive for Unmarried Daughters and Younger Sons of peers. Whereas the Younger Sons were free to supplement their income by going into a profession, the armed services, Empire Building or even Trade, such avenues were firmly closed to the Unmarried Daughters, who as time went on sank into the twilight state of aunthood.[2]

This was quite a realistic possibility to Nancy: a lifetime's dependence, resented and resentful, on her father and brother. Little had changed for the impoverished gentlewoman since Jane Austen wrote *Sense and Sensibility*: to Nancy, a lifetime's dependence on father then brother, resented and resentful, was quite a realistic possibility. Marriage would bring freedom, status and, she thought, a secure social position, and Peter was now her only prospect of acquiring them.

At first, they both decided to be madly in love. Peter wrote to Hamish, saving Nancy's dignity with an honourable fiction: 'It is absurd for me to pretend that I am sorry for taking your Nancy from you, but I know that it is hell for you and I wish it wasn't, I am so much in love with her that I can understand how you feel.' To Nancy he gushed: 'Darling, darling ... My darling I am glad this all started as a joke, I love you I love you, my darling ... I should like to see your head lying on your pillow. This Peter who loves only you.'

The Rennells were less convinced. When they read of the engagement in the *Daily Telegraph* (Peter had not troubled to tell them the news), they found it inexplicable. Lady Rennell suggested that 'as usual, it was all made up'. But Peter had manfully sat through a two-hour luncheon with Lord Redesdale at Rutland Gate and obtained his consent. He even managed to remain sober for the occasion. 'Well, the happiness,' wrote Nancy to Mark Ogilvie-Grant. 'Oh goodness gracious I am happy. You *must* get married darling, everybody should if they want a receipt for absolute bliss.' Bounding towards the altar on waves of joy, Nancy was even prepared to like her new in-laws, an opinion she was swiftly to revise. When the Rennells came to spend a weekend at Swinbrook, with Nancy in permanent terror lest Lord Redesdale explode, she pronounced them 'charming' and Lady Rennell 'really rather gorgeous'.

A pretty little house was found for the couple, Rose Cottage at Strand-on-the-Green near Kew. Nancy knew that they were going to be 'damn poor' but was clearly thrilled at the prospect of escaping her ageing-deb status and finally beginning life as an adult woman. Peter struck a rather ominous note as to his expectations of his bride when he remarked that Lord Redesdale refused to 'tie himself up about a settlement. I hope he does his stuff about your allowance even if he sours on the marriage', but Nancy was too happy to pay attention. She ordered her wedding dress, in white chiffon with narrow frills, which was to be a present from her thoughtful ex-brother-in-law Bryan Guinness, and decided on a bouquet of white gardenias and roses. The eleven page boys were to wear white satin, while the mother of the bride opted for brown velvet and a plumed hat. Lord Redesdale gave his eldest daughter away at St John's, Smith Square, on Monday 4 December 1933 and, after a reception for over two hundred guests at Rutland Gate, Nancy changed into the dark green woollen coat and skirt and the duck-egg jumper (carefully chosen to 'go with' though not to 'match' her suit) in which she was to begin married life.

Peter's parents lent their apartment in the Palazzo Giulia in Rome for the honeymoon. Although Nancy loved Italy, she never quite took to the Eternal City. To Mark Ogilvie-Grant, she wrote teasingly: 'I am having a really dreadful time, dragging a sprained ankle round major and minor basilicas and suffering horrible indigestion from eating goats' cheese. However, I manage to keep my spirits up somehow. PS And all my shoes hurt.' And to Unity: 'Why do people always say they don't enjoy honeymoons?

I am adoring mine.' The hint of the negative is just a little too strong for the joke to take. In a *Sunday Times* essay of 1952, Nancy commented that 'Arnold Bennett once said that "pavement" is the most beautiful word in the English language, a sentiment which must be echoed by anyone who has ever tottered about on Roman cobbles and splashed in and out of Roman puddles, trying to avoid death from the huge buses which squeeze their way between the palaces at ninety miles an hour'. Nancy's true feelings about her honeymoon came out in *Pigeon Pie*, her 1939 novel of the 'Phoney War'. The husband of the heroine, Sophia Garfield, is purportedly modelled on Francis Rodd, while Peter is cast as the dashing, raffish lover Rudolph, but many of the brothers' traits are conflated. Sophia ponders:

> How soon she began to realize he was a pompous prig she could not remember. He was a sight-seeing bore and took her the Roman rounds with dutiful assiduity, and without ever allowing her to sit on a stone and use her eyes. Her jokes annoyed and never amused him; when she said that all the sites in Rome were called after London cinemas, he complained that she was insular, facetious and babyish.

But in many ways, Nancy *was*. She and Peter did in fact share a sense of humour, and she would make a point of repeating his better lines to her correspondents, including Gaston, throughout his life. He made her laugh a lot, always the most important characteristic for Nancy, and one of his better-known teases, declining an invitation from Von Ribbentrop to the German Embassy in Yiddish, was a perfect example of the alignment of their humour (though Nancy did remove the letter from the post as she feared it would create unpleasant publicity). But even as early as the honeymoon, Nancy sensed that she would never prove capable of really holding Peter. Curling Hamish's hair had hardly prepared her for a full physical relationship, so one wonders about the sex. The enforced intimacies of a honeymoon (sharing a bed is one thing, sharing a bathroom quite another) lurk behind the slightly awkward cheerfulness of her letters.

Peter was an experienced lover but, like many Englishmen of his generation, and like Sir Conrad in *The Blessing*, he appeared to prefer to make love with ladies whose profession it was. A nervous twenty-nine-year-old virgin with a tendency to shriek could hardly have been an arousing prospect.

The extent of Nancy's actual sexual experience is difficult to ascertain. Peter's sister described her disparagingly as 'shop-soiled', though that may have been merely a reference to her long 'affair' with Hamish. The world of the Bright Young Things floats in a historical miasma of licentiousness, but one historian of the period notes that it was in fact one of the most 'tightly regulated' eras in English history.[3] Avid press coverage of outrageous parties disguised the fact that young women like Nancy still lived in a constrained and chaperoned society in which the sexes occupied largely separate spheres. Assuming that Nancy *was* aware of Hamish's tendencies (and Driberg's delights aside, there are enough hints in *Highland Fling* and *Christmas Pudding* to suggest that she was), had their protracted engagement been a means of evading a mature sexual relationship? Nancy's mother could not have been much help on the subject. When a friend explained to her what she might expect on her own wedding night, she recoiled in horror – 'a gentleman would *never* do anything like that'[4] – and when Nancy went on to experience gynaecological difficulties, she remarked vaguely that she thought women had millions of eggs, 'like sturgeon'. No one could mistake the physical passion that flourished between Diana and Mosley, and in a later diary entry Nancy observed that love was a 'punchy physical affair', but it seems reasonable to infer that when she married, she was unprepared for its reality and that Peter, on subsequent evidence, was a keener tour guide than he was a seducer.

Evelyn Waugh was encouraging. 'I do think it's top-hole about you and Rodd, and I foresee a very wild and vigorous life in front of you.' All the same, he added while he was glad to think Hamish would now disappear from her work, 'I won't have you writing books about Rodd because that would be too much to bear.' In fact it was Evelyn who really immortalized Peter, as Basil Seal in *Black Mischief, Put Out More Flags* and the late story, poignant in the light of what actually became of him, *Basil Seal Rides Again.*

Whether she enjoyed or merely endured her honeymoon, Nancy set about married life with gusto and continuing assertions of happiness. She declared that she was learning to be 'a rather wonderful old housewife', and though she never learned to cook anything much beyond scrambled eggs, she was successful in turning Rose Cottage into a truly pretty house. Lady Redesdale had always had a talent for charming interiors, what Alexander Mosley called a gift for *mise en scène*, which was inherited by Nancy and Diana and, on a much grander scale, by Deborah, and her taste for spare lines, delicate colours, beautiful furniture and simple, delicious food characterized her daughters' homes. As she would later at Rue Monsieur, Nancy hung festooned curtains, framing her views of the garden and the river, and with the help of Mark Ogilvie-Grant picked up cheap, effective pieces such as a sofa and a carved chimneypiece that complemented an Aubusson carpet and her beloved Sheraton writing desk. 'That little house was really exquisite, there wasn't an ugly thing in it,' Deborah commented. The *Evening Standard* even wrote up an evening of bridge-playing as 'a gay, light-hearted affair' even if Nancy did have to contrive space for her guests by cramming the tables into the bedroom.

Compared with most of their contemporaries, the Rodds were poor. 'Not poor like poor people,' Nancy admitted, but beyond providing necessities like a servant and, later, a car, their income of £500 per year – made up of parental allowance, Peter's salary, Nancy's journalism and the earnings from the shares she had bought with the profits from her two novels – didn't go far. Peter soon chucked his City job on a vague promise of a better post at £600 per year, but inevitably it never materialized, and Lord Rennell was left wondering whether 'their house is healthy and they get enough to eat and keep warm ... I should like to be reassured that these repeated attacks of flu are not the result of inadequate resources.' Lord Rennell occasionally slipped a discreet hand-out to Nancy behind his wife's back, but Lady Rennell was blithely brazen about the fact that she gave much less money to Peter than to her other children. He always seemed to get by somehow, she claimed. How he got by was mostly Nancy.

Wigs on the Green, Nancy's third novel, which she began in early 1934, caused a cataclysmic row within the Mitford family and has remained her most contentious book. Nancy herself refused to allow her publishers to reissue it after the war, when anything with her name on it was a guaranteed bestseller. 'We were young and high spirited then and didn't know about Buchenwald,' she wrote to Evelyn. But before considering the political context, the financial circumstances of its production are worth recalling. Quite early in her marriage, Nancy had to confront the fact that Peter simply didn't care enough for her to rouse himself from his over-entitled indolence. As ever, she put a good face on his incompetence, joking about what a lovely new set of bailiffs they were acquiring and inviting the embarrassed debt-collectors in for tea, but it was a horrible humiliation. Whenever Nancy did have some money Peter would 'borrow' or quite simply steal it from her in order to go off on a 'bat' in the London nightclubs. He refused to acknowledge her growing anxiety and was quite shameless about living off his wife. *Wigs* is in many ways an inadequate book, but also, in context, a brave one. There is a whiff of Grub Street about the novel, written swiftly in a cold house with the bills stacking up on the table and the duns at the door. Not quite *Richard Savage*, yet those who see Nancy as the frivolous child of privilege fail to recognize how urgent it was to her, at the time, to produce something that would permit the Rodd ménage to flounder on a little longer with some degree of self-respect.

Lord Redesdale and Hitler had similar views on make-up. Much to the despair of his daughters, the former, like his alter ego Uncle Matthew, 'liked to see female complexions in a state of nature and often pronounced that paint was for whores'. On her first trip to Paris Nancy had mourned the parental edict against powder ('the others look *too* lovely'). No wonder, then, that the younger Mitfords slapped it on with such enthusiasm when safely out of sight, to the extent that Unity, who refused to do without lipstick, even scotched her first opportunity to meet Hitler rather than give up her warpaint. In the spring of 1933, Diana Guinness had been introduced to Putzi Hanfstaengl, a press-relations officer who had known Hitler for twelve years. This 'very interesting German' promised to introduce Diana to the Chancellor if she could come to the Nazi Parteitag, the first Nuremberg rally, in September.

Tom Mosley (as Oswald was always known to family and friends) had begun an affair with his married sister-in-law Baba Curzon after his wife's death. That summer, he was on a motor tour of France with his new mistress. Diana, in need of distraction from this latest evidence of the callousness of the man for whom she had sacrificed her life, suggested to Unity that they take a trip to Bavaria. They travelled from Munich to Nuremberg, where Putzi met them at the station and reacted with horror to their heavily made-up faces, not at all the sort of thing that pure, cosmetic-free Aryan womanhood was supposed to go in for. Despite vigorous backstage wiping, Putzi was unable to make good on his promise, but Unity and Diana were nonetheless overwhelmed by the Parteitag, three days of parades, speeches and rapturous saluting which confirmed them both in their absolute belief in Fascism. The Redesdales were disgusted and furious when they discovered what Diana had done. 'I suppose you know without being told how absolutely horrified Muv and I were to think of you and Bobo accepting any form of hospitality from people we regard as a murderous gang of pests,' wrote Lord Redesdale, but Unity had already decided on returning to Nuremberg the following year to embark on her quest to meet her idol.

Given the Redesdales' views on Nazism at the time, it seems astonishing that the next year Lady Redesdale accompanied

Unity to Munich to settle her into 121 Königstrasse, the home of Baroness Laroche, who took in English girls *en pension*. From then until the end of Unity's life, Germany was her home and Hitler her obsession. On 9 February 1935, after a prolonged campaign of stalking and staring, Unity was able to write to her father describing 'the most wonderful and beautiful' day of her life. Hitler summoned her to his table in the Osteria Bavaria restaurant and they had a long conversation, at the end of which the Führer presented his twenty-one-year-old fan with a signed postcard: 'To Fräulein Unity Mitford as a friendly memento of Germany and Adolf Hitler.' Four months later, Nancy was writing to her sister:

> Darling Head of Bone and Heart of Stone,
> Oh dear oh dear the book comes out on Tuesday. Oh dear, I won't let Rodd give a party for it ... oh dear I wish I had never been born into such a family of fanatics. Oh dear ... I wish I had called it mein uncomf now because uncomf is what I feel when ever I think about it. Oh dear.

In many respects, *Wigs on the Green* is less a political novel than a 'light, accomplished comedy of manners',[6] like its two predecessors. If anything, it is less concerned with Fascism than with the problem of Peter, to whom it is dedicated. He appears as Jasper Aspect, a charming wastrel who lives 'from one day to another, picking up by fair means or foul enough cash for the needs of the moment and being dragged out of the bankruptcy courts about once every three years by protesting relations'. Nancy's narrative voice might be that of Amabelle Fortescue. Love is viewed with a fashionable, hard-edged cynicism, as an 'unethical and anti-social emotion' and Jasper's fecklessness justified by his remark that wives might as well keep their husbands, since although women have to endure pregnancy, chaps get hangovers, after all. Her marriage is dissected briskly and sharply and turned into a joke, since a joke was what she had to live with.

The Fascist parts of the novel centre on the beautiful, fanatical heiress, Eugenia Malmains, Unity to the life: strapping, blonde, with eyes like 'enormous blue headlamps' and her evangelical zeal for the 'Union Jack' movement, led by Captain Jack (who, in deference to Diana, never appears in the novel at all). Nancy was quick to protest to Diana that the novel couldn't possibly damage her beloved Mosley's cause.

> A book of this kind *can't* do your movement any harm. Honestly, if I thought it could set the Leader back by so much as half an hour I would have scrapped it, or indeed never written it in the first place ... I still maintain that it is far more in favour of Fascism than otherwise. Far the nicest character in the book is a Fascist and the others all become much nicer as soon as they have joined up. But I also know your point of view, that Fascism is something too serious to be dealt with in a funny book at all. Surely that is unreasonable? Fascism is now such a notable feature of modern life all over the world that it must be possible to consider it in any context when attempting to give a picture of life as it is lived today.

Diana and Unity were by no means the only people to be enraptured by Hitler. Despite the fact that, as a political movement, pacifism was by far stronger than either Fascism or Communism during this period, in the early Thirties Mosley was still respectable and Fascism was considered by many as a serious force for good. The *Observer* compared the two leaders in 1933: 'Where Mosley is like Hitler is in his sense of the dramatic. There is an extraordinary sense of drama about a Mosley meeting, a sense that great things are about to happen.' In January 1934, the *Daily Mail* was trumpeting 'Hurrah for the Blackshirts' from its front page.

Nancy's own declared support of Fascism was, as Diana knew, initially borne out by fact. Just before her marriage, Nancy had heard Oswald Mosley speak in Oxford and in 1934 she and Peter had bought black shirts and attended several BUF meetings, joining the 15,000 strong crowd at the notorious Olympia rally of 7 June 1934. Nancy herself chimed in that summer with an article for the *Vanguard* entitled 'Fascism as I See It'. Possibly this departure from her usual field of *Vogue* and *The Lady* was a pre-emptive strike against potential criticism of her novel, and certainly its conclusion is strikingly similar to one of Eugenia's rousing perorations. Nancy denounced a culture where 'respect for parents, love of the home, veneration of marriage ties is at a discount' and where only the authority of a great leader would be able to lift the country 'from the slough of despond in which it has too long weltered'. Nancy's article came out in July. But however sincere she may have been at Olympia, and however 'pretty' Peter looked in his black shirt, she now saw Fascism as a joke.

Unity, for once, was more prescient than the editor of the *Left Review*, who described the piece as 'a very well-developed case of leaderolatry'. Unity, though, knew a Mitford gag when she saw one and recognized the article for the parody it was. 'I'm furious about it,' she wrote. 'You might have a little thought for poor me, all the boys know I'm your sister you know.' She also warned Nancy that she had heard about *Wigs* from Lady Redesdale and threatened that she would never speak to her sister again if it was published.

But Nancy did publish, and she was prepared to risk her relationships with the Fascisters in order to do so. Hitler might not as yet have been considered a monster, and the BUF might have attracted an estimated 40,000 adherents at the peak of its respectability, but even at this stage there were dissenting voices, and those voices were audible in the Mitford sisters' circle. In the autumn of 1933, while Diana was staying in Rome with Gerald Berners after her first Nuremberg rally, Victor Gollancz had published *The Brown Book of the Hitler Terror* by a group calling itself the World Committee for the Victims of German Fascism. Containing a list of over 250 murders carried out by the Nazis since 3 March that year, it detailed, with photographs, the appalling treatment of the Jews under the Reich, the application of anti-Semitic laws and the number of German intellectuals and scientists who had been driven into exile by those laws. In her autobiography, Jessica Mitford described her passionate reaction to the book and the 'bitter rows' that ensued between herself, Unity and Diana who, according to Jessica, claimed that these atrocities were justified in pursuit of the Nazi goal.

Unity was prepared to dismiss the claims of the Brown Book even though she had experienced them at first hand. In June 1933, she had attended an Oxford production of *A Midsummer Night's Dream*, staged by the great director Max Reinhardt. Having fled Germany along with Einstein and Thomas Mann, Reinhardt was reduced to working with undergraduates. Unity was also friends with Anthony Rumbold, whose father, Sir Horace, was British ambassador to Berlin from 1928 to 1933. Sir Horace was a virulent critic of Nazism, stating in his final dispatch: 'It would be misleading to base any hopes on a return to sanity ... [the German] government is encouraging an attitude of mind which can only end one way.' His notes were shown by the then foreign secretary, Sir John Simon, to the Mitfords' cousin Winston Churchill. They were found sufficiently 'disquieting' to make them instrumental in the passing of the 1936 Public Order Act, aimed largely at restraining the excesses of the increasingly militaristic BUF. In a well-publicized incident, Anthony Rumbold himself was beaten up by a stormtrooper captain and ejected from Germany in February 1934. That same month, two manifestos on 'Liberty and Democratic Leadership' were issued, numbering Harold Macmillan, the art historian Kenneth Clark and Virginia Woolf among their signatories, while in March, the establishment of the Comité de Vigilance des Intellectuels Antifascistes in Paris was reported in the British press. In 1935, the pro-Labour *Daily Herald* reported a survey finding that millions of Britons across the political spectrum disapproved of Fascism. Closer to home, Robert Byron, a friend of both Nancy and Diana, had been an outspoken opponent of the Nazis since the early Thirties.

When she stated in her autobiography, 'it goes without saying that apart from the politicians who gave the orders and the unfortunates who obeyed them, nobody in Germany or Britain knew anything about what was happening', Diana Mosley was articulating what has become a conventional view of the Holocaust. But the fact that most evidence about what was occurring in Germany in the 1930s was dismissed as left-wing propaganda does not mean that either politicians or ordinary people were entirely unaware of what was taking place. Collective ignorance was a more effective cognitive defence when the full horror of the camps was revealed, and this justification for a crime of monstrous neglect has remained broadly unchallenged.

Nancy's biographers have been at a loss to explain the political change of heart that took place between her attendance at Fascist rallies early in 1933, her increasing disaffection by July 1934 and her evident contempt by the time of *Wig*'s publication. How had the cheering supporter at Olympia become the sharp satirist of just a month later? Nancy was not a hypocrite: she simply changed her mind, as careful consideration of the chronology of her dissent demonstrates.

Before their marriage, in May 1933, Peter had lunched at the Café Royal with Harold Nicolson. He described the atmosphere in Germany, from where he had just returned after his ignominiously brief stint as a *Times* correspondent, as one of 'complete terror'. Conceivably, Nancy and Peter might initially have thought, along with far more experienced political players than themselves, that Mosley's brand of Fascism was to be a form of National Socialism-lite, the dynamism without the brutality. Curiosity and family feeling accounted for the rest.

However, the events of the Olympia meeting soured Nancy's perception of Fascism irrevocably. As Mosley waited for the fanfares of trumpets and cheering to die down before beginning his speech, violence broke out in the crowd. Medical evidence from the sixty or so protesters who were taken to hospital showed that Mosley's Blackshirt guard had come prepared with knuckledusters and razors. In a civil yet pointed correspondence in the *Daily Mail*, Lord Rothermere firmly withdrew his support. 'I have made it quite clear in my conversations with you [Mosley] that I could never support any movement with an anti-semitic bias, any movement which has dictatorship as one of its objectives or any movement which will support a "Corporate State" for the Parliamentary institutions of this country.'

In October 1934, between the publication of Nancy's July article and the release of her novel in June 1935, Mosley addressed another crowd at Olympia in terms which were explicitly anti-Semitic. International Jewry, he stated, was mobilized six to one against Fascism, and he could prove that BUF members had been victimized by Jews, who 'owe allegiance not to our empire but to friends, relatives and kith and kin in other nations, and they know that Fascism will not tolerate anyone who owes allegiance to a foreign country'. He concluded with the well-known statement that Britain would not fight Germany in a Jewish quarrel, a tacit admission of the persecution his followers were elsewhere so keen to deny as left-wing propaganda. In March 1935, in a speech at Leicester, his remarks were self-avowedly even more anti-Semitic, so much so that he received an encouraging telegram from the rabid German anti-Semite Julius Streicher.

Nancy had learned enough to turn her gushing support for Mosley's charisma into what became an increasingly fervent hatred. The fact that in *Wigs* Fascism is seen as a joke has led her to be accused of political shallowness, an inability to react to the proximity in her own family of 'a grotesque and sinister political movement'[7] with anything other than schoolroom in-jokes. Yet as the German newspaper *Der Spiegel* recently commented: 'The ultimate way to shrink a myth is to make it laughable.' Nancy recognized an innate silliness in Fascism and ruthlessly sent up the pompously childish posturing, the uniforms and the marching that so enthralled her sisters.

'The Union Jack movement is a youth movement,' Eugenia cried passionately, 'we are tired of the old ... We see nothing admirable in that debating society of old and corrupt men called Parliament.'

At this point a very old lady came up to the crowd ... 'Eugenia, my child,' she said brokenly, 'Do get off that tub ... Oh! When her ladyship hears of this I don't know what will happen.'

'Go away, Nanny,' said Eugenia.

Nancy was not the only Mitford to perceive an inherent absurdity in Fascism. Pamela, in spite of her own distinctly right-wing politics, also objected to Mosley's 'ridiculous, play-acting behaviour'.[8] Even in her letter to Diana describing the early Oxford rally, where she described him as a 'wonderful speaker', Nancy couldn't resist exposing her sister to the reality of what Mosley's supporters were doing. 'There were several fascinating fights, as he brought along a few Neanderthal men with him ... One man complained afterwards that the fascists' nails had pierced his head *to the skull.* Bobo was wonderful, cheering on we few, we happy few. Longing to see you, darling ...' At this stage, Nancy's absolute refusal to take her sisters' politics seriously, employing a tone which permitted their relationships to continue in that arch, teasing Mitford style, was the only means she had of expressing her dismay to them, but there is an urgency to the comedy of *Wigs on the Green*, an attempt to defuse the myth before it went too tragically far. She herself regretted this attempt to reduce Fascism to nursery silliness, an approach that has taken three-quarters of a century to become palatable.

What would she have made of the fact that in 2009 storm-troopers once more paraded along the Unter den Linden in the guise of the tapdancing showgirls of Mel Brooks's 1968 musical comedy *The Producers*? Doubtless she would have relished the detail that in publicity for the show the swastika, which is still banned as an unconstitutional symbol in Germany, had to be replaced with a large pretzel. Or of Daniel Levy's film *The Truest*

Truth About Adolf Hitler, featuring a dog in Nazi uniform, a joke anticipated by Nancy in Eugenia's pet, Reichshund? Or of the rap 'Cool Mein Führer', featuring Hitler going street in a baseball cap? The novel's picture of Fascism in the 1930s does not demonstrate a 'failure of imagination,'[9] rather the hope that the movement would be recognized as the ridiculous showing off it then was. Perhaps what is really discomfiting about *Wigs* is that Nancy got there first, and the immeasurable pity that Europe took so long to get the joke.

Nancy had offered to let Diana see the book and excise any offensive passages, but she was not prepared to scrap it. She did make some amendments, observing to her sister, with her allowance from Bryan Guinness of £2,500 per year, that the Rodds' finances had already been seriously affected by the novel's having missed the spring list as a result. The sisters had a last day in Oxford together before publication on 25 June, after which Nancy had to endure the clouds of Diana's displeasure. The estrangement begun by the book did not really end for ten years. Nancy and Diana met occasionally and wrote to one another, but after Diana married Mosley in 1936, Nancy was forbidden to stay at their Staffordshire home. The sisters did not really become close again until the Mosleys moved to the Temple de la Gloire at Orsay in the early 1950s.

6

THE PURSUIT OF HONOUR

I n 1919, Prince Antoine Bibesco brought his fiancée, Elizabeth Asquith, to the bedside of his dear friend Marcel Proust. Proust, somewhat embarrassed to receive Miss Asquith *en déshabille*, nonetheless pronounced himself enchanted by the encounter. Many of Proust's circle, however, disapproved of the bourgeois Jewish doctor's son whose only object in life seemed to have been to ingratiate himself in the Faubourg. Although Proust had already published two volumes of *A la Recherche du Temps Perdu*, they felt that he would make much better use of his genius if he were not so fond of society. A decade later, Maurice and Rose Palewski, whose son was also a close friend of Bibesco, were having similar thoughts. In 1927, Maurice had bought a property at Louveciennes, west of Paris in the Seine-et-Oise. He and Rose devoted their retirement to improving the property, but though Gaston had a room there, he rarely used it. He preferred strolling round the Invalides in intense discussion with his friend Marcel Fouchet, or talking vaguely about a thesis he intended to write on English painting, which never got further than the title. His concerned parents felt that having made such a promising beginning under Lyautey, their talented son was settling into eternal studentdom.

Proust's *Pastiches et Mélanges* notes the encounter with Antoine and Elizabeth, whom he compares to a beauty stepped down from an Italian fresco. He also added a late subplot concerning a parvenu First Empire family and the attempts of 'Saint-Simon', convinced that the most vital interests of the state are founded on the rights of dukes, to undermine them. The irony of the pastiche is not so much Saint-Simon's absurdity, but that it is 'Proust himself, "the little Proust", who had travelled the Guermantes way and emerged far beyond', who is speaking of the Faubourg Saint-Germain 'from the standpoint of a social superior, with the bitter diction and violent syntax and in the haughty person of the great memorialist'.[1] Gaston never aspired to despise, but he yearned desperately to belong.

Gaston's connection with Proust was through Jacques-Emile Blanche, the painter whose Sunday afternoon salons formed an important centre for his early Parisian social life. The décor of Persian rugs and chintz gave Gaston an advance taste of the 'artistic' houses he would come to know later in Chelsea. Proust had contributed the preface to Blanche's *Propos de Peintre*, but this friendship, 'an amity armed to the teeth',[2] collapsed when Proust's star outshone that of his friend. Chez Blanche, Gaston came to know many of the living prototypes for Proust's characters; while his parents fretted about his idleness, he was setting out on his course *du côté de chez Guermantes*.

It was through Blanche that Gaston met Antoine Bibesco, who lived on the enchanted Ile St Louis, at 45 Quai Bourbon. His mother, Princesse Marthe Bibesco, played duets with Fauré and knew Liszt, Wagner and Debussy. She became a friend and lifelong correspondent of Gaston's. There were Vuillards on the gold-leafed walls which, with their antique mirrors, presented a mosaic appearance that Proust compared to San Marco; Odilon Redon and Bonnard were regular visitors. Antoine and Elizabeth lived above, amid eighteenth-century vases and panels by Boucher. Their parties were international and political. Antoine, who would have been in his forties when Gaston first knew him, was a successful diplomat. Gaston met Leon Blum, the poetess Anna de Noailles, Lord Lloyd, in an atmosphere which, he wrote, 'was one of those privileged environments where one can capture the essence of a civilization: it was that of French Europe'. It was this 'essence', in which Nancy and Gaston shared such a fervent belief, that coloured both their lives with joy and melancholy.

Gaston was fascinated by Antoine's family in much the same manner as he was later fascinated by the Mitfords. They used a private language – secrets for example, were 'tombs' and anyone who violated them 'hyenas' – and, of course, he 'tutoyed' Proust.

The Bibescos knew everyone, including the originals of Proust's impossibly grand Guermantes family, derived from the Castellanes and the Talleyrand-Périgords. Boni de Castellane, who contributed some aspects of the character of the Marquis de Saint-Loup, had been 'the most brilliant young man in Parisian society' until his American wife grew tired of his extravagance. Boni's mother was a model for the Princesse de Guermantes, his aunt, the Princesse Marie de Radziwill (*née* Castellane, her mother was a Talleyrand-Périgord) once thanked him for taking her to luncheon at the Ritz by saying she was particularly grateful as she had never before dined at an inn. Gaston obviously remembered Boni's anecdotes about Aimery de la Roche-foucauld, nicknamed 'Placement' for his addiction to etiquette, as this makes its way into *The Blessing*. Marriage for love is all very well, but why exchange a few nights of passion for a whole lifetime at the wrong end of the table?

Gaston's attitude to his own family was ambivalent. He was proud of his father and had a close relationship with his Diamant-Berger cousin Marcel. He never concealed either his Polish or his Jewish roots, but nor did he ever emphasize them. Jean-Paul was much more interested in his family history and visited Poland several times, persuading Gaston to accompany him there in 1921, when they visited an aunt at Wilno on a trip which also included Poznan and Warsaw. Presumably both Palewski boys knew Polish, though their parents had not insisted that they follow the Jewish faith, and they both converted to Christianity. In 1923 in the chapel of Saint Joseph de Cluny in Paris's four-teenth arrondissement, Gaston was received into the Catholic church by Abbé Mugnier, a fashionable priest who was much sought after as a confessor by smart Parisiennes. His godfather was Henri Bremond, a former Jesuit and distinguished literary critic. Gaston's choice of spiritual counsellors does not appear uncalculated – this last step to assimilation contained an element of social ambition – but in his own writing he reveals himself on occasion as a sincere, if somewhat sentimental Christian.

Through the diaspora of the Polish intelligentsia in which his uncle Michel Rabbinowicz moved, Gaston came to know Jean Godebski. Jean's father, the sculptor Cyprien Godebski, lived in a sixth-floor flat whose extreme modesty was the inverse of the glamour of his guests. Ravel was Jean's godfather, Gide and Poulenc were intimates and the walls of the scruffy apartment were hung with portraits of Cyprien by his friends Manet and Renoir. Gaston was on his way to being a crashing snob, but he had too much respect for genuine talent and sensibility not to admire the Godebskis, who devoted their lives to their brilliant friends. He was as thrilled to share a glass of orangeade with Stravinsky or Satie as a dish of Belle Epoque champagne with the Princesse Bibesco.

Moving in such exalted circles, it was unsurprising that Gaston seemed disaffected by his own relatively modest life, so his family were astonished when he found a job at Boivin, a small, conservative publishing house near the Place Saint-Sulpice. He tried to interest the director in a series of his own devising, 'What you need to know about . . .' (if only he had known Prod then). It was not accepted; still, he stuck it out for two years. When Jean-Paul visited him in his gloomy office he remarked cheerfully: 'See how low I've sunk!' Eventually his boss offered him a partnership in the business, but Gaston admitted with relief that he hadn't a penny to invest and resigned. Rose Palewski stepped in and wangled him a job at a prototype think-tank through her friend Mme Raymond Poincaré, with whom she took singing lessons. The *Bulletin Quotidien*, whose office was at 282 Boulevard Saint-Germain, produced daily reports on the political and economic situation with a right-wing bias. The atmosphere was young, energetic and provocative, and Gaston loved it, remaining there until 1928, when one of the editors who also headed the *Journée Industrielle* offered him the job of secretary of a centre-right parliamentary group, the Democratic Alliance, led by the gifted fifty-year-old Paris deputy Paul Reynaud. At first, Gaston scrabbled about to make ends meet, writing odd articles in the afternoons when the Chamber was sitting, then joining his boss in the late afternoon to work on finance briefs. In 1930, Reynaud became finance minister in the second Tardieu government, and Gaston accompanied him to the Rue de Rivoli, following his minister to the Colonial Office in the government of Pierre Laval in 1931 as *directeur de cabinet*.

With a serious political job came Gaston's first adult home: the apartment at 1 Rue Bonaparte that Nancy later gave to Fabrice de Sauveterre. Although his means were limited, Gaston immediately began to collect the pictures and *objets* with which the flat was soon filled. Collecting was a taste he shared with Nancy. When she gave this shared delight to Louis XV and Mme de Pompadour it was a realistic reflection of both relationships. Her letters are full of treasures discovered in the *antiquaires* to which Gaston introduced her, she understood that relationship with things that made Gaston call his paintings his companions and confidants. Later, when she was rich, she tried to buy things for him, though even the idea, she joked, would cause him to knock her flat on the floor. Like Nancy with her fittings for couture clothes, Gaston loved the process of acquisition, 'the ardent duel with the dealers, who didn't blame me because they saw that I loved their things, and that I bought them not as a speculation, but to cherish'. Gaston's relationship with the dealers becomes Charles-Edouard de Valhubert's in *The Blessing*. 'Here are the vases, not bad ... but the price is the funniest thing you ever heard. M. Dupont does love to make me laugh. Now what of this bronze? I am thinking of it seriously. I do love Louis XIV bronze, so delightfully solid, so proof against housemaids ... As soon as M. Dupont has mentioned the real price I shall buy it.' The Rue Bonaparte flat, a few doors along from where his first inspiration, Maréchal Lyautey, lived, was most convenient for other activities. 'If this bed could talk ...' Gaston once boasted to a friend. Not the remark of a gentleman.

For a year, Gaston's boss remained in the ascendant. A trip

to Saigon, Bangkok and Calcutta was followed by Reynaud's promotion to minister of justice. In February 1932 Gaston formed part of the French delegation to the League of Nations Disarmament conference in Geneva. Here he claimed to have heard, faintly, the sound of boots marching over Europe. Germany was to leave the league the next year. Gaston found himself exasperated by the weaknesses of a parliamentary system that spent more time making resolutions to take resolutions than taking action and he was perturbed by the French government's insistence that further disarmament would produce greater security. Even more disappointing was Reynaud's fall in the elections that May. After only three months at the Chancellery, he returned to the back benches.

Perhaps it was not a coincidence that Gaston met Charles de Gaulle in 1934, the same year that Maréchal Lyautey died. He immediately saw the light. After their first encounter, 'I decided from now on to use all the means and relationships I had at my disposal in the service of this man ... Everything he said was of an incomparable force and originality. I entered totally into his crusade, because it was a crusader, a preacher, that he made me think of.'

Charles de Gaulle was either a fraud, a saint, or the greatest political gambler of the twentieth century. After six years of screaming rows, Churchill inclined towards the latter view; Roosevelt definitely took the former. Saint-like, De Gaulle was stubborn, singleminded to the point of bigotry, capable of extraordinary self-sacrifice, often terrifyingly mystical and extremely irritating. In many ways, this archetypal Frenchman possessed a certain sort of Englishness, in his respect for a 'law of extreme reticence that was both a pride and a desire not to allow the pure order of the family to interact with the impure order of family life'.[3] God was a fact, not a discussion; the Catholic bourgeoisie, like the English, simply did not speak of certain matters. Spotless honour and service to the nation were the only worthy masculine ideals. De Gaulle never got on with the English, though, neither liking nor understanding them, and without Gaston Palewski's contribution to his self-imposed crusade at its most feeble pass, it might well have failed.

The deep traditionalism of De Gaulle's family was evident in the fact that although they were Parisian, his mother returned to her home town of Lille to give birth to him. Henri and Jeanne de Gaulle were monarchists who did not acknowledge the rights of the French Revolution, Catholic, puritanical, worthy without ever being generous or cheerful. Henri de Gaulle taught philosophy and literature at the Jesuit college of the Immaculate Conception on the Rue Vaugirard. Like Maurice Palewski he educated his children in their history by walking them through the Paris streets, to the Arc de Triomphe and the tomb of Napoleon. De Gaulle knew his vocation early. At fifteen he sat the examination for the officers' academy at St Cyr which he entered in 1910. Already conspicuous for his great height – fellow students called him 'The Asparagus' and an aloof, superior manner, he graduated thirteenth in his class of 210, progressing to the 33rd Infantry Regiment, where his colonel was one Philippe Pétain, the future hero of Verdun. After the First War, he trained Polish officers near Warsaw, returning in 1920 to take up a teaching post at St Cyr, the same year he married Yvonne Vendroux, known as 'Tante Yvonne' to the Free French.

It was something of an arranged match, but the marriage was a devoted one and they had three children, Philippe, Elisabeth and Anne. Anne, the youngest, was mentally handicapped and her illness forged an important bond between the couple, who cared for her tenderly and bravely in a much less tolerant time. It would be a cliché to say that Anne brought out De Gaulle's most gentle, human qualities were it not also true. Speaking to his military chaplain as he prepared to lead his tank division into battle in 1940, De Gaulle said: 'For a father, believe me, it is a very great trial. But for me, this child is also a blessing, she is my joy, she has helped me to rise above all setbacks and all honours, and always to aim higher.'[4]

What De Gaulle was to do – that solitary escape to England after the fall of his country in 1940, that Shakespearean insistence

that he, like a mediaeval king, contained France in his person –
was 'an action that has scarcely had any precedence since
the appearance of sovereign states'.' Its magnitude has been
smoothed by history, one heroism in a period of great heroism,
yet it is worth pausing to consider. One man alone defied the
orders of the government he was sworn to serve and declared to
another, on the basis of no authority whatsoever, that it was he,
and only he, who represented his country. His conviction was
such that this single act, which could so very very easily have
been taken as no more than the delusion of a madman, won him
the support of the world's greatest empire, a support that was
vindicated when he returned to govern his country four years
later. His was an entirely spiritual rebellion, and only the strength
of his imagination succeeded in turning it into fact. Like
Châteaubriand, he led his people by dreams; like Napoleon he
'made his plans out of the visions of his sleeping soldiers'.

Gaston first came to know De Gaulle through his writing. In
the summer of 1934, in the journal *Le Temps*, he came upon an
extract of a new book by a Colonel de Gaulle, *Vers l'armée de
métier.* Following on from his previous publications *La discorde
chez l'ennemi* and *Le Fil de l'epée*, De Gaulle argued powerfully
for a new, more efficient army of armoured divisions which could
work in close co-ordination with the air force. He emphasized
that it was crucial for French industry to start producing tanks
and planes at a time when, as Gaston had observed at Geneva,
the policy of the French government was directed towards disarmament. Reynaud was sympathetic towards De Gaulle's new
approach to strategy and asked for a meeting.

This eventually took place in December, three months after
Lyautey's death. Palewski welcomed De Gaulle into Reynaud's
office at the Rue Bremontier, where the colonel's head almost
touched the ceiling. Gaston mentioned his cousin, Marcel
Diamant-Berger, De Gaulle's companion in the attempted escape
of 1917, and De Gaulle visibly relaxed. They went on to discuss
Morocco, Lyautey and Pétain, for whom De Gaulle's initial liking
and respect had dissipated: 'a great man who died in 1925' was

his comment. Reynaud was then introduced and the three men spoke for an hour. Reynaud had another engagement, but instructed Gaston to work with De Gaulle on preparing a report which would pinpoint the weaknesses in current strategy at the Ecole de Guerre. Gaston and De Gaulle repaired to Poccardi's restaurant on the Boulevard des Italiens. The food was mediocre, but their conversation lasted well into the afternoon. De Gaulle subsequently visited Rue Bonaparte on several occasions where, propped against the wall between the two windows of Gaston's salon, he outlined his thoughts for the 'effort' to come. Further discussion took place at the De Gaulles' flat on Boulevard Raspail, where Yvonne hosted a black-tie dinner once a month. Both men favoured an alliance between the British, the French and the Russians to counter the potential for German aggression. Two days after their first encounter, De Gaulle wrote the first of the sixty-two letters he addressed to Reynaud up to 1939. The three men would remain closely connected until the man Churchill called '*l'homme du destin*' was summoned to his fate in 1940.

Reynaud's commitment to armoured divisions and a pact with the Soviets would during the following years place him in opposition to his former allies on the right. Gaston prepared his speech for a foreign policy debate at the end of 1935, shortly after Mussolini's invasion of Abyssinia in which. Reynaud spoke of the danger of German imperialism and the threat it posed to smaller nations allied with France. The speech received strong support from all spectra of the left, diminishing noticeably (Gaston counted those who were applauding) across the right and extreme right. Reynaud's attempts to instigate production of an armoured division that would be ready to go into action by 1940 met with repeated failure throughout 1935, at the end of which Laval's government was replaced by Albert Sarraut's. Reynaud remained on the Finance Commission, where his speeches, researched by Gaston, formulated many of the ideas which later became known as Gaullist. The feebleness of the party system was a consistent theme: 'We can no longer remain where government depends on the vote of one or another parliamentary factions ... The dangers threatening democracy are too great for us to be able to remain subject to the exclusive regime of party.'[6] Despite a theatrical showdown with Daladier in 1937 and the promised support of Leon Blum for an alternative alliance which would include moderate Communists who supported De Gaulle's reforms, Reynaud's efforts came to nothing. He returned to power as minister for justice in 1938, but Gaston estimated that it was already too late. After Munich and the annexing of Austria, Gaston believed that the British were keen for Reynaud to continue in office, but there was already the sense that the proto-Gaullist faction was a spent force in French politics.

Like Nancy, Gaston was greedy for beauty. 'I live a great deal by my eyes,' she told Evelyn Waugh, and so did he. On his daily walk from Rue Bonaparte to the office on the Rue de Rivoli, where Reynaud succeeded as minister of finance in November 1938, Gaston 'filled his eyes' with the vista of the Pont des Arts and the façade of the Louvre. 'It was,' he remembered, 'the only happy moment of my day.' That ominous sound of marching was coming inexorably closer, and still the French government seemed incapable of action. Gaston referred to this period as the 'pre-Resistance', a political climate in which traditional party lines regrouped according to those who believed on one side in the threat of 'the monstrous evangelism of totalitarianism' propagated by Hitler and those who argued that the best defence lay in appeasement and the Maginot Line. Many of the latter favoured the policy of leaving Germany to expand against Russia in the east, ignoring the possibility of a mooted Nazi–Soviet pact. Nonetheless, the Communists, who were now Reynaud's unlikely allies, agreed with the right that such a thing could never happen, producing dissent even among those who acknowledged the threat of Germany. Pétain, despised by Gaston since his displacement of Lyautey in Morocco, emerged as a popular representative of the conservative view.

Even as he reached out to unlikely supporters on the left,

Gaston was making enemies within Reynaud's circle. The Comtesse de Portes, Reynaud's mistress, loathed him and plotted with her friend, the sardine heiress the Marquise de Crussol, to have him dismissed. Gaston was in charge of Reynaud's press campaign, meeting newspaper editors daily to try to place articles linking French financial policy with the need for industrial and military initiatives. Using Reynaud's funds, he contributed secretly to a daily socialist journal, *Populaire*, which earned him the hostility of Hélène de Portes and Daladier. The need for reform was blindingly obvious, yet still the nation seemed deaf. Gaston wrote later of how he lay awake at night, maddened by the inability of his colleagues to recognize that invasion was coming. In his view, France was already lost.

7

LOSING

As Gaston embarked on his Gaullist crusade, the Rodds moved back into London, to 12 Blomfield Road, Maida Vale, which was not quite the chic *quartier* it became after the war. Lord Norwich, who lives there now, recalls that it was 'brothel, brothel, brothel, Nancy, brothel, brothel, brothel'. Peter was working again, but appeared to be drinking his wages as fast as he earned them, and aside from the attractions of the local amenities, he had found himself a mistress, Mary Sewell, a married writer who lived near the Redesdales in Rutland Gate. Nancy pretended to be *insouciante*, writing to her brother-in-law Simon Elwes: 'It's lovely being in London because now Rodd can go out with his girlfriend who has a spoon face and dresses at Gorringes [a sharp stab – Gorringes was an auction house]. Also I can go out with people like Raymond Mortimer and Willie Maugham who like the sound of their own voices punctuated by giggles, but who hate being told about the origins of toll-gates by Rodd.' The bridge parties continued, but they were far from gay. Mary and her husband came often, Peter flirted, Nancy sniped and when the atmosphere became too gruesome would pretend to faint, a pathetically desperate way to seize attention. Peter would dump her on the drawing-room sofa and go back to the game and his lover.

For all the sophisticated posturing of *Christmas Pudding* and *Wigs*, Nancy was quite unable to distance herself from the embarrassment her marriage was becoming. Rather than leave Peter to get Mary out of his system, she even agreed to a holiday in

Brittany with the Sewells, accompanied by Jessica, whose adolescent blindness to the situation could not have been com-
forting. 'We went to an extraorder nightclub,' Decca wrote from
Saint-Briac, 'run by an ex-Folies-Bergere lady called Popo ...
And she did a dance and took off her jersey. Wasn't it extraorder?
And then she waltzed with Mary Sewell. Nancy didn't come
because she thinks nightclubs boring and the Sewells (evidently)
thought it was because she was shocked by them.'

Jessica was preparing an 'extraorder' shock of her own for her
family. She had come out in 1935 and was mired in the boredom
of Swinbrook, waiting for adult life to happen. Now a committed
Communist, Jessica was fascinated by the doings of her cousin
Esmond Romilly, Winston Churchill's nephew, who had run
away from Wellington, where he had published a leftist magazine, *Out of Bounds*, and then signed up to the party. In January
1937 he had been invalided home from the front in Spain, where
he had joined a unit of international volunteers and seen action
against the Fascists. At the time, he appeared to adults the worst
kind of self-righteous schoolboy prig. Philip Toynbee described
him as an intolerant fanatic, and Nancy, later, as the most
horrible human being she had ever known. But to Jessica, frustrated by her family's concurrent attitude of both evangelism and
apathy towards Fascism, he was an idol. They met at a house
party in Wiltshire soon after Esmond had returned to England
and within twenty-four hours had decided to run away to Spain
together. (Esmond appeared less interested at this point in Jessica
than in the £50 running-away money she had saved. He was the
worst of hypocrites when it came to appropriating other people's
funds.)

In early February, on the pretext of a motor tour in France
with two girlfriends (and, of course, a suitable chaperone), she
bolted. Esmond declared his love the day after they arrived in
France; from then on they travelled as a couple to Bayonne,
where Jessica needed to obtain a Spanish visa. After a period of
frantic anxiety, the Redesdales learned that they had reached
Bilbao and planned to marry. The Mitfords, including Unity,

who had rushed back from Munich, assembled at Rutland Gate to consider what should be done. By this time, the elopement was all over the press – 'Peer's Daughter Elopes to Spain', 'Mixed Up Mitford Girls Still Confusing Europe'. Prod wrote an article for the *Daily Mail* in which he claimed Jessica had become a Communist only to score points off Unity and suggested that she be made a ward in Chancery to compel her to leave Spain. Prod's desire to play 'the heroic brother-in-law' was a great bore, according to Unity, who had loathed him ever since he had written to her parents pointing out the inevitable disaster that would ensue if they continued to give rein to her obsession with Hitler. Nonetheless it was agreed that he and Nancy, with permission from Anthony Eden at the Foreign Office, should be allowed to travel to Spain to try to talk Jessica out of it.

They arrived on a naval destroyer, disembarking in a cannonade of flashbulbs. Both Jessica and Esmond were adamant that they would be married and would not return home. Nancy pleaded with her sister, describing Sydney and David's misery, as well as resorting to the codes of their class – English society could 'make things pretty beastly to those who disobey its rules'. Was she also hoping to prevent Decca from confusing love with her desire to escape, as both she herself and Diana had done? Nancy and Peter left in exasperation the next day. With her usual political sophistication, Unity wrote to Jessica: 'I naturally wouldn't hesitate to shoot him if it was necessary for my cause, and I should expect him to do the same to me, but in the meantime I don't see why *we* shouldn't be quite good friends.' This went further than Nancy's mealy-mouthed expressions of support for Diana in the Thirties. However, she was now increasingly coming round to Esmond's position: 'I realize that there will never be any peace, or any of the things I like and want, until that mixture of profit-seeking, self-interest, cheap emotion and organized brutality which is called fascism has been fought and destroyed forever.'[1] Nancy was by this time no fool about Fascism, though when it came to her own sisters she was still unable to reconcile the ever-greater hatred and anger it provoked with her love for them. When, in 1941, she was forced to choose, she did her duty, like Unity, and chose Esmond's side.

Jessica was soon pregnant and she and Esmond were married on 18 May in Bayonne with Lady Redesdale as a sorrowful witness. The Romillys felt that the Rodds had betrayed them by siding with the grown-ups. Nancy continued to write to Jessica, who was prepared to forgive her, but insisted that she had been rather disloyal in disapproving of her living with Esmond unmarried, or marrying him. Nancy expressed her relief and sent 'a narst little diamond ring, as I know it is nice to have things of popping value'. She didn't think Jessica would make much of a mother after her dreadful behaviour, but luckily 'Aunt Nancy' would be on hand to help.

In the late Thirties, Nancy was hopeful that she might have a baby of her own. Childbearing was not easy for all the Mitford women. Pamela, rather unkindly described as the least maternal of the sisters, in fact underwent several operations in an attempt to have a child. Deborah, as she has recently recorded in her memoirs, suffered a stillbirth and Nancy herself was treated with curettage in an effort to help her to conceive (hence, perhaps, the rather bald Mitford slang for babies – 'scrapages'). Despite her fastidious warnings to Jessica about the horrors of nappies, Nancy was not, as has sometimes been surmised from her novels, hostile to children. Quite the contrary. That some were unloved and unloveable, like Linda Radlett's first daughter Moira Kroesig in *The Pursuit of Love*, or Polly's baby in *Love in a Cold Climate* which, according to the Radletts, took one look at its father and died in despair, she recognized. She was realistic, too, about the drudgery and boredom involved in bringing up young children, to a degree which reads as shocking in our own late-breeding, child-fetishizing culture. Nevertheless she writes with great sympathy of the physical satisfaction mothers derive from their children when small and equally of the sometimes bewildering transformation of this relationship as they grow.

Nancy was very fond of her friend Billa Harrod's son Henry, and proved a 'perfect' godmother to Evelyn Waugh's daughter

Harriet when she was young, choosing just the sort of charming, imaginative, 'grown-up' presents little girls adore. Perhaps she liked small children best – heaven from two to six and then rather dreary until they become civilized adults – but again this is a not uncommon, if unfashionable view. That Nancy acknowledged later in life that she might not have become the writer she did had she had children does not mean she didn't want them, though her comment to Evelyn that her infertility was 'God's idea, not mine' is maybe the nearest she got to expressing her sadness on the subject. Inevitably, her infertility coloured her relationship with Gaston, though initially not negatively; indeed, the fact there was no risk of pregnancy might well have lent a certain abandon to the proceedings. But Nancy was later forced to confront her belief that since a child was one thing she could not give him, he was entitled to look elsewhere.

In the summer of 1938, though, Nancy was thrilled to find herself pregnant. To Robert Byron she wrote that while it was madness from the financial point of view, 'one must never be deterred from doing what one wants for lack of money'. Nancy had been warned to rest in bed, and the first weeks of her pregnancy proceeded calmly, first with her friend Helen Dash-wood at West Wycombe and then in London, where she was cared for by a nurse. Despite these careful precautions, in September she lost the child. In 1941, she conceived again, though by this time proof that the Rodd marriage had broken down irrevocably was provided by the fact that the father was not Peter. Much of Nancy's attitude to suffering, her immense personal courage, is shown in her behaviour as she lost this second baby. The pregnancy turned out to be ectopic, and she began to suffer pain during a visit to her friends the Harrods in Oxford. Dismissing it as possible appendicitis, she carried her own suit-case to the bus stop, rode to the station and returned to London, where she checked herself in to the University College hospital. Before the anaesthetic, she apparently asked the surgeon to preserve her fertility, but he had no choice other than to perform a hysterectomy. When Nancy came round, it was to the news that she would never now have a child.

Lady Redesdale was in no position to be supportive. She produced her airy remark about ovaries and then, when Nancy said she was saddened by the scar on her abdomen, wondered why she minded, as nobody was ever likely to see it. To Diana, Nancy wrote of this 'horrible', 'depressing' experience, but outside the family the 'shop-front' was strictly maintained. Nancy went to beautiful West Wycombe to recuperate, where she found her friends James Lees-Milne and Cecil Beaton in a lively house party of 'evacuees' which also included her cousin Clementine, Sibyl Colefax and Eddy Sackville-West. As at other times of great stress in her life, she took refuge in somewhat hysterical and savage teasing. James Lees-Milne's diary is rather impatient with her incessant 'shrieking', but then he did not know the physical and mental agony she was trying so bravely to conceal. The operation had taken place in December and Nancy was too unwell to return to London until the following March, but with the exception of her letter to Diana, she made no fuss and demanded no special treatment. Peter showed very little concern for his wife's health, as had been the case when she had lost their first baby. The Rodds, Nancy wrote, had been 'wonderfully true to form – my mother-in-law was told by the surgeon I should be in danger for three days and not one of them even rang up to enquire, let alone send a bloom or anything. I long to know if they bothered to look under R in the deaths column – very much doubt it however.'

This tight-lipped, very English stoicism is now viewed as a perverse suffocation of healthy emotion; sentimentally, at least, we're all American now. Yet to Nancy's generation, the generation of the war, it was a badge of honour, a conquest of the self based on not imposing one's own suffering on others. In his diaries, Cecil Beaton writes admiringly of their mutual friend, the famous hostess and musical connoisseur Emerald Cunard, when she learned that her long-term lover Sir Thomas Beecham, on whom she had spent much of her life and fortune, had married a Miss Betty Humby, despite having denied the engagement to Emerald's face just two days before. Beaton comments on how bravely she rallied, never showing her pain or speaking ill of the man who had hurt her so profoundly. When Nancy was told of the death of her brother Tom in 1945, she was staying with Lord Berners at Faringdon. After he had broken the news, her friend kindly asked if she would prefer to remain upstairs, but Nancy appeared, immaculately made up, to sit through dinner with no outward show of grief. Similar examples abound among Nancy's peers – the 'shop-front' was by no means unique to her – but there is no reason to mistake the want of manifest pain for its lack. In the case of her infertility, there is no doubt that Nancy minded deeply. But the codes of her time and class provided a means of coping with grief, a certain grim courage, which later generations have been perhaps too ready to misread or dismiss.

Nancy's first miscarriage occurred at the same time as the Munich crisis. With the exception of Deborah and Jessica, all the Mitfords were at this point pro-Fascist in varying degrees. Nancy herself was opposed to the Munich agreement, which she discussed in a letter to her friend Billa, the wife of the Oxford economist Roy Harrod, expressing her disappointment at the result of the Oxford by-election where Quintin Hogg had beaten the anti-Munich independent candidate. For someone who was supposedly capable only of making jokes about politics, she was thoughtful about the inadequacy of a strong anti-appeasement figurehead on the liberal left, while her impatience with appeasers is manifest: 'The young prospective candidate . . . [said] that he was glad of the Nazis as they will prevent by their menace the young of England from becoming decadent . . . I think ordinary people are at last getting sufficiently interested in politics to prevent all these half-witted young public schoolers from being returned so easily in the future.' For all her sisters' much-vaunted political convictions, it was Nancy, of them all, who engaged most practically with her beliefs in the year before the war.

Peter had failed to get a job at the BBC, his brother Francis having warned the corporation against hiring him (Nancy put his name in a drawer, the Mitford family curse) and decided to go to France as a volunteer to help the Republican refugees, numbering an estimated half a million, who had fled from Franco over the Pyrenees. Nancy, pretty, frivolous, apolitical Nancy, followed him. In Perpignan, Prod was for once in his element. The French government had no idea how to deal with this sudden mass immigration, so they herded the unfortunate Spaniards into barbed-wire enclosures and more or less left them to rot. When Peter arrived, they were dying at a rate of four hundred a day. 'The thing that is happening,' he wrote to his wife, 'is so appalling that it amounts to the cold blooded murder of thousands of chaps. It is impossible to get at the mortality figures, but the dying has not even properly begun. They've got typhoid and possibly cholera as well now.'

The refugees needed to be fed and provided with medical supplies, dispersed families had to be reunited and boats, tickets and visas arranged to Mexico and Morocco, where those who had relatives there might join them. The situation was utterly chaotic, and Nancy was impressed not only by seeing her husband's long-wasted abilities finally put into action, but by his deep and sincere concern for the frightened, desperate people he was helping. He worked round the clock, barely seeing Nancy, and she too threw herself into the task, driving a wheezing supply van in a distinctly unchic straw coolie hat and organizing the passengers on a ship for Mexico departing from Sete. A long letter to Lady Redesdale captures the frantic atmosphere, pitched between grief and rejoicing.

Well, we got our ship off ... There was a fearful hurricane and she couldn't get into Port Vendre, so all the arrangements had to be altered ... at an hour's notice, special trains etc etc the result was Peter was up for *two whole nights* ... I was up all yesterday night as the embarkation went on until 6am and the people on the quay had to be fed and the babies given their bottles. There were 200 babies under 2 and 12 women are to have babies on board ... The women were on the quayside first and then the men arrived ... you never saw such scenes of hugging. The boat sailed at 12 yesterday, the pathetic little band played first God Save the King for us, then the Marseillaise, and then the Spanish national anthem. Then the poor things gave three vivas for Espana which they will never see again. I don't think there was a single person not crying – I have never cried so much in my life.

Nancy had come to know many of the refugees personally, as some had helped with the office work. Jessica had idolized the working class so long that when she actually met a member of it who didn't work for her family (during a job as a saleswoman) she was horrified to find them dirty, coarse and unpleasant. Like George Orwell, she felt terribly let down when she saw the noble proletariat close up. Nancy had no such naïve expectations and therefore no such prejudices. She took the refugees as they were, embraced their concerns and understood them – for example, criticizing the Red Cross for issuing shorts, which the Spaniards found undignified and humiliating to wear. Unlike Diana or Unity, Nancy had first-hand experience of the human wretchedness Fascism produced, and Perpignan annealed her hatred for it. To her mother she wrote: 'If you could have a look, as I have, at some of the less agreeable results of Fascism in a country I think you would be less anxious for the swastika to become the flag on which the sun never sets. And whatever may be the good produced by that regime, that the first result is always a horde of unhappy refugees cannot be denied.' To Nancy, no ideology was worth the cost she had witnessed. When she returned to England in June 1939, she was more than ever convinced that Fascism had to be fought.

The Perpignan experience had also brought about a rare moment of closeness and collaboration in the Rodd marriage. Until Lord Redesdale's dramatic recantation ('like Latimer in the *Daily Mirror*') Peter and Nancy presented a united front against both the milder pro-appeasement beliefs of the Rodd family and the ever-more obsessive devotion of the elder Mitfords. In the six years between their first visit to Nuremberg and the outbreak of war, Diana and Unity had spent much time with Hitler. Diana's personal friendship with the Führer was coloured by her practical aims of obtaining help for her husband's cause; Unity was evangelical. Her life was lived with no other object than seeing Hitler, her time organized around the possibilities of meeting him. Far from heeding Peter's warning as to the disastrous consequences of her idolatry, the Redesdales had accommodated it, first in visiting Munich and being introduced to Hitler, subsequently in espousing Fascism in both the House of Lords and the British press and attending the 1938 Nuremberg rally. Pamela and Deborah were largely unimpressed by their presentations to the leader of the Reich. Pamela described him as looking like any ordinary farmer while Deborah giggled at her mother's earnest attempts to engage him in a discussion of laws regulating the quality of bread flour.

In terms of the family allegiances, though, Pamela was ranged on the Fascister side through her marriage in 1936 to Derek Jackson, a rich and distinguished physicist and a supporter of Fascism. Jackson attracted less opprobrium than other sympathizers, both within and without the family, partly because of his extreme brilliance and partly because when the time came he served with great valour in the RAF. Tom's position was complex. While contemporaries disagree as to whether or not he approved of the Nazis, he was unequivocally pro-German. As a near-professional-level musician he admired German composers above all others and he was an extremely serious student of German philosophy and literature. He had a spiritual affinity with Germany as Nancy had with France. When the time came he elected to be drafted to the East, rather than Europe, because, in the words of his friend James Lees-Milne, he was better able to face killing the Japanese, whom he did not like, than the Germans, whom he did. Of the latterday Mitford conversions to National Socialism, Lady Redesdale's was the most enduring. It infuriated Nancy that her mother openly declared she hoped Britain would lose the war, and that she seemed to regard Adolf as her 'favourite son-in-law'. According to her personal logic, it was British opposition to Fascism that destroyed not only her marriage, but the life of her daughter Unity.

The relationship between the Fuhrer and the young English aristocrat had made Unity the most notorious of the Mitford sisters by the end of the Thirties. She was mentioned a good deal in the press, for example on 18 March 1939, after the occupation of Czechoslovakia, in a piece run by the *Daily Mirror* entitled 'What Miss Mitford Would Like to See'. Lady Redesdale published her own opinions on National Socialism in a *Daily Sketch* article on 10 June, her connection with Unity making for engaging copy. Whatever the reality of Unity's political influence (which appears, on balance, to have been negligible), it is understandable that the interest and controversy she provoked, which she monitored in fat scrapbooks of press cuttings, not only fuelled her passion for all things Nazi but contributed to a belief that she was possessed of a unique destiny. Rudi von St Paul, a friend of Unity's, claimed to her biographer David Pryce-Jones that 'she put her life and ambition into avoiding a war between England and Germany ... She could not admit to herself and the public that she had failed to prevent the war. She had been on a pedestal and was therefore mistaken into thinking she had influence.'[2]

In 1938, Lord Redesdale had purchased the isolated Hebridean island of Inch Kenneth from a chap at his club. The Redesdales, Nancy and Deborah were summering there when war was declared on 3 September. Nancy immediately set off for London, followed the next day by Deborah, who made the journey to Blomfield Road accompanied by one of her mother's goats. None of the family could have been aware that Unity was by this time lying in a Munich hospital with a bullet lodged in her brain. During her last visits to England, she had told Diana, Tom, Deborah and Jessica that she intended to commit suicide if war was declared and after leaving a suicide note and a sealed letter for Hitler had driven to the Englischer Garten and shot herself in the temple.

On 15 September, Nancy wrote to Violet Hammersley that Unity 'on fairly good authority is in a concentration camp for Czech women which much as I deplore it has a sort of poetic justice'. Peter, she claimed, would use his diplomatic connections to have her released when she had come to her senses. The first real news came on 2 October, but it was not until December that Lady Redesdale and Deborah were able to set off for Switzerland, where Hitler had arranged for Unity to be transferred, to bring her home. They arrived back in England in early January to a hostile furore in the press. Unity was to live for another eight years, an overblown, incontinent wreck, unmanageable, pathetically furious and piteously needy. Lady Redesdale sacrificed herself to her care and her condition dealt the final blow to the Redesdale marriage. After Unity's return the Mitford parents chose to live apart. Nancy later described her 'beautiful, charming, odd' sister as a 'victim of the times'. 'Am I mad?' Unity had asked her plaintively. 'Of course you are, darling Stonyheart,' Nancy replied, 'but then, you always were.' Unity was the first family casualty of the war, her lumbering ghost the nexus for all the guilt and grief that no amount of Mitford jokes could ever quite appease.

8

WAR

Nancy began her war work the day she returned to London. Peter was already commissioned in the Welsh Guards and while waiting to be called up joined a first-aid post in Chelsea. Nancy was to drive an ARP van every night. Driving in the blackout was not a success – she crashed almost immediately – so she found more suitable work at a first-aid post in Praed Street, near Blomfield Road. Sitting around rolling bandages in anticipation of casualties, indelible pencil poised to write on their foreheads, she began her fourth novel, *Pigeon Pie*.

The satirical effect of inverted context had already been exploited by Nancy in *Wigs on the Green*, where Fascism is parodied by its transposition to rural England. The technique owes something to Pope's *Rape of the Lock*, where a petty society squabble is elevated to mock-Homeric epic; in *Pigeon Pie* Nancy did something similar, reducing the paranoia of the 'Phoney War' to a spy story set in a Mayfair drawing room. Considering the novel later with Evelyn Waugh, Nancy thought it 'extremely evocative' of those first tense months of the conflict, when no side seemed anxious to begin.

England picked up France, Germany picked up Italy. England beckoned to Poland, Germany answered with Russia. Then Italy's Nanny said she had fallen down and grazed her knee ... England picked up Turkey, Germany picked up Spain, but Spain's Nanny said she had internal troubles and must sit this one out. England looked towards the Oslo group, but they had never played before, except little Belgium, who had hated it, and the others felt shy. America of course, was too much of a baby for such a grown-up game, but she was just longing to see it played. And still it would not begin.

This approach, it has been suggested, is 'horribly compromised by its flippancy'. Nancy 'simply does not know how to respond to an event of this magnitude'; hence *Pigeon Pie* is 'less an exercise in detachment than straightforward evasion, an attitude to life forged in that artificial late-Twenties crucible in whom the events of a decade later can only raise a kind of forced inanity'.[1] That the Twenties produced a generation incapable of coping with war seems a fairly specious point, given that they fought it, but the critic is completely missing Nancy's technique. Comparing the first months of the war to a children's round game captures exactly the horrible diplomatic team-picking of those first months. It was not Nancy but the governments of Europe who were unable to contemplate the magnitude of what they had done. The consistent theme of the novel is the error of appeasers, those English people (like Nancy's acquaintance Henry 'Chips' Channon and indeed her own parents) who were flattered by 'being made a fuss of' and trips in Mercedes–Benzes into believing the Nazis fundamentally benign. Nancy does not gloat, rather it is the childish, the blind, the venal, the conceited, who have brought Europe to this pass and it will be up to the adults, like her pretty, dizzy but ultimately sound heroine Sophia Garfield and her soldier lover Rudolph, to get it out.

Pigeon Pie is also the first of Nancy's novels to touch on America. The anti-Americanism which was to become almost a fixation with her has its roots in what she perceived as the attitude of the US government in these first months of the war. Americans are portrayed as dull, money-grubbing hypocrites, their proud boast of democracy belied by their obsession with class and their apparent hope that Germany would win the war. In general, British people were unaware

of Roosevelt's ardent behind-the-scenes manoeuvrings to overcome the restriction of the neutrality acts passed in the USA
in the mid-Thirties, acts which he did not begin to publicly
circumvent until September 1940. Senator Joseph Kennedy,
the US ambassador to Britain who remained en poste until
late 1940, made no secret of his pro-appeasement views or of
his belief that democracy was 'finished' in Europe. Kennedy's
opinions were well known to Nancy, as Deborah Mitford was
at the time close to Andrew Cavendish, whom she married in
1941. Kennedy's daughter Kathleen would become Deborah's
sister-in-law in 1944, on her marriage to Andrew's elder brother,
the Marquess of Hartington. Nancy's views of America were
thus both informed and representative of what many people
thought in that first period of the war.

The political framework of the novel is slight yet solid, deftly
raised beneath the comedy of Sophia's attempts to deal with her
unruly lover and her hopes of being a 'glamorous female spy'.
Unwittingly, she outwits the sinister Boston Brotherhood, an
American religious cult populated by German spies, who have
kidnapped Ivor King, 'the King of Song', an affectionately
bewigged portrait of Mark Ogilvie-Grant derived from an earlier
story, *The Two Old Ladies of Eaton Square*. Rudolph and Luke,
Sophia's husband, are, as noted, a compound of Peter Rodd and
his brother Francis. Rudolph comes out well – brave, clever and
equal to his duty – but there is none of the fascination Nancy
betrays in *Wigs* with his earlier incarnation as the brilliant,
guileful Jasper Aspect. Sophie keeps Rudolph very effectively in
his place, and is resigned to the view that while he is an ideal
lover, he would be a disastrous husband. 'Women are divided
into two categories, those who can deal with the men they
are in love with and those who can't.' Sophia, like Amabelle
Fortescue, is very much the former type. Dealing with men was
becoming Nancy's perennial question, one that was to dominate
her next four novels, as well as her biography of Mme de
Pompadour, and the elements are all there in *Pigeon Pie*: when
and how to make a scene, how to cope with infidelity and

jealousy, how to reconcile romantic idealism and the pragmatism required for an enduring marriage.

By the time the book was published, however, these eternal questions seemed trivial. The Phoney War was at an end, the Blitzkrieg had begun and France had fallen. 'Poor sweet charming Sophia. She is, alas! an unimportant casualty,' concluded the *Spectator.* (When the book sold 10,000 copies on its reissue fifteen years later, Nancy reflected ruefully on how much that success would have meant to her during those 'penniless' years.) But she was about to make a more significant contribution to the war effort than a cheerful comic novel. On 20 June 1940, she visited Gladwyn Jebb at the Home Office, at his request, and denounced her sister Diana. 'I regard her as an extremely dangerous person,' she told the under-secretary for economic warfare. It was not, as she wrote to Violet Hammersley, very sisterly behaviour, but she believed it was her duty.

And she truly did. Unlike her three stridently political sisters, Nancy has never been permitted partisan passion of her own. With her, it was always about the jokes. Nancy was always better prepared to lose a friend than a good laugh and the sharpness of her teasing brought her enemies as well as admirers. Nevertheless she did have political convictions. She was extremely well read in history, she had been at the very centre of political debate in Europe through her family for years and her hatred of Hitler and belief in Britain's duty to fight the war was shared by millions of British people. Perhaps she was not politically sophisticated, but none of her sisters was renowned for the profundity of her views. Yet somehow, with Nancy, it has been made personal. One biographer suggests that her denunciation of Diana came down to nothing more than jealousy of her beautiful, brilliant sister, who had been loved by one adoring husband and left him for another equally enraptured, who had the children and the money so painfully absent from her own life. Another suggests that it was due to Nancy's 'increasing bitterness' at the rift over *Wigs on the Green*, 'proved' by the 'waspishness' of her letters at the time (was Nancy ever anything other than waspish?).[2]

If there was anything personal about Nancy's hatred of Fascism, it stemmed from what it had done to her own family: Unity was a wreck and her parents were tearing one another apart. She had experienced a form of political awakening in Perpignan, her husband and many of her beloved friends were fighting. Moreover, Hitler's creed was the antithesis of everything she believed about civilization, promising nothing but ignorance and cruelty. A convinced anti-appeaser, she was disgusted by the surprise expressed by those who had been pro-Munich at Hitler's consistent failures to keep his word 'as though he had ever behaved any other way'. Nancy's declaration was made four days after the capitulation of the Pétain government to the Nazis. With France in Hitler's power, invasion became a strong possibility. She had every reason to sincerely believe that her much-loved sister, her closest friend, was a genuine threat to her country.

This opinion was based on both Diana's avowed close friendship with Hitler and the visits she had been making to Germany since 1933. These had begun when she accompanied Unity to the first Nuremberg rally. On her return in 1934, she took a flat for three months in Munich. In January 1935 she went again, with Lord Redesdale, was introduced to Hitler in February and presented him to Mosley in April. In 1936, she attended another Nuremberg rally and in October she and Mosley were married in Munich. In total she made five trips to Germany between April 1936 and February 1937. She was at the Parteitag that autumn and continued to visit Hitler in Berlin through 1938. Three more journeys to Munich took place in 1939, the last for the Bayreuth Festival in August, less than a month before Britain declared war. Nancy could hardly be blamed for finding this extremely sinister, and the fact that the authorities were clearly anxious (why else should she have been summoned? It was not her own initiative) endorsed her own suspicions. The paranoia she had mocked in *Pigeon Pie* seemed more plausible after the fall of France and with posters proclaiming 'Careless Talk Costs Lives!' displayed everywhere. Unsurprisingly, according to

Diana's biographer, 'In this climate, British Fascism was inevitably seen as a vehicle for future Nazi influence in Britain.'[3]

What Nancy could not have known was that the purpose of Diana's visits had been the establishment of a commercial radio station which could raise money for the BUF (or, as it had become in 1936, the British Union of Fascists and National Socialists). After the riots of Mosley's notorious march in Cable Street in London's East End, the government had passed the Public Order Act, giving police the power to break up demonstrations and forbidding the wearing of uniforms. The act removed the basis of much of the party's popular appeal, while Cable Street discouraged Mussolini, who had been donating to it for several years. After Il Duce's financial support was withdrawn in 1935, Mosley was looking for alternative funding. Recognizing that his name might put off both potential advertisers and listeners, he took on two partners, Bill Alan and Peter Eckersley. Eckersley and his wife Dorothy were committed Nazis (they had been taken by Unity to gaze on Hitler in Munich in 1937) and Dorothy Eckersley would eventually be imprisoned for broadcasting propaganda from Germany between 1937 and 1941.

Diana's persistent requests for permission to set up a radio station were finally granted in 1938. She and the company's lawyer, Frederick Lawton, travelled to Berlin to meet the minister of posts and telegraphs, who granted the concession for the wavelength, and the station was registered as a company in December that year. During this visit, which took place a few months after the Munich agreement, Lawton heard Diana describe a dinner with Hitler and Goering at which they had discussed their plans for the takeover of Czechoslovakia. Diana did not consider it her patriotic duty to report this to the British government, and Lawton finally decided it would be a betrayal of his client's confidentiality to do so.

Special Branch had been investigating the BUF for some time. Two days before war was declared, Mosley had set out the BUF's official line.

The Government of Britain goes to war with the agreement of all Parliamentary parties ... Neither Britain nor her Empire is threatened, therefore the British government intervenes in an alien quarrel. In this situation, we of the British Union will do our utmost to persuade the British people to make peace ... Our members should do all that the law requires of them and, if they are members of any of the forces ... they should obey their orders and, in every particular, obey the rules of their Service. But I ask all members who are free to carry on our work to take every opportunity within your power to awaken the people and demand peace.

This statement would have seen Mosley prosecuted had it not been for the convenient timing. The authorities did not yet consider him a direct threat, despite their present knowledge of the radio station. The agreement that Lawton had drawn up stated that 'programmes shall contain no matter which can reasonably be construed as political propaganda or cause offence in Greater Germany or Great Britain'. However, anti-Nazi jokes were to be forbidden and a Nazi official present in the studio to supervise broadcasts. 'Greater Germany' might have been a further hint, in 1938, to the hapless Lawton. Special Branch also reported a private meeting of top BUF officials in January 1940, at which Mosley explained: 'Reward and victory are in sight ... You must bring in new members ... reliable men and women who would take their place in the ranks when the time came for the sweep forward ... as their brother parties in other countries had made when their hour of destiny struck.'[4]

In April Vidkun Quisling helped the Nazis to power in Norway, placing himself at the head of a collaborationist government. Writing to Mark Ogilvie-Grant on 24 May, Nancy observed: 'I'm glad Sir Oswald Quisling has been jugged, aren't you, but think it quite useless if Lady Q is still at large.'

Mosley had been arrested two days after the government had pushed through an amendment to the Emergency Powers Act, known as '18B'. Under the new clause, the home secretary was empowered to detain anyone who was a member of an organization believed to be 'subject to foreign influence or control' or whose leaders 'have or have had associations with persons concerned in the government of, or sympathetic with the system of government of, any power with which His Majesty is at war'. Special Branch had reported to Sir Alexander Maxwell that the BUF was 'not merely advocating an anti-war policy, but a movement whose aim it is to assist the enemy in every way it can'.

Nancy opened the letter to Mrs Hammersley in which she admits to denouncing Diana with the 'heartbreaking' thought of all 'our' refugees, no doubt now destined for execution under Franco. She wrote that Peter was back for a brief visit before joining his battalion, then describes the visit to Gladwyn Jebb. She says she really knows very little about Diana's activities, but had advised Jebb to examine her passport. There is a narrative of justification in this letter: first the refugees, then Peter, then the admission that she has done her unsisterly duty. Diana's home had already been raided (luckily she had the presence of mind to hide the photograph of Hitler she kept by her bed) and on 29 June she was taken to Holloway, where she remained for the next three years. She did not learn of Nancy's actions until after her sister's death.

Diana was not imprisoned because her sister betrayed her. Her former father-in-law, Lord Moyne, had written to Lord Swinton, the chairman of the Security Executive, about his concern at her 'extremely dangerous character'.[5] His letter was passed to MI5 and the Home Office and the order for Diana's detention had been countersigned by Alan Harker, the acting head of MI5 and a member of Swinton's secret committee. Sir Alexander Maxwell at the Home Office, conversely, advised caution, but by then it was too late. Diana's own unrepentant testimony when she was questioned by Norman Birkett on 2 October led the advisory committee to conclude that: ' It would be quite impossible, having regard to her expressed attitude and her past activities with the leaders of Nazi Germany, to allow her to remain at liberty in these critical days ... Lady Mosley could be extremely dangerous if she were at large.'

Nancy has been accused of the most grotesque hypocrisy in writing to her sister when she was permitted to do so, for sending her books and accepting gifts, including the money to buy a rare Guerlain lipstick, for playing the supportive sister. But she had done her political duty, and now she did her family duty. She was unrepentant about the conditions Diana had to endure: the dirt, the squalor, the confinement and the terrible pain of being separated from her eleven-week-old son Max. True, Diana had committed no crime and had not been tried, but under 18B there was nothing illegal about her imprisonment. Diana herself was appalled to find herself condemned for nothing more than her political beliefs, but then she did not seem able to make the connection between this and the regime she supported. In Nancy's view, Diana unequivocally deserved prison, and her feelings of sympathy for her sister could not be allowed to get in the way. She wondered what Diana did after 5pm lights-out in Holloway – 'I suppose she sits and thinks of Adolf.' Such remarks are quoted as more evidence of Nancy's callousness, her attempts to joke her way out of her own treachery. They were written at a time when London was suffering the worst of the Blitz and Nancy was caring for Jewish refugees at the Redesdale town house in Rutland Gate. In that context, they appear quite restrained.

9

LE PREMIER DES GAULLISTES

Gaston Palewski had joined up as soon as war was declared. His brother Jean-Paul was mobilized with his infantry regiment in August, but Gaston requested a transfer to the air force. Perhaps his experiences at the Salon d'Aviation, where he had attended his father's stand as a teenager, suggested that the air force might be more congenial to him than the infantry. Paul Reynaud agreed to obtain him a commission, writing to Guy la Chambre, the minister for the air force, on 29 September 1939 to request a place for his 'close collaborator', though with the caveat that the post should be such as would allow Gaston to remain in permanent contact with him. Accordingly, Gaston was commissioned in the reserves, and in January 1940 he resigned from his employment to take up an active commission in the 34th Bombing Squadron.

Acquiring his pilot's licence at Villacoublay, he had his wings by 22 March and began to fly his first missions, which he reported in regular telegrams to Reynaud. At first these expeditions were no more than observational tours, or, rather absurdly, used to drop pamphlets with news of the latest papal encyclical over the Ruhr, but by May, the leaflets had been replaced with bombs. 'Finally,' Gaston recalled, 'we received authorization to bomb Germany ... it was about time.' He spoke vividly of his first night mission, of seeing a sudden light in the sky and hoping that it was a star, in which case he would live, or if not, wondering whether he would have the strength to escape his burning Amiot and plummet to the ground 'a nocturnal animal condemned by its weight'. He also evoked the unbearable tension as the airmen scrambled their planes, and the overwhelming relief of landing after a completed mission. He described his 'anguish' as the squadron flew over the battlefields of the First War, their names unbearably poignant to every Frenchman, the sight of Amiens, Arras, Sedan once more aflame 'like great braziers' beneath them a torture to their eyes, a hellish firework display of failure. Gaston was mentioned in dispatches on 4 June for flying a particularly dangerous mission as far as Brussels, where he saw a huge camp near the city, brightly illuminated, which he rightly surmised was the central supply depot for the advancing German troops. In an infuriating vindication of everything his party had been arguing for years, it was judged impossible to bomb the depot due to a shortage of air power, and the enemy supply line remained intact.

On 5 June, the Germans launched the final phase of their attack. At first it seemed there might still be hope, as the Aisne, the Oise and the Somme still held, and on 6 June De Gaulle received a telephone call from Reynaud asking him to join the government as under-secretary of state. As soon as he arrived at Rue St Dominique, De Gaulle began to denounce the spirit of defeatism that prevailed among the ministers, arguing passionately that Pétain should be excluded from the government. He was prepared to concede that metropolitan France was lost, but insisted that the fight should continue throughout the colonies. Both Pétain and Weygand were furious at De Gaulle's inclusion, complaining about his 'vanity', ingratitude and 'boundless ambition'. Unfortunately for De Gaulle, much of this bile was poured into the ears of Sir Edward Spears, recently appointed by Churchill as his personal representative to the French government. By 8 June, the London *Times* had noticed Reynaud's latest, maverick appointment: 'Rather aggressively right-wing, a powerful theoretician, and an almost fanatical advocate of the massive use of tanks, he is a man with an enlightened and penetrating mind, a man of action and at the same time of dreams and abstraction.'

Churchill had the chance to inspect Reynaud's 'interesting innovation' for himself on 9 June, when he received De Gaulle at Downing Street. The purpose of the visit was to cement collaboration with the British for the continuance of the war, as Reynaud, retreating from the tentative suggestions of armistice that he had made to Churchill in late May, was now emphasizing French determination to fight. He explained to De Gaulle that 'it is a matter of convincing the British that we shall hold out, whatever happens, even overseas if necessary'.[1] After reviewing the potential for transferring troops to North Africa, De Gaulle concluded that with the aid of the British fleet and swift action from the French navy and air force, it would be plausible to withdraw half a million men to continue the struggle. Yet De Gaulle's first political mission as a minister was a failure. Churchill refused to countenance the redirection of the Royal Air Force to the battle for France, arguing that as the front moved further away from the British Isles, it was more efficient for RAF bombers to engage the enemy near the coast. Five German planes could be destroyed at close range, he asserted, for every one shot down far away. Nevertheless, on a personal level, the two men produced favourable reactions in one another. In his *Mémoires*, De Gaulle claimed as his first impression that:

> Churchill seemed to me equal to dealing with the most arduous task, so long as it was also grandiose. His character fitted him for action, for running risks, for playing his part wholeheartedly and without scruple . . . From the beginning to the end of the drama, Winston Churchill appeared to me as the great champion of a great undertaking and the great actor in a great History.

He might have added that, in his own estimation, it takes one to know one.

On 10 June, back in France, De Gaulle recorded 'a day of extreme anguish'.[2] The northern front was crumbling, the Germans had attained the Seine, Mussolini had decreed Italy's entry into the war and Paris was under threat. Late that night, after a bitter confrontation with Weygand, who claimed that armistice was now the only solution, De Gaulle accompanied Reynaud to Tours, where the French government was to establish itself in retreat.

They travelled through a landscape already given over to nightmare. The exodus had begun on 10 May, as the Germans advanced, when 25,000 Luxembourgeois had set out for the fragile safety of France. The stream of refugees swelled with the surrender of Belgium on 28 May and now the French were among them. As many as 25 per cent of French people are estimated to have quit their homes by June. As the cities of the north emptied, those of the south found themselves faced with impossible numbers of migrants – 8,000 at Orléans, 47,000 at Cahors, 70,000 at Brive, 100,000 at Pau. Any vehicle that could move had been dragged into service, bicycles, farm carts, perambulators and wheelbarrows as well as bronchitic lorries and elegant private cars. Railway stations were in a state of near riot. On and on they trudged, this mass of 'terrified and miserable humanity',[3] abandoning first their transport, when fuel ran short, then even their pathetic, hastily gathered possessions. They slept in the open, huddling in church porches and marketplaces, and, slowly, they began to starve.

Arriving at the Château de Muguet for what would be the penultimate conference of the Inter-Allied Command, De Gaulle encountered Pétain.

'You are a general,' observed the marshal. 'I don't congratulate you. What's the use of rank during a defeat?'

De Gaulle responded with contained distaste. 'But Maréchal, it was during the defeat of 1914 that you received your first stars.'

'No comparison.'

On the evening of 11 June, Reynaud, Pétain, Weygand, De Gaulle and Général Georges met their British allies, Churchill, Anthony Eden, General Spears, General Sir John Dill and General Ismay. Weygand complained vigorously about the isolation of the French army and the lack of support from the British.

Observing De Gaulle, Spears noted his calm demeanour as compared with the other Frenchmen, who 'really looked like prisoners who had been brought out of their cells to hear the inevitable verdict'. At dinner, where De Gaulle was placed beside Churchill, the prime minister gained the impression that Reynaud would give him the command if the French lines failed to hold their present position. De Gaulle was not present at the next sitting of the meeting as he left early next morning for Rennes to discuss the possibility of establishing a redoubt in Brittany. De Gaulle was in favour of this, but the idea came to nothing due to lack of resources. He had to rush back from Brittany, arriving an hour late at the meeting at Tours, where Reynaud announced that Weygand considered an armistice necessary and that therefore the French government asked to be released from the agreement of March that year at which he and Chamberlain had each forbidden the other the conclusion of a discrete peace treaty. Pétain added his support for capitulation that evening, declaring that the government ought not to leave metropolitan France and that he, personally, was prepared to stay and share the necessary suffering of the French people, from which the country would be reborn. De Gaulle felt he had no choice but to resign, as Pétain's wholehearted support for the armistice signalled defeat for those who felt France should continue the fight, but Georges Mandel, the minister of the interior, persuaded him it was his duty to remain in his post.

By 14 June, the French government was on the move once more. On arrival at Bordeaux, De Gaulle made a last attempt to rally Reynaud. 'For three days now I have seen how fast we are moving towards capitulation ... I refuse to submit to an armistice. If you stay here you are going to be overwhelmed by the defeat. You must reach Algiers as soon as possible. Are you determined to do so, yes or no?'

As ever, when directly confronted by the adamantine conviction of his minister, Reynaud convinced himself that he, too, could stand firm. He charged De Gaulle to go immediately to London to obtain the help they would need for the projected transport to North Africa. He assured De Gaulle that they would meet in Algiers. Pausing at Paimpont, where De Gaulle visited his dying mother, and at Carantec, where he saw his wife and daughters, the general made his way to Brest, where he boarded the *Milan* to sail for Plymouth, landing at daybreak on 16 June. Once at sea, De Gaulle gave the first indications of his break with the official French government line by ordering another ship, the *Pasteur*, to divert with its cargo of weapons from a French to a British port, a measure which caused several members of the Reynaud government to demand that he be court-martialled.

As a last resort, De Gaulle and Churchill thought it might be possible to adopt Jean Monnet's plan for an Anglo–French union in which the two countries would operate as a single political unit. De Gaulle wrote ten years later that neither he nor the prime minister had any illusions about this as a pragmatic solution, but they believed that if Reynaud could be persuaded to accept it his resolve would be stiffened in the face of the increasing pro-armistice feeling in the French Cabinet. Pétain declared the proposal no better than 'marriage with a corpse', and though Reynaud claimed he would prefer to collaborate with France's allies than with her enemies, the proposal was rejected.

Colonel Palewski knew nothing of the dramas occurring within the Cabinet, but he had no intention of giving up the struggle. Along with his squadron leader, Colonel François, Gaston now took the first of the maverick steps which were to lead him to London. Without any orders, they took off for Bordeaux, arriving on 15 June and making their way directly to the Prefecture, now the headquarters of Président Lebrun. Despite managing to penetrate the council chamber, where, he later claimed, the only talk he heard was of capitulation, Gaston was unable to find De Gaulle, who had already left on his twenty-four-hour mission to London. He soon learned that the 34th Air Squadron was ordered to North Africa, with the aim of bombing southern Italy from its new base.

In the words of the editor of his *Mémoires d'Action*, Eric

Roussel, Gaston Palewski possessed an extraordinary gift, 'the rare ability to distinguish always, with a sort of faculty of divination, not only what were the superior interests of France, but also what was most apt to serve them and to consecrate himself to their cause'.[4] Général de Gaulle himself put it more effectively: 'He is always where History is made.' Gaston had shown signs of this prescience throughout the Thirties, now he wrote a letter to the general which he cast into the whirlpool of history 'like a message in a bottle', uncertain whether it would ever reach its destination, but convinced of its desperate justice. 'I have to leave with my planes for North Africa. It is an order from which I cannot extricate myself. But I am sure that you will do something. You can count on me. I will join you as soon as I can.' It was with perfect accuracy, then, that even before the legendary broadcast of 18 June, Gaston Palewski could call himself 'the first of the Gaullists'.

Before he left Bordeaux that evening, Gaston was able to have a meeting with the Spanish ambassador, Lequercia. He was anxious to protect his mother, who was still át Louveciennes, though he prudently gave as his reason his intention to join De Gaulle in London rather than the fact that Rose was Jewish. If the families of those who had joined De Gaulle were persecuted, he asked the ambassador, could he help Rose with a visa to Spain? Lequercia agreed to do all that was necessary, but encouraged him not to leave, declaring airily that the Germans were only 'savages' because they were poor. Now that they should be rich, their spirit and their methods would become more moderate. It should be perfectly possible, he continued, to live easily alongside the new conquerors of Europe. Concern for Rose forced Gaston to swallow his fury, but he could not resist remarking to the Chinese ambassador, as he left, 'Sans doute vous allez me voir arriver chez vous?'

More promising was an interview with the British ambassador, Ronald Campbell, not least as it was conducted in the elegant surroundings of the famous Chapon Fin restaurant. Campbell, who had heard of Gaston's decision to join De Gaulle, assured him that he would be welcome in London, whether or not he managed to bring any of his planes with him. Flying the fifty modern aircraft of the 34th Squadron to London had been Colonel François's original plan, but the new orders rendered it impossible. The air force attaché to Campbell's embassy managed to whisper to him, as he left despairingly for the aerodrome, 'Go to Africa. From there, you'll be able to escape to England.' By dawn of 16 June, just as De Gaulle reached the English coast, Gaston was in Casablanca.

Reynaud, described by Georges Mandel with that very French use of litotes as 'easily influenced',[5] was incapable of holding out any longer. His domineering mistress, Gaston's old enemy Hélène de Portes, was pushing him towards armistice and he was, in the words of the American ambassador William Bullitt, 'completely under her influence'. On the evening of 16 June, as De Gaulle flew back to Bordeaux, he tendered his resignation to Lebrun, who accepted it. On arrival at Merignac airport at 10pm, De Gaulle was informed that since the Reynaud administration was dissolved, he no longer held ministerial office. Half an hour later, Maréchal Pétain was appointed head of the French state. De Gaulle recorded: 'It was certain capitulation. I made my decision at once. I should leave the next morning.'

That night, as Pétain called on his new ministers to approve the armistice, a measure passed in less than twenty minutes, De Gaulle called on Reynaud. They agreed that De Gaulle should go to London and Reynaud undertook to provide immediate funds and passports for Yvonne De Gaulle and the children. At midnight, the general met Spears and Ambassador Campbell at the Hôtel Montre. They agreed that De Gaulle might use the plane Churchill had put at his disposal and next morning at seven, De Gaulle, Spears and Jean Laurent (equipped with 100,000 francs from Reynaud) drove in two cars for the airport. No document has ever been produced to validate the claim that De Gaulle had been given an official 'mission' by Reynaud, who the previous day had still been in a position to continue immediate government business: De Gaulle was effectively deserting his military post. There was a real danger, then, that he could be arrested, but in the chaos of the airfield 'an indescribable mass of people, something between a scrap metal fair and a gypsy encampment',[6] there was little likelihood that the small party would be noticed. De Gaulle appeared serene, 'lost in his thoughts', even as the plane took off and banked over the ports of La Rochelle and Rochefort, where the clear summer sky was fogged with the drifting smoke from the firing ships of France's new ally. They touched down briefly on Jersey, where Spears recalled De Gaulle asking for a cup of coffee. After one taste, he declared it to be tea. 'It was his first introduction,' wrote Spears, 'to the tepid liquid which, in England, passes for one or the other. His martyrdom had begun.' 'It was awful,' De Gaulle wrote later, 'awful.' Though presumably he was referring to the gravity of his position, not the coffee.[7]

As the four-seater RAF plane came in to land at Heston, Maréchal Pétain was delivering 'a heavy-hearted' message to the French people informing them that they must cease to fight. Churchill, in a telephone conversation with Pétain two days before, had attempted to shame the marshal into continuing to resist, but the only thing Pétain appeared capable of resisting was the prime minister's 'roars'. Churchill greeted De Gaulle in the Downing Street garden that afternoon with friendly warmth, and agreed to permit the general to broadcast to the French, though as neither man was as yet informed of the contents of Pétain's speech, it was decided to wait until the terms of the armistice were clarified. Perhaps an eleventh-hour surge of French pride could still preserve the country from capitulation. That evening, De Gaulle denounced Pétain's treasonable behaviour at dinner with Jean Monnet before settling down to write the speech that, more than anything else, would earn him his place in history.

It was largely thanks to Duff Cooper, then minister of information, that the 18 June speech was allowed to go ahead at all. When the War Cabinet met at 12.30pm that day, they concluded that it was ill advised to permit De Gaulle to broadcast while there remained the possibility that the new French government might still act 'in conformity with the interests of the alliance', notably with regard to the French fleet. Cooper consulted Churchill, exhausted after delivering his own great speech to the Commons:

> But if we fail, then the whole world, including the United States, including all that we have known and cared for, will sink into the abyss of a new dark age made more sinister, and perhaps more protracted, by the lights of perverted science. Let us therefore brace ourselves to our duties, and so bear ourselves, that if the British empire and its common-wealth last for a thousand years, men will still say, This was their finest hour.

Cooper and Spears, authorized by a sleepy Churchill, went to each member of the Cabinet in turn and convinced them to allow De Gaulle to go ahead, though Cooper graciously gave the general no indication of the effort this had required when they met for lunch that day. At 6pm De Gaulle took a cab to Oxford Circus, his boots gleaming with polish. There is some disparity between the BBC's records, which state the broadcast was made at 8.15 and transmitted at ten, and De Gaulle's *Mémoires*, where he claims he spoke shortly after six. Churchill's 'finest hour' peroration was broadcast from 9pm until 10pm; it seems prob-able that De Gaulle followed him.

In the concierge's lodge of the Institut Charles de Gaulle on the Rue de Solferino, a little cartoon is pinned to the wall. It shows two BBC recording engineers in a sound box, chatting as De Gaulle reads his speech. One asks the other if they should bother switching on the tape. No, his colleague replies, 'not worth it, he'll be gone soon enough'. The text of De Gaulle's speech is preserved on the wall of the institute lobby, and though it is now as famous and beloved to the French as Churchill's wartime speeches to the British, it deserves to be quoted in full.

The leaders who have been at the head of the French armies for many years have formed a government.

This government, alleging the defeat of our armies, has entered into communication with the enemy to stop the fighting.

To be sure, we have been submerged, we are submerged, by the enemy's mechanized forces, on land and in the air.

It is the Germans' tanks, planes and tactics that have made us fall back, infinitely more than their numbers. It is the Germans' tanks, planes and tactics which have so taken our leaders by surprise as to bring them to the point that they have reached today.

But has the last word been said? Must hope vanish? Is the defeat final? No!

Believe me, for I know what I am talking about and I tell you that nothing is lost for France. The same means that beat us may one day bring victory.

For France is not alone. She is not alone! She is not alone! She has an immense Empire behind her. She can unite with the British Empire, which commands the sea and is carrying on with the struggle. Like England, she can make an un-limited use of the vast industries of the United States.

This war is not confined to the unhappy territory of our country. This war has not been decided by the battle of France. This war is a worldwide war. All the faults, all the delays, all the sufferings do not do away with the fact that in the world there are all the means for one day crushing our enemies. Today we are struck down by mechanized force, in the future we can conquer by greater mechanized force. The fate of the world lies there.

I, General de Gaulle, now in London, call upon the French officers and soldiers who are on British soil, or may be on it, with their arms, or without them, to get into contact with me.

Whatever happens, the flame of French resistance must not and shall not go out.

10

FLIGHT

The 34th Squadron had received further orders to regroup on Tunisia. In Tunis, Gaston was received by the new governor, Marcel Peyrouton. He tried to persuade Peyrouton that there was still hope in resisting, but the governor was convinced that Britain would fall and that negotiation was the only possibility. Palewski reported this to the British consul, who cabled London for instructions and received the expected response that no negotiation with the Nazis was to take place. Gaston presented this to Peyrouton, who then claimed he could do nothing without the agreement of Général Noguès, the military commander of French North African troops. Gaston drove to Alger to confront the general who, despite having received telegrams from De Gaulle in London, was determined to wait. He could only hold North Africa with warships, he insisted, and these Darlan had refused him.

With the armistice negotiations under way, the war was obviously over for the 34th Squadron. Gaston made his way via Meknes to Rabat, where he sought out an old acquaintance, Christian Funck-Brentano, later amongst the founders of the newspaper *Le Monde* in 1944, who was then the curator of the national library. Gaston was encouraged to finally encounter the defiant morale he had so vainly been trying to incite in others. 'There was a marvellous atmosphere of courage, of intelligence,' he remembered, so much so that he wondered whether his duty really lay in remaining in North Africa. He did what little he could to support the resistants' cause, producing pamphlets from the library with Funck-Brentano's help to spread the Gaullist word through the coastal towns. Yet any hope the Free French had of support from the region was destroyed in the tragic assault of Mers el-Kebir.

Among the principal anxieties of the British in the face of French surrender was the fate of the French fleet. As late as 18 June, Admiral Darlan had given his word at Bordeaux that his ships should never be taken by what still remained a mutual enemy, but the British were unconvinced. Some time during the days immediately preceding the armistice, Operation Catapult was formulated. Its end was the destruction of much of the French navy. Under the terms of the armistice, the French ships had not been handed over either to Germany or to Italy. However, to Churchill's anxiety, there were conditions that required them to return to their peacetime bases. In Churchill's view, this made an invasion of Britain even more likely. Two thirds of French ports were in the newly established Occupied Zone, and therefore at the mercy of the Wehrmacht. The risk was simply too great. De Gaulle's biographer, Jean Lacouture, also suggests that in insisting on implementing Operation Catapult, Churchill was 'flinging down an irrevocable challenge to Hitler', casting himself as a latterday Robespierre (Churchill was almost as passionate about French history as De Gaulle) in a blow against both the lingering disappointments of Munich and the Pétainist capitulators. It was nevertheless, in Churchill's own words, 'a hateful decision, the most unnatural and painful in which I have ever been concerned'.[1]

On 3 July, Admiral Somerville, in command of Force H at Gibraltar, sent an ultimatum to Amiral Gensoul, the commander of the French fleet at Mers el-Kebir. He offered five choices: join the British navy to continue the fight against the Axis powers, moor in English ports, sail to the United States or the West Indies, or scuttle the fleet. He warned Gensoul that the port at Mers el-Kebir was mined and that if none of his demands was met, then at 5.30pm Force H would attack. Amiral Darlan was on leave in Gascony, so it was to Amiral LeLuc that Gensoul communicated Somerville's threat. However, he gave LeLuc only two options, internment in British ports or 'battle'. With LeLuc's authorization, Gensoul rejected the ultimatum and Force H opened fire slightly before the deadline in a battle that lasted less than sixteen minutes. Three French ships were sunk, with only one battle cruiser managing to escape and steer for Toulon, 1,380 French sailors were killed and another 370 wounded. At Portsmouth and Plymouth, the French men-of-war were commandeered by the Royal Navy and their crews interned, while the pride of the French fleet, the battleship *Richelieu*, was bombed by British planes.

The effect on French morale was, of course, terrible. There was already much resentment among French sailors at their perceived abandonment by the British at Dunkirk. The theme of 'perfidious Albion', that atavistic hatred of France's old enemy, which had always bubbled beneath the alliance, burst out in a geyser. From Bordeaux to Casablanca, the talk was of British treason. De Gaulle, hearing the news on the evening of 3 July, recognized that Operation Catapult rendered the position of the Free French almost untenable. His grief and rage as a Frenchman were augmented by his position as the leader of a rebellion supported by the British. Worse still, Vichy was quick to capitalize on this relationship, claiming that Mers el-Kebir was De Gaulle's brainchild, devised to eradicate any threat to the Free French movement by destroying the possibility of an understanding between London and Vichy.

In Rabat, Gaston's grief over Mers el-Kebir was compounded by the news that his brother Jean-Paul had been captured and interned in a camp in Silesia, where he was to remain until 1941. Another blow was the death of Marcel Diamant-Berger, who had been wounded fighting in the Vosges mountains with the 82nd Infantry Regiment. Gaston was now desperate to leave North Africa, and telegraphed De Gaulle to that effect. Destiny called in five words: 'Come as soon as possible.' But how? Through a former ministerial colleague, Yvan Martin, he managed to obtain a pass which allowed him to spend a weekend

in Tangiers. The city at that time was a parody of a Graham
Greene novel, its hotels – including the grand Minzah, whose
paintings Gaston characteristically took the time to admire –
chock-full of spies of every nationality, frantically spying on one
another.

Evading the boozing spooks was not easy, but Gaston made
contact with the British consul-general, Gascoigne, who provided a plane. At dawn on an August morning, Gaston took off
for Lisbon, where he found a former companion of his Sciences
Po'days, François de Panafieu, second secretary to the French
Embassy. Evidently infected by the atmosphere of Tangiers, when
his university friend suggested he come to the Embassy, he
replied with mysterious relish: 'I'm still visible, but soon I won't
be.' They met instead at François's home and agreed on an official
story, assiduously gossiped about by the Embassy staff, that
Palewski would shortly be returning to Vichy. Gaston was so
disheartened at this point that he asked if he would have time to
reach London before the Nazis did, but the British ambassador,
Sir Walford Selby, reassured him and showed him the plane in
which he would escape. The next day at dawn, he was in England
where, almost immediately, Winston Churchill summoned him
to Downing Street.

As Gaston stepped into the Cabinet office, Churchill launched
into a eulogy for the honour of France 'with a passionate and
poetic eloquence, as a lover addressing a lost mistress – "La
France! La France! How could she have let herself be conquered?
. . . how could she have so abandoned herself?"' The effect was
rather spoiled by the fact that Churchill was wearing a peculiar
pair of blue combinations, but for a few moments both men
gave way to their emotions. The prime minister then asked
Gaston's opinion as to the responsibility of the British in the fall
of France. They discussed the effects of German propaganda,
the implications of Mers el-Kebir, and Gaston stressed the
importance of a British promise not to appropriate the French
colonies. Churchill then became confidential, lit a cigar and
asked Gaston whether the former minister Camille Chautemps,

presently at Lisbon, ought to be permitted to come to Britain. Gaston argued forcefully that Chautemps, instrumental in the removal of Reynaud, was responsible for the idea of the armistice and the institution of the Vichy regime. He added that all those who had retained a friendship for Britain in their hearts would be disgusted by Chautemps's appearance in London. Churchill thanked him, and took his advice.

Gaston's next call was paid to Sir Orme Sargent, the director of political affairs at the Foreign Office.

'Finally!' Sir Orme greeted him. 'Someone who knows De Gaulle.'

English civil servants, he told Gaston, were confused by and sceptical of the general. They saw Free France as little more than a fantasy which could not endure for long. Gaston explained urgently that De Gaulle was the only French general with any real grasp of the political situation, and that during the period of defeat, when the French government had fled, he had been the only man who had stood firm. Working himself into a splendid fit of rhetoric, Gaston declared: 'I have always seen our only hope in him … At Bordeaux, I met old friends, destroyed by the defeat. They bowed their heads and said to me "It's finished." I answered them "No! Nothing is finished! For there is De Gaulle! De Gaulle! De Gaulle!"' His rousing speeches performed an essential service to De Gaulle, whose fanatical hauteur had given the impression to many that he might be more than a little mad. As an old friend, who had believed in the general's cause for so long, Gaston was able to use his excellent English, his urbane charm and his knowledge of English culture to convince the British of De Gaulle's credibility.

He had missed De Gaulle by days. On 31 August, the general had embarked at Liverpool for Dakar. De Gaulle was adamant it was essential that the Free French begin their fight as soon as possible on French soil, explaining to his staff on 15 July that he planned to establish the capital of the 'empire at war' in Africa. Several French colonies had already declared for him: Tahiti, Chandernagor, New Caledonia and New Hebrides. On 27 July he put out a call to the remaining territories of the French empire to join him. By the end of August Chad, Cameroon, the Congo and Ubangi-Shar had rallied to the general, who had recognized rather before Hitler did the crucial role that Africa was to play in the war. Free French territory had suddenly expanded from the space occupied by De Gaulle's feet to immense swathes of Africa, of which De Gaulle believed Dakar to be the crucial locus.

De Gaulle's attempt to take Dakar was a disaster. Arriving with his pathetic little mongrel fleet, he tried the first phase of his plan (unfortunately codenamed Happy), which was to take the port without violence. The governor general turned a machine-gun on the Free French negotiators and imprisoned the leaders of Gaullist demonstrations in the city. After some halfhearted shelling of the Vichy ship *Richelieu*, a small landing party was put ashore, and three Free French were killed. De Gaulle had no wish to pit Frenchman against Frenchman and he and his British colleague, Admiral Cunningham, agreed to retreat. Churchill countermanded this, goaded by the British press and the scorn of Washington, and Dakar was shelled, resulting in severe damage to a ship from each side and the loss of 2,000 lives, half of them inhabitants of Dakar, 200 of them French. Some observers suggested that De Gaulle came to the brink of suicide at this point, though Churchill had defended him in the Commons, taking full responsibility for the debacle and reaffirming his trust in the general. The African adventure did produce some successes. De Gaulle was greeted by enthusiastic crowds in Cameroon and Chad on his way back to London, Vichy troops surrendered to Philippe Leclerc de Hautecloque (abruptly renamed Leclerc) at Gabon and the general felt confident enough to create the first Free French decoration, the Ordre de la Libération.

Gaston and De Gaulle were reunited on 18 November 1940. De Gaulle beamed with joy when he saw his old friend and immediately asked him if he would take the role of director of political affairs of Free France. It was a dauntingly broad portfolio. Reporting directly to De Gaulle, Gaston was to be responsible for gathering and exploiting information concerning the political situation in France and its empire, with the aim of penetrating every aspect of 'political, social, religious, economic, professional, intellectual' life and emphasizing the necessity of a united national interest. Foreign affairs, insofar as they had an impact on French politics, were also to be closely considered. Accordingly, Gaston's bureau was to be divided into three sections: liaison with the Allied information services, action in France and the empire and liaison with the direction of foreign affairs.

Strategically, the rallying of the African territories had greatly strengthened the position of the Free French with their allies. They could offer air and land routes to the Sudan, Libya and Egypt, favourable trade in essentials like coffee, rubber, palm oil and cotton and protection for Southern Atlantic naval bases. Less positive was the effect of Dakar on the already precarious relationship between De Gaulle and Roosevelt.

If Nancy Mitford's subsequent vociferous loathing for Americans had a political source, it was Gaston's accounts of the contempt with which De Gaulle believed he had been treated by the American president. When Gaston had first arrived to join the Free French in London, the general had remarked: 'The London French, my dear fellow, fall into two groups: those who are in the United States and those who are getting ready to leave.' From the first, as America continued to recognize Vichy France, the States represented a threat to De Gaulle's authority, the French empire and the potential legitimacy of France's position in a post-war Europe. Though their views on the enervated state of the French body politic in the Thirties were essentially similar, the mutual suspicion and dislike that prevailed between the two leaders, compounded by what De Gaulle saw as a lengthy chronology of affront, culminating in the exclusion of France from the 1944 Dumbarton Oaks summit and her absence from the Yalta, San Francisco and Potsdam conferences, compromised their collaboration throughout the war and De Gaulle's

American policy after it. Gaston had strong views on American cultural depravity and the nastiness of 'le high grade' pork supplied in rations after the liberation, but his attitude was affable compared to De Gaulle's aggrieved aggressiveness, while his genius for diplomacy contributed significantly to the maintenance of this most fragile, volatile and crucial of relationships.

11

POOR FROGS

'They're a dirty lot. I used to be in a hotel as a chambermaid and we had to take them. They ruined all the nice rooms in no time.' This comment, recorded by Mass Observation from a Cricklewood resident, was typical of the dislike and prejudice faced by many of the 4,000 French refugees who had managed to make their way to London between May and June 1940. Prior to the war, MO reports suggested that the Germans were regarded more favourably by many British people than the French. Throughout the Thirties, the Francophobe stereotype of the bearded, lubricious Frenchman had been associated with a suspicion of aggressive militarism; after May 1940, this was replaced with a contempt for their effete passivity, though the lubricity remained. The bureaucratic chaos the refugees found in Britain after Dunkirk was little better than that they had fled. The British authorities' response was well intentioned but badly organized, accommodation and billeting allowances had been planned for but not yet put in place.

The majority of refugees were mothers with children and young men, predominantly from reserved occupations, and the latter, in the Phoney War atmosphere of paranoia about fifth columnists and parachuting nuns, were immediately perceived as a potential threat. Most were rounded up into ill-staffed camps in the south-east, Midlands and north-west, where enforced idleness and insanitary conditions had a deleterious effect on morale. De Gaulle toured several such camps, where the men slept under canvas, observing that they felt betrayed after

Dunkirk and were conscious of ill treatment. In particular they were distressed by the compulsory presence of armed guards and barbed-wire fencing. 'I feel ashamed of being a British woman,' wrote one camp visitor, 'every time I go to the camp and see ... that awful infirmary.'[1]

The fall of France had come as a profound psychological shock to the British. 'Bleeding French' was a remark heard by many Mass Observation reporters. The British didn't want the refugees, and the refugees didn't want to be there. For many Londoners, the arrival of escapees at the capital's stations was the first evidence, in the eerie calm of those first months, that a war was being fought at all. George Orwell described the silence with which they were greeted, a silence remembered also by the diarist Mollie Panter-Downes, who noted that the French defeat was so overwhelming it could not be spoken of. Paul Johnson vividly recalls the plight of servicemen who had fled Dunkirk, 'destitute, with nothing but their greatcoats'. While MO reports suggest that the overwhelming attitude to the French, including their suspiciously unknown leader, was negative and mistrustful, many did express pity for the refugees' plight. Station porters carried their pathetic belongings for nothing, and advertisements for missing family members were placed free of charge. In the French press, at stations and in reception centres, heartbreaking announcements began to appear: 'Grillot, Françoise, age 2 and a half (family of 12), from Luyères was with her elder sister in a military bus. Her sister was very seriously hurt ... she fainted and since that moment, no news of little Françoise, who has disappeared.'[,]

No statistics exist as to the number of children, of a total of 90,000 who were separated from their parents after the invasion, arrived orphaned in Britain.

One of Gaston's first duties was liaising between the Free French and Vere Ponsonby, the 9th Earl of Bessborough, head of the newly created Department of French Welfare. Bessborough supervised propaganda concerning De Gaulle's movement, the welfare of French civilians and refugees and the occupation or repatriation of members of the French armed forces if they chose not to join the Free French. Recruitment was initially poor. Of 11,550 French sailors in Britain at the outbreak of war, only 882 opted for the Free French and just 300 from a permanent expat population of 10,000. The military was better represented, with 2,000 joining by July 1940. What to do with the remainder was Bessborough's headache, and it quickly became Gaston's. Their job was complicated because the French Welfare department was the administrative centre for no fewer than twenty-eight separate charities and associations that concerned themselves with the French, as a consequence of which Bessborough's days at his headquarters at the Savoy were mostly spent arbitrating internal quarrels.

The atmosphere was not much better at 4 Carlton Gardens, the Free French headquarters. Outwardly, the general's routine revealed him as a giant be-jodhpured automaton, arriving punctually from the Connaught Hotel at nine, proceeding straight to his office next to Gaston's, overlooking St James's Park, returning to the Connaught at 1pm for a heavy luncheon, including *digestif* and cigar, then heading back to the office to work until eight. To the MP and diarist 'Chips' Channon, who spied him strutting 'insolently' along Jermyn Street, De Gaulle appeared serene in his self-proclaimed role of saviour of France. Within the eccentric, extremist atmosphere of Carlton Gardens, his friable self-esteem and obsession with French dignity could produce an atmosphere of near hysteria.

Within the broader context of the war, the British government's principal problems with France in 1940 were reconciling their support of the Free French with Roosevelt's mistrust, relations with Vichy, De Gaulle's status and that of the nascent French Resistance. De Gaulle's goal was to achieve united control of all French resistant movements while negotiating their volatile relationships within the Allies. Gaston's principal problem was controlling De Gaulle. The general had 'never pretended to like the English. But coming to them as a beggar, with his country's wretchedness branded on his forehead and in his heart, was unbearable.'[2] Harold Macmillan, who knew De Gaulle during the North African campaign, described him as a combination of 'terrible inferiority complex and spiritual pride'.[3]

Gaston loved political prestige, but found its milieu lugubrious. Much as he worshipped the general, he never claimed De Gaulle was much fun socially. Much more to his taste were the society acquaintances he had developed during his period at Oxford, and as often as he could he escaped from Carlton Gardens, which shared 'that heavy atmosphere which envelops all power' to spend time with '*les gens du monde*'. Not everyone was thrilled with his society airs. Georges Boris, former Cabinet director to Leon Blum, remarked: 'We needed an administrator, what we got was a dancer.'[4] Many names familiar to readers of the *Tatler*, including Nancy Mitford, were keen to show their support for the Free French. Lady Peel opened a hotel in her house in Baron Square, Lady Spears donated funds for a Free French hospital, a Churchill cousin set up a restaurant at Olympia for Free Frenchwomen and Olwen Vaughan established the Petit Club Français in St James's Place.

Officially known as the Canteen of the Allies, the Petit Club was one of the landmarks of Free French London. There were never enough funds, the food, cooked at first in a converted lavatory, was famously dreadful, even by wartime standards, and Olwen, in alice band and unfortunate lipstick, could be a terrifying hostess, unceremoniously flinging out anyone to whom she took a dislike, but the ambience was remembered happily for years by Free Frenchmen. Olwen loved the cinema as much as she loved France, having been secretary of the British Film Institute when it opened in 1933, and her colleagues in the film industry came over to Piccadilly from Soho, lending much bohemian glamour. The club was described in Irwin Shaw's novel *The Young Lions* as 'merely three small rooms decked with dusty bunting with a long plank nailed on a couple of barrels that did service for a bar. In it, from time to time, you could get venison chops and Scotch salmon ... It was the sort of place where all ranks could fraternize on a mildly alcoholic basis with the certain knowledge that the cold light of day would erase the military indiscretions of the previous night.' Olwen served red Algerian wine at legal prices to her homesick guests, on Bastille Day she decorated with *tricolores* and the party spilled out into the street. Thanks to her film connections, the Petit Club became the place where, 'if you knew Rita Hayworth was in town, you went to look, before the Savoy'.

The general would dine at the Ritz, the Connaught, the Savoy, or the RAC Club on Pall Mall; Gaston preferred parties at Emerald Cunard's suite at the Dorchester or the Travellers' Club, where he became a member, presented by Harold Nicolson. He particularly admired the staircase, a gift from Talleyrand. At a lecture given by Nicolson on Proust, he met a Parisian acquaint-ance, the Marquise de Ludres, at the door, and asked her, since she had known Proust so well, if she had divined his genius in their conversations. 'If I had, I would have kept his letters,' she replied. He discovered several other old *gratin* friends, including the Princess de Polignac and Leo d'Erlanger, by whom he was introduced to the foreign minister Lord Halifax. In turn, Halifax presented him to Major 'Fruity' Metcalfe and his wife Baba, sister-in-law to the imprisoned Diana Mosley. Gaston's social life was an essential means of publicizing the Free French and getting influential people on the general's side – several dinners were organized, including one with Cecil Beaton, who photographed De Gaulle, and Noël Coward.

For all Boris's accusations of frivolity, Gaston never lost sight of the reason for his presence in London; for all the determinedly cheerful gaiety of the Petit Club or the aristocrats in exile, France remained lost, and the future horrifically uncertain.

In London ... the light was grey. We were Frenchmen and we walked about the streets of that London like so many broken toys, useless and shamefaced spectators on the rocks of a beach being covered by an irresistible tide. There was a collapse of all standards, the ground giving way under one's

feet, the unspeakable bitterness of the present, the inco-
herence of the imagined future.[5]

Leo d'Erlanger, with whom Gaston was lodging in Mayfair, later
showed him the rug which had lain before the fireplace in his
bedroom, worn out by long nights of pacing, as Gaston walked
sleepless, 'obsessed by the sadnesses of the present and the memories of the past'.

12

LOVE

After seven months in London, Gaston became weary of the petty, backstabbing culture at Carlton Gardens. As an experienced, professional politician, he was equally frustrated and irritated by the pomposity and incompetence of many of his colleagues who took their titles too seriously and their jobs not seriously enough. Knowing that De Gaulle made it a point of honour never to refuse a man who wished to return to active combat, he requested a transfer to Africa. He suggested that Maurice Dejean, who before the war had served as *chef de cabinet* to the minister for foreign affairs, replace him and in March 1941 he was delegated in turn to the command of Free French forces in East Africa. Departing from Glasgow, Gaston took an enforced six-week holiday as his ship, evading German submarines, crawled to the Cape, before crossing South Africa and Angola to Ethiopia. The port of Djibouti, which remained loyal to Pétain, gave the country its principal access to the sea and was of great strategic importance in providing a 'ladder' for ships to the Horn of Africa, to the south of the Suez Canal. Gaston's aim was to bring French Somalia over to the Free French and to support the British blockade of the port, which would considerably weaken Vichy forces in the region. After visiting Aden and Cairo for negotiations with the British, he arrived in Addis Ababa on 11 June.

The resources of the Free French were very meagre. Gaston had one infantry battalion (the BM4), recently arrived from Syria, at his disposal, as well as a group of deserters from Djibouti.

He set about raising two more Somali companies and distributing leaflets by air over the port to encourage French soldiers to abandon Vichy, flying many of these missions personally. He also set up a Free French mission to Kenya under Lieutenant Henri Girard which would oversee the situation in Madagascar, La Réunion and the Comoros Islands. In November, he achieved a small success when Free French troops fought alongside the British at the taking of the Ethiopian town of Gondar.

Christmas found Gaston in pensive mood. The sparkling chill of the desert nights reminded him of 'the time when the Ethiopian king turned with the two other *magi* towards the stable at Bethlehem'. The soldiers of the BM4 sang carols 'fervently' and 'our hearts went out with desolate ardour towards those families and loved ones of whom, lost in this corner of Africa, we had no news. How far away France seemed in those times when victory was as yet uncertain.' It was as well, perhaps, that news was so scarce, as learning that he had been deprived of the French nationality his father had struggled to attain would have made a wretched Christmas present. Gaston's brother Jean-Paul, who had been able to return to France, had received a visit from an official at Louveciennes informing him that Gaston had been stripped of his citizenship as a consequence of his joining the Free French, and that all his possessions were to be sequestered awaiting confiscation. Luckily, the inspector sent to deal with the division of the brothers' property agreed to permit Jean-Paul to act as conservator for Gaston's share and conveniently disappeared, a gesture which made it clear where his own sympathies lay. The next summer, Jean-Paul was informed by friends that Gaston's apartment in the Rue Bonaparte was also to be sequestered and for a month he smuggled his brother's furniture, books and beloved *bibelots* out of Paris to safety.

Gaston grew more and more frustrated with the complexities of his role in Ethiopia. Early in 1942, he had met Haile Selassie, restored to his imperial title by the British after the brief Italian occupation. Selassie was alert to the potential of co-operation with the Free French and their powerful allies against the continuing threat of Italian expansionism, but though he promised to do all he could to facilitate Gaston's mission, Gaston himself was sceptical of the British position. He voiced his concerns to De Gaulle, claiming it was obvious that the British, obliged to evacuate Ethiopia, were as anxious as possible to remove any foreign influence, particularly that of the Free French in Djibouti with its vital railway. In response, De Gaulle blamed the State Department in Washington for its 'protectionist' strategy towards Vichy, which was preventing the Free French from bringing the province of the Somali coast into the war and handicapping Vichy through the Djibouti blockade.

Gaston did manage to extract the confirmation of the concession of the Djibouti railway in favour of the Free French (it had belonged to France before the war), but he also learned that a simultaneous treaty between the British and the Ethiopians would risk consigning the concession to the Allied Military Government for Occupied Territories (AMGOT), that great Gaullist bugbear. Selassie responded to Gaston's protests by claiming that he perfectly understood the difficulties of the Free French and asked only that they understood his. Worse still, Gaston heard that the British and Vichy had come to a secret accord whereby the territory of Djibouti would not be attacked in return for Vichy leaving the ships in the port alone, and making no attempt upon Aden. Gaston attempted to block this agreement, but the attentions of the British, and indeed De Gaulle, were frankly elsewhere.

Djibouti would not be definitively claimed for the French until January 1943, when Général Paul Legentilhomme was installed as high commissioner for the Indian Ocean after an offensive involving 1,800 troops the preceding November. By then, Gaston had been back in London for several months, having achieved little more than a medal for his efforts. Despite his extremely limited success as a diplomat, he had ventured to ask De Gaulle for an embassy, but the general, looking rather hurt, asked plaintively: 'Do you not wish to work with me?' and offered him the post of director of his Cabinet. From then on, they worked together in 'perfect understanding'.

Nancy Mitford's involvement with the Free French began in August 1940, when she took a job in a canteen at White City established for French soldiers who had been interned after Dunkirk. She stayed in North London with Julian Huxley, a biologist, and his Swiss wife Juliette. Writing to Gaston in 1963, she remembered how much she hated Mrs Huxley for her cruelty to the French troops in their time of despair. Nancy decided that she adored them. 'I never knew what hard work was before, I only hope I can stand up to it,' she told Mrs Hammersley. '... but am perfectly happy and simply love the frogs more and more.' She returned to Blomfield Road that September, as the Blitz was beginning. 'The nights!' she exclaimed. 'Nobody who hasn't been in it can have the smallest idea of the horror one is going through. I never don't feel sick, can't eat anything and though dropping with tiredness can't sleep either ... last night I shall never forget as long as I live.' Maida Vale was particularly badly affected, as the Luftwaffe aimed for Paddington station, and Nancy's descriptions are a moment-by-moment account of what it was like to endure the bombing.

Peter had appeared with the two small children of one of the men in his unit who had been bombed out. Their mother was dying of a miscarriage and the soldier had no leave. Nancy put them to bed in the kitchen where she was sleeping with her maid, Gladys, and at two o'clock that morning the house next door was hit. Nancy took the children through the blackout in a taxi to Hampstead – 'it was like leaving Sodom and Gomorrah, great fires the whole way and fearful explosions' – where her old governess Zella found them a bed. The Home Guard fired on her returning cab and she awoke to find five more Blomfield Road homes destroyed. The children, Gladys, Nancy's bulldog, fur coat and linen were sent to the country later that morning in another cab. 'I think every living thing that can be got out of this hell should be ... the screaming bombs simply make your flesh creep ... the great fires everywhere, the awful din which never stops and the wave after wave of aeroplanes, ambulances tearing up the street and the horrible unnatural blaze of light from the searchlights all has to be experienced to be understood.' (According to Nancy, Gladys nonetheless loved air-raids – in a BBC interview she recalled her maid popping her head round the bedroom door towards the end of the war and remarking, 'Isn't it a *treat* to hear them again?') At White City, some of her earlier enthusiasm for the divine frogs had turned to exasperation at their spoiled behaviour. She had gone to considerable trouble to procure a cardinal to offer a little spiritual succour, but they *would* persist in grumbling that the bombs kept them awake and that they hadn't been taken to the theatre even once: '*Ça je trouve un peu exagéré quand même.*'

Maida Vale was impossible, so the Rodds moved back to Rutland Gate, which was being used to house Jewish refugees from Poland evacuated from the East End. ('Isn't it killing?' wrote Deborah to Diana.) Nancy was impressed by their quiet bravery and did what she could to cheer them, buying them Christmas presents (she looked up the Feast of Queen Esther first so as not to give offence) and organizing a dance. Lady Redesdale was foul about the Jews, claiming she would never again want to live at Rutland Gate and criticizing Nancy, doing her best in a huge house full of people with only one maid, for the dirt and mess. One girl of sixteen was pregnant. Nancy suggested a strenuous walk and a hot bath, but was anxious it might not take. 'Shall I be obliged to wield a knitting needle and go down to fame as Mrs Rodd the abortionist?' She was quick to see the comic potential in the other unlikely wartime hats she wore. She volunteered to give a course of lectures on fire-watching, but the organizer had to explain after the first that the audience found her voice too irritating. The peculiar high-pitched drawl which characterized the speech of Nancy and her peers was apparently developed to carry over the sound of Bright Young gramophones; Nancy's listeners failed to appreciate its gaiety and wanted to put her on the fire. In 1941, she was hired to arrange holidays for ARP workers, a great success – They come back saying how the wife and I couldn't have been better treated if we were King and Queen. They are such heaven – but, she added to Jessica, 'The other people in the office think I'm a sort of joke and when there's a quiet moment do imitations of me on the telephone.'

Much more exciting was the request Nancy received in March 1941 from 'a friend of mine at the War Office' to infiltrate the Free French officers' club. She, too, was to have her chance of being a glamorous lady spy. The idea, Nancy explained to Mrs Hammersley, was to 'try to find out something about them. They are all here under assumed names, all splashing mysteriously large sums of money about and our people can't find out a thing about them and are getting very worried.' Having so little experience of French society, Nancy was nervous and declared rather disingenuously that it would bore her to work in an officers' club. Nevertheless she was intrigued. The *espion*-riddled Free French were both glamorous and enigmatic. Two neighbours in an expensive flat at Rutland Gate called themselves the Selliers and claimed to work at the Quartier Général, though another acquaintance, whose *nom de guerre* was Violette ('Why not Pansy?' asked Nancy, forgetting her Napoleon), insisted she had never heard the name.

Nancy became a Gaulliste before she ever met Gaston. Within weeks of her successful penetration of the club, she was describing to Jessica her approval of the general's plans for post-war settlements. She also approved of the way French officers kissed one's hand without having to be 'rendered gaga with love first like the English ones', their heroic stories, their love of chatting. Being amusing in a foreign language is always a boost to the self-esteem and if Nancy liked her 'wonderful' Free frogs, they liked her back, appreciating her knowledge of their country, her prettiness and her chic, simple clothes. Their company was all the more soothing as Nancy was beginning to accept the fact that her eight-year marriage to Peter was effectively over.

Inside the cover of her day diary for 1941, Nancy wrote a sad meditation on the state of her relationship.

Waiting for love: Nancy spent five hopeless years 'engaged' to Hamish St Clair Erskine.

Nancy's wedding to Peter Rodd – handsome, feckless and famously boring.

Gaston Palewski, 'the
Colonel', Nancy's
great love.

The Connaught Hotel – Nancy and
Gaston were caught here together
and it remained a codeword ever after.

Rue Bonaparte. Gaston's beloved flat was sequestered as punishment for his having joined De Gaulle.

Immortal in France, General De Gaulle's speech of 18 June 1940 was not thought worth recording by the BBC.

Piccadilly and Leicester Square: Nancy's eyewitness accounts provide a devastating description of the Blitz.

Nancy spent some of her happiest times with Gaston at Rue Monsieur.

'Good clothes are a matter of health' – Nancy was an enthusiastic devotee of the New Look.

Gaston's daily walk across the Pont Royal. Nancy and Gaston were both 'greedy for beauty'.

Nancy spent many happy summers in Venice, for whose preservation she and Gaston campaigned.

The 'Pal Exquis', home to 'l'Embrassadeur'.

Gaston and Nancy were devoted to the spirit of 'l'Europe Française'.

Nancy was a Gaullist even before she met Gaston.

Gaston in action as a politician.

Gaston's achievements commemorated at Rue Bonaparte.

ICI VÉCUT
GASTON PALEWSKI
COMPAGNON DE LA LIBÉRATION
MINISTRE D'ÉTAT
AMBASSADEUR DE FRANCE EN ITALIE
PRÉSIDENT DU
CONSEIL CONSTITUTIONNEL
GRAND-CROIX
DE LA LÉGION D'HONNEUR
1901 – 1984

Louise de Vilmorin was a fixture at the Embassy, a lover of Duff Cooper and – possibly – Gaston.

Did Gaston seduce Nancy's American friend Susan Mary Alsop?

The Sun King's great house was the source of several of Nancy's most successful books.

Paris at his feet and a
beautiful woman in
his arms – Gaston's
scalophilia began with
l'Escalier Daru.

Nancy spent the last years
of her life at Versailles.

Marriage is the most important thing in life and must be kept going at almost any cost, it should only be embarked on where there is, as well as physical love, a complete conformity of outlook. Women, as well as men, ought to have a great many love affairs before they marry as the most critical moment in a marriage is the falling off of physical love, which is bound to occur sooner or later and only an experienced woman can know how to cope with this. If not properly dealt with, the marriage is bound to go on the rocks.

At the beginning of the war, the Rodds' union had enjoyed a brief renaissance, with Peter, so handsome in his scarlet-lined coat, so brave, so keen to do the right thing and Nancy happy to play the adoring wife keeping their home going in Blomfield Road. But her determined hopefulness was, as ever, shattered by the reality of Peter's utter disregard for her feelings. The miscarriage does not seem to have ignited any tenderness in him. When he returned on leave he usually stayed at his club, the Savile, warning any friends he bumped into not to tell Nancy. She was, he told James Lees-Milne, 'a very difficult woman'.[1]

Perhaps he thought this justified his affair with Adelaide Lubbock, a cousin of Nancy's on the Stanley side, with whom he preferred to spend his time in London, visiting her at her first-aid post in Chelsea. Nancy does not seem to have taken the affair very seriously. She continued to mention Adelaide in her letters and invited her to dinner on at least one occasion. What pained her was more that Peter didn't bother to conceal his neglect with good manners. When they did meet, he would cheerfully remind her that widows' pensions were very small, and little of his army pay made its way to his wife. His legendary dullness took on an increasingly bullying tone: Lees-Milne described a dinner at the Ritz in 1944 where Prod's droning became aggressive and Nancy tried pathetically to placate him. Whatever 'physical love' they had shared was dead and there was very little else left. Nancy's letters from this period suggest she was depressed, felt old and ugly and was incapable of taking an interest in her life which, for her, was the worst sign of all.

Perhaps a solution was to take a lover of one's own? Roy André Desplats-Pilter (*nom de guerre* André Roy) had joined the Free French in October 1940 and worked as a liaison officer in the Quartier Général. He was clever and charming and rich and he and Nancy were soon involved in a very adult love affair, visiting Nancy's friend Helen Dashwood in her lovely house at West Wycombe and trying to enjoy what social life the shattered capital had to offer. Roy was clearly a kind man. In 1942 Nancy gave a party at Blomfield Road to which she invited Unity, who was now overweight and distinctly eccentric-looking. Nancy stuffed her into a black dress of her own, with a coat over the top to cover the open fastening, but Unity refused to make up her face. Roy took her to the bathroom and did it for her, rendering poor Unity 'awfully pretty'. Not many men would have been capable of such tactful and skilful gentleness. The affair was clearly physical – it was during this relationship that Nancy suffered the ectopic pregnancy that destroyed her fertility – and again, Roy was kind, visiting her in hospital (he thought her choice of reading matter there, Châteaubriand's *Mémoires d'Outre Tombe*, positively narcoleptic). After Nancy's convalescence in the country they continued to see one another on her return to London in March 1942, when she began her job at Heywood Hill's bookshop in Curzon Street.

It was odd that Nancy didn't meet Gaston at Heywood Hill, as the shop was popular with the Free French. It was there that Gaston bought the gift of Saint-Simon's memoirs which Général de Gaulle later kept in his study at Colombey. The Curzon Street shop was already a nexus for social London – handy for the Ritz, Trumper's barbers a few doors down, and a hop from the clubs of St James's, not to mention the brothels in Shepherd Market (one of Nancy's favourite stories was of the tart whose wartime business was going so well she wished she could open a second front). When Heywood Hill was called up at the end of the year, his wife Ann, an assistant, Molly Friese-Green, and Nancy managed the business. Nancy walked over from Maida Vale every day, sometimes running to keep warm, 'very thin and upright, her arms folded over her chest, and her long legs jerking to left and right of her like a marionette's'.[2] She was a cold body. With the stove cranked up 'her' shop, as Evelyn called it, was a much more sympathetic salon than dismal, bombed-out Blomfield Road. Everyone came – Harold Acton, Cecil Beaton, the Sitwell brothers, Cyril Connolly, Lord Berners (a great friend of both Nancy and Diana, and the model for Lord Merlin in *The Pursuit of Love*), Gerry Wellesley, Waugh, Raymond Mortimer. For many, the shop was an oasis of delight in wartime London. Nancy was actually a rather good bookseller, though she concealed it well – 'A little less darling and a little more attention, please!' rapped out one customer, wearied by the endless shrieks. 'Even the books,' wrote Harold Acton, 'seemed to join in the laughter during their exchange of gossip.' Today a blue plaque on the site records her time there.

Gaston, too, has a blue plaque to commemorate his achievements: at 1 Rue Bonaparte in Paris. There is nothing left, now, of the garden at the Allies Club where he and Nancy met, but the geography of their affair can still be traced through Mayfair and St James's, Hyde Park Corner, Maida Vale. From that first evening, for Nancy, for ever, this was love. In *The Pursuit of Love*, Linda describes the sensation.

> She was filled with a wild, strange, unfamiliar happiness, and knew that this was love ... she knew that never before, not even in dreams, and she was a great dreamer of love, had she felt anything remotely like this. She told herself, over and over again, that she must go back ... but she had no intention of going back, and she knew it.

Ann Rosse, Oliver Messel's sister, was a close friend of both Nancy and Evelyn Waugh. She was part of the set of upper-class habitués of London's smartest air-raid shelter, the 'Dorch'. In 1942, she lent Gaston a house at 27 Eaton Terrace. And so, one morning in September, he returned there at dawn from dinner at Blomfield Road, got into bed and picked up the telephone. It rang across the Park, in the house he had just left.

'Alors, racontez.'

Nancy asked him to pronounce her name the French way, like the town. She liked the sound of her name in his heavy accent. He agreed, and she recounted the first of the stories of her life, her family and friends that kept him fascinated for thirty years. From September until May, Gaston dined with her and slept at her house, returning in his car to Belgravia to telephone her for a long, deliciously silly conversation before setting off to Carlton Gardens for another day of liberating France.

Gaston was unlike any man Nancy had ever known. As is the case with many men who genuinely like women, there was a feminine side to his character. His interest in lovely things, in chatting, in jokes, was seductive in an entirely different fashion to the rather aggressive (indeed comic) masculinity of Tom Mosley. One can't really imagine Noël Coward calling him 'chéri' as he did Gaston. Mosley, whose relationship with Diana Nancy has been represented as envying, was sexual Marmite – strong, unsophisticated, something one either craves or hates. Unlike Mosley, who never had and never did amount to anything politically from the day he left the Labour benches, Gaston was also someone Nancy could admire, a decorated hero, illuminated by the halo of 'le Grand Charles' fighting to save the country she worshipped. She had a very handsome husband already, so his lack of looks didn't matter a bit (she sticks to the truth with Fabrice de Sauveterre, though admittedly, by the time she gets to Charles-Edouard de Valhubert the colonel resembles a film star). And, there is no doubt, his lovemaking was an education and a revelation.

In his family memoir *The House of Mitford*, Jonathan Guinness suggests that Nancy was never very interested in sex. His brother Alexander agreed, but then young men rarely find their aunts sexy. Jonathan's argument is based on Nancy's portrayal of Mme de Pompadour in her biography of Louis XV's mistress as physically a cold woman who found lovemaking exhausting. To infer from this that Nancy felt the same seems odd – characters like Polly Hampton and the Bolter adore 'rolling and rolling' with their lovers and Jonathan never suggests, correspondingly, that Nancy went in for that. She was completely relaxed about sex – in her correspondence with Waugh she happily discusses 'fucking' and masturbation – Lady Jane Grey was an early, if improbable favourite, and she is quite fascinated by lesbianism ('Lizes') and homosexuality ('buggers'). She described herself as 'ferociously normal' and in an interview at an age where women are supposed to be past that sort of thing she pronounced lovemaking 'delightful'.

Before she met Gaston, Nancy plainly hadn't met anyone who was much good at sex. (Poor Capitaine Roy died of tuberculosis just after the war, and may not have been very vigorous.) A *Spectator* reviewer, Alistair Forbes, who knew them both put it quite bluntly: 'To a beguiled and consenting party like Nancy his pleasure-giving skills in the sack made her conclude that ... Peter Rodd had quite simply been ignorant of the facts of lovemaking life.' Nancy's letters to Gaston only go so far as to refer to her longing for him, but they employ a code, 'Connaught hotel', that alludes to a mortifying incident in which Nancy was caught by an officious concierge on her way up to Gaston's room. It is used between them well into the Sixties, to tease, but also, given the content of the letters in which it appears, as a shorthand for a reminder of pleasure shared.

Nancy was acknowledged as a pretty, even beautiful woman, but her particular allure didn't captivate Englishmen. She was not what she herself called a 'romper'. What Harold Nicolson described as her 'hoydenish Roedean quality' was in her manner, which was extremely sharp, vicious even. Tom Mosley once remarked 'poor brute' when Nancy teased Gaston after a hard day's work. Presumably he cared for women who were better at being gazed on (Diana was not, and she minded). Men, at least the heterosexual Englishmen Nancy knew, weren't wild about clever girls. Throughout Nancy's writing on France, she praises the way in which French conversation keeps one up to the mark, one is always obliged to produce an aperçu about Gide or Proust, to sparkle rather than simper. Frenchmen admire prettiness, but they also expect cleverness. And Nancy's particular sort of prettiness, her attention to elegance, even as she kept strictly to four inches of tepid bathwater and bemoaned the lack of wearable clothes, was ideal to Gaston's eye. He always said that he could never love a woman who wasn't elegant. Seduce them, perhaps, but a companion who had no gift for 'arranging herself' would be too damaging to his self-image.

Later, Cyril Connolly told her, 'The trouble with you, Nancy, is one can't imagine you sitting on one's lap. Have you ever sat on anyone's lap?' 'No, and nor have I ever allowed anybody to kiss me.' This is turned into a joke entirely at 'Smartyboots's' expense in *The Blessing*, when Connolly's alter ego the Captain is thwarted by his inability to grasp Grace at the waist. The remark has been read as indicative of Nancy's virginal primness. In truth she would have been horrified at the idea of sitting on Connolly's lap. She deplored the grubby, bohemian women he found sexy, and if her starched Dior skirts kept his like at bay, so much the better. That doesn't mean she wasn't quite happy to sit on Gaston's. And, like many people in the first throes of love, she liked to flaunt it. In June 1944 she wrote to Gaston: 'Osbert Lancaster said at luncheon on Friday that Aly Forbes told him you were so frightened in that raid on Thursday that you kept ringing him up – I said furiously that is a total lie, I was with Palewski all night. Sibyl Colefax said, "All night?", N.R. "Well you know what I mean."' As this slightly embarrassing boasting shows, Nancy had no intention of keeping her relationship with Gaston secret, even though she was still a married woman. 'The Col' was now part of her life and her friends seem to have accepted this without question or any particular surprise. In a letter of 1944, Gaston writes formally to Georgia Sitwell (the wife of Nancy's friend Sacheverell, 'Sachie', and a former mistress of Mosley's) to thank her for a weekend visit he and Nancy had enjoyed. In the manner of Nancy's class and the urgent, *carpe diem* mood of the times, they were acknowledged as a couple.

In her own way Nancy was as much of a *bon viveur* as Gaston. She never drank much alcohol, except for brandy when she was ill, at the end of her life, but she adored food. Her later, much-exaggerated, letters from France are simply swimming in cream and butter. Maybe *gourmandes* can be bad at sex, but women who don't like food are never good at it. Nancy was only cold in as much as she was sensitive to it; very slim with poor circulation, she liked to heat her houses to tropical levels when she could. In Paris, she imitated her sister Diana in sweetening her home with expensive scent carried burning through the rooms on a spoon. Gaston would arrive in the perfumed heat and promptly 'do the death of Chatterton'. During his time in Morocco, he would have been familiar with the quaint thermometers used in colonial buildings there. At 75 degrees, the temperature gauge is marked '*vers de soie*', and accordingly he would call Nancy 'his silkworm'. Rather a sexy nickname.

After eight months of perfect happiness for Nancy, her Colonel was swallowed up by the war. In May 1943, Gaston left with the General for Algiers. Nancy was not entirely abandoned, as a Paris friend of Gaston's moved into Blomfield Road (perhaps as a chaperone?). Marc, Prince de Beauvau-Craon, had escaped via Spain to join the Free French. He was younger than Nancy, in fact the son of one of Gaston's old flames, Mary-Grace Gregorino, and Nancy joked that people thought he was their son. Marc was an ideal companion, taking her to suppers and the theatre, though there was no question of romance between them, although Marc clearly found her very attractive: 'Nancy darling, don't you think of me a little bit?', ran one rather plaintive letter. Marc remained a friend after his marriage in 1952 to Albina-Christina Patino and became something of an adviser to Gaston in his later political career, but though Nancy may have enjoyed flirting with him, there was never the merest question of her so much as looking at another man. While Gaston was away, she deluged him with letters, using all the charm her pen could conjure to keep their relationship alive. If Gaston was not quite such an assiduous correspondent, he might be forgiven, for the future of post-war France was still very much in abeyance.

It had always been the General's aim to establish Free French sovereignty on French soil; now, with the whole of metropolitan France occupied and Vichy's credibility destroyed, it seemed to him that the moment had come. So far as the Americans were concerned, though, nothing had been decided. Roosevelt was pushing his preferred candidate, Henri Giraud, to lead a future administration, and his solution, as tastefully expressed to Churchill in advance of the meeting between the Allies at Anfa, near Casablanca in January 1943, was a 'shotgun wedding', with Giraud as the bridegroom and De Gaulle as the bride. The American perspective is summed up in the Anfa declaration, which stated that:

> France no longer possesses a government. In the interests of the French people and in order to safeguard the past, present and future of the country, the President of the United States and the British Prime Minster recognize that the French Commander-in-Chief, whose headquarters are at Algiers, has the right and duty to act as the director of the French military, economic and financial interests that are or shall be associated with the liberation movement at present established in North Africa and French West Africa . . .

The commander-in-chief was of course Giraud. 'Thus Roosevelt', De Gaulle's biographer concludes contemptuously, 'that paragon of democracy . . . who so firmly maintained the theses of France as *res nullius* against De Gaulle solemnly handed over the authority to a man without the slightest evidence of popular support.[3] De Gaulle confounded Roosevelt by appearing agreeable to an alliance with Giraud, describing the American president's solution as that of a 'great statesman'. He had no intention of allowing Giraud to take over, proposing the establishment of a national committee of French liberation (CFLN) which would operate harmoniously from Algiers. The ostensible aim of De Gaulle's trip was the organization of the command of the North African territories; its purpose was the routing of Giraud. When Duff Cooper, who had been offered the position of British representative to the CFLN, arrived in 1943, the situation was chaotic.

There had been no question on De Gaulle's arrival in Algeria as to which general the people preferred. After meeting Giraud on 30 May, De Gaulle attended a memorial for Algerian combatants where he and his entourage were carried by cheering crowds to the monument to the dead. The next day, De Gaulle held a press conference where he read a statement emphasizing the importance of French sovereignty and the impossibility of working with men appointed by Vichy, who the Americans and Giraud were prepared to retain. The CFLN was announced on 3 June, De Gaulle had now to establish it at the head of the military. Eventually, Giraud was given the North African command, derived from Vichy's troops, and De Gaulle that of the Free French forces, though he was also to oversee the military committee which would have ultimate control. Technically, Giraud was co-president of the CFLN, but not even Roosevelt really believed it by July. In August, Moscow, London and Washington, with varying degrees of reservation, recognized the CFLN.

Duff and his wife Lady Diana had met Gaston in London, where he had dined with them at the Dorchester. Beautiful, unconventional, capricious Diana was a friend of Nancy and close to Evelyn Waugh. Gaston took time out from unravelling Gaullean knots to welcome Diana at the airfield and appointed himself her guide to the 'hub of the free world'.[4] She was soon calling him her 'Laughing Cavalier' (more flattering than her husband's nickname for him, 'Wormwood', as in 'gall and'), as he refused to be fazed by the deplorable conditions in which they found themselves. There was simply nothing to buy, no plates, candles, not a sheet of paper, a hammer or a nail, no soap, no matches, no lightbulbs. Gaston took Diana to the Inter-

Allied Club, where 'all the upper homeless', who hadn't seen butter for months, cheerfully drank sour wine from cut down beer bottles with jagged, lipstick-smeared edges. If Diana complained of the cold, he encouraged her to skip to get warm, still chatting away, he took her to the Kasbah and the old palaces of the city and did his best to cheer her, though he wasn't much help with Mme de Gaulle, 'rather a pathetic little woman . . . she is obviously forbidden to put on any make-up',[5] whose hatred of public life was equalled by Diana's relish for it. The relationship between Duff and Gaston was to veer between affection, admiration and outright contempt, inevitably compromised by both the vagaries of their political missions and the difficulty of the General's personality, but he and Diana always remained close, and she was to be instrumental in Gaston's relationship with Nancy in the immediate aftermath of the war.

PART TWO

1944–73

13

LIBERATION

In May 1944, the telephone rang in Blomfield Road. The operator asked Nancy to hold the line. Then, for the first time since his departure for Algiers, she heard Gaston's voice. She was overcome with emotion, barely able to speak coherently, and afterwards worried that she had been foolish and inarticulate. On 5 June, at 7.30 in the morning, she received another call. Gaston was there, in London, on his way from Northolt, where he had just landed with De Gaulle. Several hours later, after so very long, he was with her, for one brief, perfect night. In *The Pursuit of Love*, Linda hears Fabrice's voice emerging from the maelstrom of war, and waits in calm ecstasy for him to arrive. He has come to tell her he loves her. Perhaps Gaston did the same, perhaps he did not, but surely it is a measure of his regard for Nancy that it was to her he came, at the climax of the Free French struggle, just as the Normandy landings promised to deliver all that the general had for so long fought to achieve.

De Gaulle had been told of the date of the invasion at lunch with Churchill in the prime minister's private railway carriage near Portsmouth. Initially, the encounter went well, and De Gaulle described his admiration of 'the policy of courage that [Churchill] had personified since the darkest hours' as now 'brilliantly justified'. 'Esteem and friendship' wafted round the carriage like the steam from Churchill's perennial baths. Things went sour when the two leaders got down to brass tacks. Churchill endeavoured to encourage the general to meet Roosevelt, a proposal the latter loftily dismissed. 'The French government exists. In that area, I have nothing to ask of the United States of America any more than of Great Britain.' Churchill declared his unequivocal preference for Roosevelt, should he be obliged to divide his loyalties, but Ernest Bevin discreetly added that the prime minister was speaking personally, and not for his Cabinet. The row was smoothed over and Churchill politely proposed a toast to 'De Gaulle, who never accepted defeat', answered by his guest, who proposed 'To England, to victory and to Europe'.

The party then proceeded to Eisenhower's temporary head-quarters, a hut in nearby woodland (there is a touch of bathos in the choice of meeting places for these men who were about to determine the future of the world). De Gaulle was shown a 'draft' (in fact it had already been printed up as leaflets) of a speech Eisenhower was to broadcast at the moment of attack. It was unfortunate that Gaston was presently in bed with Nancy Mitford, as never had his diplomatic skills been more urgently needed. De Gaulle exploded. Eisenhower was named as having entire responsibility for France and no mention was made of De Gaulle, the Free French or the Resistance. That evening, De Gaulle drew up a broadcast in which he called on the French to 'comply with the orders of the qualified French authority', which would allow them to choose their representatives and their gov-ernment once the Germans had been expelled, but when he discovered, on the evening of 5 June, that Eisenhower had dissembled, De Gaulle refused to broadcast after the supreme commander, explaining that this would make him appear to be endorsing Eisenhower's authority – effectively a direct denial of the principles on which the Free French had been operating since the broadcast of 18 June 1940.

Despairingly, Alexander Cadogan described the behaviour of Roosevelt, De Gaulle and Churchill at this juncture as like that of 'girls approaching the age of puberty'.[1] The quarrel between Churchill and De Gaulle, who continued to refuse to send the required military liasion mission to the invading force, was so severe that the two men almost came to blows. Pierre Vienot and

Anthony Eden shuttled between the War Office and Carlton Gardens trying to find a resolution, but Churchill was now so enraged that he dictated a letter expelling the general from British soil. This was subsequently burned, but at 1am, with just three hours to go before Eisenhower launched the invasion, both leaders remained furious and intransigent. Churchill, who, according to Vienot, was even more drunk than usual, accused De Gaulle of treason, claiming that he saw the lives of British and American troops as worthless; De Gaulle denounced Churchill as a gangster.

Finally, on the afternoon of 6 June, De Gaulle spoke on the radio. He talked of the supreme battle that France was now facing and the 'sacred duty of the sons of France to fight the enemy with all the means at their disposal'. His endorsement of Allied authority was vague but sufficient. 'The orders of the French government and by the French leaders it has named for that purpose [must] be obeyed exactly. The actions we carry out in the enemy's rear [must be] co-ordinated as closely as possible with those carried out at the same time by the Allied and French armies.'

Between 6 and 12 June, by which time the invading force had succeeded in establishing a bridgehead stretching 100 kilometres along the coast and 20 inland, Churchill departed to visit the troops at Bayeux. In a rare example of misjudging the press, he did not invite De Gaulle to accompany him. Both the newspapers and the Commons were indignant on De Gaulle's behalf. With the exception of the Netherlands, the governments-in-exile in London now recognized De Gaulle, and there was also pressure from the intelligence services, who reported that the only name being heard in France was the general's. Churchill's attitude to De Gaulle at this point was shamingly truculent. He conceded that the general should be permitted to land and be treated courteously, but explained to Anthony Eden that no meetings ought to be held or crowds encouraged to gather. De Gaulle's principal biographer notes: 'Let it be remembered that the person in question was the head of a government of a country whose armed forces were fighting in the war, whose maquisards were everywhere giving their lives to help the Allies' advance, and whose people, in many places, were being massacred by way of reprisals for the landing.'[2]

On 13 June, Gaston boarded the destroyer *Combattante* with Vienot, Koenig, Boislambert, d'Argenlieu and De Gaulle. They sailed the next morning, landing just after noon near Courseulles. De Gaulle seemed withdrawn and glum, though he explained later that he had been too choked with emotion to speak. One of his entourage tried to start a conversation by observing that it was four years since the Nazis had entered Paris. De Gaulle's laconic response? 'They made a mistake.' Gaston's reaction was more romantic: 'I picked a rose at Bayeux. It stayed a long time on my night table as a message of sweetness and hope.'

Otherwise, the first footsteps on French soil were something of an anticlimax. A few old ladies dressed in black appeared and failed to recognize De Gaulle, two bicycling gendarmes dropped their *vélos* in surprise when they realized whom they were speaking to. For his own part, Gaston knew that the day was won when he spied the scuttling cassocks of the bishops of Lisieux and Bayeux fluttering down the beach. The party was received enthusiastically at Bayeux, where the crowd soon warmed up when they understood who was addressing them, but for De Gaulle it was Isigny that provided the most poignant and sobering sight of the day. The Americans had taken the town and De Gaulle's jeeps were obliged to drive through the wreckage from which bodies were still being dug out. Despite the intense emotions of the day, it was no time for triumphalism.

Gaston departed for Algiers with De Gaulle on 16 June to prepare for the anticipated visit to Washington. Churchill was still smarting from the quarrel, but Eden and Vienot had continued their discussions and arrived at a consensus, reported in a letter from Vienot of 30 June, which seemed to promise a tripartite agreement of recognition of the provisional government, a categoric assertion of French sovereignty, the affirmation of the provisional government's equality with that of their allies and the dismissal of the concept of 'supervision' by the commander-in-chief. Yet from the moment the plane touched down on US soil, it was clear that Roosevelt remained unconvinced. In a snubbing gesture worthy of Louis XIV, De Gaulle was met with a seventeen-gun salute, as accorded to a high-ranking military leader, as opposed to the twenty fired for a head of state. Although the military commanders Marshall, King, Arnold and Vandegrift were summoned to welcome him, Cordell Hull and Sumner Welles were conspicuously absent. Hull awaited him along with Roosevelt at the White House, whence he was conducted in what could only have been a display of outright malignance by Admiral Leahy, the former ambassador to Vichy. Roosevelt greeted his guest in French, and then, in case anyone had missed the point, offered tea to De Gaulle, suggesting that Leahy might prefer Vichy water. For a moment, it was unclear whether De Gaulle intended to leave the room or assault the President of the United States in his wheelchair. Gaston clenched his hand around the General's arm. A frigid cordiality prevailed throughout the dinner, where Gaston remembered the only thing worse than the food was the orchestra, but discussions did begin the following day, 7 July.

In America, public opinion had turned virulently against De Gaulle after his refusal to make the military liaison broadcast. Encouraged by the White House and the State Department, the press portrayed the general as a presumptuous imposter who had actively impeded the Allied advance and sacrificed American lives for the sake of his own status, a position Roosevelt had affirmed at press conferences. De Gaulle surprised his critics by addressing the United States in English, declaring himself happy to be meeting the president once more and paying tribute to 'all those American men and women who at home are working relentlessly for the war and also those brave American boys, soldiers, sailors and airmen, who abroad are fighting our common enemies'. By the end of his trip the *Chicago Daily News*, the right-wing *Nation* and *The New York Times*, as well as the London *Times*, were much more positive.

De Gaulle's manifest enthusiasm for the prosperity and modernity of America was obvious to all who met him. Fiorello

La Guardia, the mayor of New York, had skilfully aligned De Gaulle's success as a popular leader with Roosevelt, who was facing an election; thus his triumphal reception at City Hall served as a Democratic endorsement. Since in terms of metropolitan provincialism the self-satisfaction of Parisians is equalled only by that of New Yorkers, De Gaulle judged his audience perfectly. Taking the microphone from La Guardia, he once again spoke in English. 'From the very first, your city, which is literally a world, perceived where France had its being . . . It is up to us Frenchmen to show that we can return help for help, faithfulness for faithfulness.' If he was dumbstruck when the black singer Marion Anderson sang the 'Marseillaise' at a concert at Madison Square Garden, altogether his public reception in the States could not have been more promising. Gaston's description was 'heartwarming'.

Gaston arrived back in France with the general on 20 August. On 31 July, the Third Army under General Patton had moved westward from Avranches to Argentan, 167 kilometres from the French capital. The race for Paris was on. Gaston recalled that they had almost not made it to Normandy at all. Sleepless in their plane, while De Gaulle dozed beside him, he wept as the pilot enumerated the names of the towns over which they flew. At dawn, a lone German fighter was spotted. The plane had lost contact with its accompanying squadron and Gaston was forced to make a decision. He felt that for those few moments, as the enemy plane circled, the destiny of France was in his hands. The thought that they might be shot down was unbearable, but he knew the general well enough to be certain that he would not consider turning back. So De Gaulle slept on while Gaston watched breathlessly through 'the longest half-hour of my life'. From Cherbourg they arrived via Rennes at Rambouillet, where a doctor was summoned to deal with the general's croaking voice, exhausted by roadside speechifying.

The news from Paris was confusing. On 15 August the city's police had gone on strike in response to a German move to disarm them. Two days later the Communist-dominated

COMAC (Comité Militaire d'Action) met to discuss their options for an uprising. De Gaulle had emphasized that no popular insurrection should begin without his authority, but even as his prefect of police, Charles Luizet, arrived to take up his post the same day, the city appeared to be out of control. The general desperately needed to reach Paris, as a citizens' revolt could mean his authority would be compromised by another popular (that is, Communist) leader, with the implication that Communist government would lead to the imposition of AMGOT. However, his strategy also required that the city should be freed by the Deuxième Division Blindée, under the command of Général Leclerc. He therefore had to convince Eisenhower and Patton to divert a planned thrust northwards towards the Rhine in favour of moving on Paris with the armoured division in the vanguard – and he had to do it before the Parisians established an alternative government.

The Nazis were already fleeing. 'Along the Rue Lafayette, coming from the luxury hotels around the Etoile, sparkling torpedoes pass by containing purple-faced generals accompanied by elegant blonde women, looking as if they are off to some fashionable resort,' described Gaston's great friend, Jean Galtier-Boissière.[3] Despite a chronic lack of Resistance ammunition – the actors of the Comédie Française gallantly planned to revolt with the aid of four shotguns and two dummy pistols from the prop room – fighting had broken out all over the centre of the city, encouraged by the call to arms of the Communist paper *L'Humanité*. An unlikely hero in the preservation of Paris was General von Choltitz, the German commander of the region. Like De Gaulle, Choltitz needed the Allies to arrive swiftly. His orders from Hitler were to defend Paris to the last, and if forced to retreat, to leave the city in ruins. Choltitz procrastinated in the hope of being able to surrender, but he knew that if the Führer learned of this, it would mean the Luftwaffe.

Fretting at Rambouillet, De Gaulle learned at last that Eisenhower had authorized the advance. Covering 240 kilometres in under forty hours, Leclerc arrived in the southern suburbs. Eight kilometres from the Porte d'Orléans, Leclerc learned that General Omar Bradley had given the order for the US 4th Division to advance: There was now a strong possibility that Paris would be freed by Inter-Allied troops rather than French ones. Leclerc ordered Raymond Dronne, the captain of a tank detachment, to push forward into the city by any means possible and accept no command to stop. At around 9.30 on the morning of 24 August Dronne found himself, spent and bewildered, outside the Hôtel de Ville in the fourth arrondissement. A triumphant crowd carried him into the building to the waiting arms of Georges Bidault, the president of the National Council of Resistance. As the news spread, by radio, cycle messenger and frantic telephonists, the bells of first Notre-Dame and then more and more churches began to ring. For many Parisians, this was the unforgettable moment; the moment when the skies above their city swelled with church bells after four years of silence. The historians Artemis Cooper and Antony Beevor note that 'with the occasional boom of a heavy gun and the constant refrain of the Marsellaise ... the Liberation of Paris started to sound like the 1812 Overture'.[4]

At his headquarters at the Hôtel Meurice, General von Choltitz heard the bells and knew that it was over. Paris was saved. On the afternoon of 25 August he was driven through an aggressive crowd to sign the surrender at the Prefecture on the Ile de la Cité. Few of those who jeered and spat at Choltitz were aware of what they owed him. In 1940, Paris had been spared by an American, William Bullitt; now, in 1944, it had been rescued by the last commander of the hated occupiers.

General de Gaulle, accompanied by Gaston, arrived at the Gare Montparnasse shortly afterwards. After saluting Leclerc, they were driven to the old headquarters in the Rue St Dominique, then to the Prefecture and, finally, at eight o'clock, to the Hôtel de Ville. De Gaulle's speech was short and choked with emotion. 'Paris! Paris outraged, Paris broken, Paris martyred, but Paris liberated! Liberated by herself, liberated by her people, with the help of the whole of France, that is to say the France which fights, the true France, the eternal France.'

His promise of 18 June 1940 had been kept. Those who deride De Gaulle, who claim that he was deluding himself as to the actual role the French had played in the liberation, who criticize his blindness, his arrogance, his absurd insistence on his role as the leader of an illegitimate government of a shattered state, are in great measure correct, but they miss an essential psychological point about the general. True, he was fanatical, even ridiculous. His self-consciously mystical identification with Joan of Arc was absurd. True, he had consistently placed the honour of France above the strategies of his allies. But only a fanatic could have done what he had done. Only a fanatic could have defied the state he had sworn to serve, convinced a government at war that he, and only he, alone and almost entirely unsupported, embodied the true spirit of a nation that had capitulated. Only a fanatic could have been possessed of such immovable conviction of the justice of his cause. The quality which had first captivated Gaston, that spiritual separation from other men, was the source of his triumph. De Gaulle *was* in some senses a saint, not because he was good, but because of the extraordinary and unswerving faith in himself as the rightful leader of France that had brought him to this point. And even now, with France at last in his hands, he refused to betray his conviction. Bidault requested him to proclaim the Republic from the balcony of the Hôtel de Ville, and De Gaulle, dumbly, offensively, refused. To proclaim the Republic would be to lend legitimacy to the Pétain regime, to suggest that Vichy had been something more than an illegal aberration. 'Why should we proclaim the Republic?' he asked. 'She has never ceased to exist.'

One wonders where Gaston slept that magical night. The Catholic press may have distributed hurriedly printed leaflets reminding young women of the importance of preserving their virtue even amid the intoxicating joy of the liberation, but no one appeared to take much notice. True to their national reputation, the French celebrated by making love. In what Simone de Beauvoir described as a '*debauche de fraternité*', they rejoiced in the shrubs along the Champs Elysées, in the Tuileries, in the gardens of the Invalides and along the quays of the Seine. One historian suggests that Gaston might have taken the time to go to Louveciennes and hold his mother in his arms, but it does seem rather unlikely there was a vacancy there.

By the afternoon of 26 August, over a million people had gathered along the route from the Arc de Triomphe to Notre-Dame. At three o'clock, De Gaulle arrived to take the salute and relight the flame of the Unknown Soldier, cold and dead since 1940. Then, with Gaston a few steps behind him, the general set off along the Champs Elysées, arms raised in victory, to walk the mile to the Place de la Concorde. In one image, Gaston appears just behind De Gaulle's left shoulder, radiant. When they reached the top of the Rue de Rivoli, De Gaulle got into an open car to travel the last couple of kilometres to Notre-Dame. As he did so, gunfire broke out, and the crowd threw themselves to the ground. It has never been ascertained whether this was a last-minute assassination attempt or a trigger-happy Resistant unused to his weapon, but De Gaulle was imperturbable. The cavalcade moved off, down to the Hôtel de Ville and across to the Ile de la Cité and the cathedral.

What took place at Notre-Dame was a moment of apotheosis, an improbable piece of symbolic theatre that burned into the hearts of all who witnessed it. As the general entered the church, shots were heard once more. His guard returned fire, aiming up at the towers and bringing down lumps of masonry. Again, the crowd hit the floor, those inside the cathedral crawling to shelter under pews or behind pillars. Quite calm, De Gaulle continued his progress, walking alone towards the high altar with the mystical solemnity of a crusader presenting the Oriflamme. Malcolm Muggeridge, serving in British intelligence, was an eyewitness and his account perfectly captures the essence of the man: 'The effect was fantastic. The huge congregation who had all been standing suddenly fell flat on their faces. There was a single exception; one solitary figure, like a lonely giant. It was, of course, De Gaulle. Thenceforth, that was how I always saw him – towering and alone, the rest, prostrate.'[5]

14

THE ADVANCE ON PARIS

Like the rest of the world, Nancy followed the liberation on the BBC, where she also heard of Gaston's appointment as *chef de cabinet*. He wrote to her that Paris was admirably beautiful, that the smoke of the factories was gone, leaving a 'ravishing' sky. Not quite an invitation, but it was enough for Nancy. Just over a year later a 'Mrs Rodd' appeared without warning at De Gaulle's headquarters at Rue St Dominique and asked to see M. Palewski. The doorman was quite used to such requests. André Malraux spitefully described the secretaries on the ground floor whispering respectfully 'Mme la Duchesse pour M. le Directeur'. 'Send up the Duchess!' was the enthusiastic response from upstairs. If Gaston's present arrangements were discommoded by this eccentric arrival, he was far too kind to show it. 'So, what's the news?' he greeted her, and Nancy, having had a year to rehearse, launched into a stream of shriek-making anecdote. Gaston was moved, charmed, delighted to see his '*chère amie*', and if he was obliged to point out to Nancy that he really did have a lot of serious obligations, he also found the time to take her to Versailles to look at the Bouchers.

Nancy had been planning her move for some time. 'Oh, to live in Paris, I'd give anything,' she had written to Lady Redesdale in September 1944. 'I am angling like mad for a job.' Her initial scheme was to establish a Parisian branch of Heywood Hill. While the war dragged on, though, this could only remain an idea, and while she waited it out, Nancy wrote her masterpiece, *The Pursuit of Love*.

'*Et j'ai compris que tous ces matériaux de l'oeuvre littéraire, c'était ma vie passée,*' wrote Proust. It would be absurd to suggest that Nancy Mitford might lay claim to the literary status of Proust, but the 'key' to her novels – who was really who – exerts a similar fascination. The originals of Proust's characters, many of whom were known to Gaston, were kept alive by their literary fame long after the prototypes were dead; Hamish St Clair Erskine, Lord Redesdale, Louise de Vilmorin, Billa Harrod, Peter Rodd, too, are only really of interest now as models. Gaston's fame as Fabrice was both a delight and a curse to him. Cyril Connolly never quite made it as a novelist, but is unforgettable as the Captain in *The Blessing*. Nancy's central character in *Pursuit*, Linda, is a blend of her sisters and herself. Idina Gordon, the inspiration for Fanny's mother, the deliciously unrepentant Bolter, has had a whole biography devoted to her. For Mitford fans, the novels provide an endlessly diverting game of who's who.

Nancy herself was both irritated and amused by the insistence that everyone she knew saw themselves in her books, including her own in-laws and Deborah's. When she wrote her biography of Mme de Pompadour, A.J.P. Taylor insisted that she had merely taken Fabrice and plonked a wig on him. Nancy delighted in this view, wondering if anyone would be convinced by Fabrice as Voltaire – 'exactly like you, all his meals are TAKEN', she wrote to Gaston – but *Pursuit* is a great deal more than a felicitous cobbling together of the anecdotes she recounted to Gaston in the course of their affair. In some measure, the book is wish fulfilment. The Radletts' furious quarrels never end in prison or suicide, Aunt Sadie's vagueness is charming rather than irritating and Uncle Matthew, storming through the story with his stock whip, is a far cry from the battered Lord Redesdale who emerged from the war.

What it is not is the fantasy of a disappointed mistress. When Nancy wrote *Pursuit* she *did* have her colonel, he *had* come back to her from the blue skies above Algeria, and she was preparing to embark on a life with him in the city she loved best in the world.

In July 1945, Lord Redesdale agreed to give Nancy £3,000 to buy a partnership in Heywood Hill, selling French books (which, naturally, she would go to Paris to acquire), for a 30 per cent markup. Nancy raced through the bureaucracy, obtaining a licence from the Board of Trade and an exit permit from the Foreign Office. Her new hat caused a sensation at the passport office. 'The typists and clerks got such terrible giggles, they were paralyzed and couldn't attend to anything, it must have made their day.' English to the core, she set off equipped with dozens of oat-cakes as provision against nasty foreign breakfasts and arrived to find her beloved in her beloved city in glorious sun. She stayed first at the Hôtel Jacob et d'Angleterre, 'the kind of hotel that Oscar Wilde died in', before moving to the Hôtel Pont Royal whose rackety bar was a great feature of ex-pat life. After two weeks she wrote to her mother: 'I am so completely happy here ... I must come and live here as soon as I can, I feel a completely different person as though I had come out of a coalmine into daylight.'

At last Nancy was able to see Gaston's beloved flat in the Rue Bonaparte, which had finally been released from sequestration. He lived on the first floor. The spiral staircase, that essential feature, was late eighteenth century. It led to three succeeding rooms overlooking the courtyard, high-ceilinged, filled with so many treasures of years in the sale rooms. One friend described it as a 'submarine grotto, original, personal, wonderful'; another, less kindly, as 'a souk'. There was a bust of Talleyrand's mistress, several good *terre-cuite* pieces by Clodion, Second Empire fur-niture, pictures by Longhi and a suspicious Magdalen by Simon Vouet, a minor Corot, a marquetry table from the Rothschild collection, a Rodin, landscapes by Narcisse Diaz, a portrait of Pope Benedict XIV by Subeyras and a Louis XV sofa. Gaston had an office, a drawing room and the bedroom which doubled as a dining room, the bed conveniently placed near the table. He blamed the 'cold respectability' of his new position for the impossibility of Nancy staying at his apartment, but within a month, she had found a flat just along the street, at number 20. Once she is installed a few doors away from the tempting *salle à manger*, Nancy's letters sing with happiness. Diana Cooper is angelic, the concierge is angelic, the maid is lovely, the rowing

French neighbours better than a film, the food is lovely, always champagne, even at luncheon. When she returned to London in November 1945 – 'In floods of tears, I do so love it here' – Nancy had decided to leave England for good.

When she came back in April 1946, she was a rich woman. *The Pursuit of Love* had earned £7,000 in its first six months. '*Vive la litterature!*' cried the colonel when he arrived at her hotel to be greeted by a bottle of champagne. Nancy had resigned without regret from Heywood Hill and could afford to start househunting.

The only drawback to Nancy's lovely new wealth was that it made it difficult to get rid of Prod. His relationship with Adelaide Lubbock continued until the 1950s, and they were as accepted in their own way as a couple as were Nancy and Gaston by their friends, but Peter refused to give Nancy a divorce. She was not terribly troubled about the morality of her situation, despite Waugh's grumblings about the indecency of her happiness, but Peter was an encumbrance and an expense. He knew Gaston, of course, and appeared quite amiable towards him – in a letter from Blomfield Road in 1946, Nancy reported to Gaston that Peter wouldn't mind if the Colonel came to stay while he was away on a projected trip to Spain. 'I said to him, about my will, would it hurt your feelings if I left some money to the Colonel. Peter said, hasn't he got any money? NR No PR Then I think it is a good idea, he ought to have some. But the trouble is I'm not dead.'

Nancy was kind to Peter, cooking him breakfast and fussing over his plans, but there is a sense in which she has sailed beyond him, floating in a couture balloon. None of the racking sense of failure that haunted her earlier remarks about their marriage remains. She was in love, her life was blossoming, and perhaps she felt, if anything, sorry and a bit embarrassed for him. Cynthia Gladwyn noted that Nancy was devoted to Prod but she must have found him a crashing bore. By 1948, he was hanging around her Paris flat 'making my life hell', as she wrote to Diana. The prospect of maintaining him indefinitely was a worry – 'even Linda can't pay for that' – but Nancy never seriously considered retreading the thorny path of duty. Though Peter had fought bravely and honourably in the war, peacetime saw a return to his old dissolute habits. He cut a pitiful figure, the bright, beautiful Balliol boy, purposeless, debauched, broke, doing all he could to prey on Nancy's sense of guilt even as his overdraft gobbled up her hard-written funds.

Nancy's biographer Laura Thompson suggests that Prod's refusal to grant her freedom in a sense did her a favour. Just as he had saved her face by pretending to have stolen her from Hamish, now he was her alibi in the 'case of the Unwanted Englishwoman'. So long as she was married, she did not have to face the fact that Gaston wouldn't have her even if she were free. And it was convenient for Gaston to bring up the threat to his political respectability when it suited him. It is impossible, however, to say whether or not he would have married Nancy had he been able to do so in the mid-1940s. Nor indeed whether she would have wished to exchange the freedoms of her own life – her work, her friends, her travels – for the role of a dutiful Yvonne De Gaulle. Prod may have cared enough for Nancy to want to spite her when she spurned him, but his reasons for hanging around were purely mercenary. Had she not been such a professional success, she might have had a chance at becoming Mme Palewski; as it was, Prod, perennially unemployed and full of improbable schemes, had no intention of releasing his meal ticket. He was quite shameless, continuing his habit of stealing any cash Nancy might have left lying about. When he made one of his odd marital visits to Paris, she was forced to have Marie, her housekeeper, sew money into the hems of the curtains to prevent him finding it. Nancy bore no grudge against him, even remained fond, in her way, of the man she had once thought 'heavenly', though he remained the fly in her Guerlain cold cream until any chance she may have had of marriage with Gaston had passed.

For a year Nancy lived like a proper Paris bohèmienne, moving between hotels and borrowed flats, before settling in December 1947 at 7 Rue Monsieur. The perfect introduction to the flat is provided by Evelyn Waugh:

You cross the Seine and penetrate the very heart of the fashionable quarter of Paris, the Faubourg Saint Germain. You go into a quiet side street, so exclusively aristocratic that few taxi-drivers know its name and ring at a great, white shabby door, which in due time opens, revealing a courtyard surrounded on three sides by low buildings of the period of the restored Bourbon monarchy. Straight in front, on the ground floor, with its glass doors opening into a garden behind, lie the apartments of Miss Mitford.[1]

Unlike Gaston, Nancy had no taste for clutter. Her rooms – hall, dining room, drawing room, bedroom, bathroom – (Marie slept several flights up, as was conventional, in the *chambre de bonne*) were furnished with her favourite London pieces, set off by softly draped pink taffeta curtains and new finds from the *antiquaires* of the sixth arrondissement: a damask-covered chaise-longue, a Dresden clock. Her bedroom was white, with an enormous bed and a rather alarming portrait of Gaston, the drawing room was French grey, with the lamps crinolined in ribboned muslin petticoats, which one visitor recalled gave an enchanting light. One of the loveliest pictures of Nancy shows her with Jessica, having tea in a room so sunny it seems like a garden, with white wicker furniture and the walls dappled by the shadows of ivy leaves.

Once she had a flat of her own, Nancy and Gaston could spend more time together, though he never stayed the night, continuing his London habit of going back to bed in the Rue Bonaparte and telephoning her at breakfast time. For a while, at least, it can only have seemed to Nancy that everything she had dreamed of – financial independence, a beautiful home, an admirable, desirable man who loved her, with whose voice she began her days – had been attained. Too many of her biographers, determined to spy out the shadows beneath the sunlight, have been unwilling to grant her this period of unalloyed bliss, but that is what it was.

Pursuit had bought Nancy her new life in Paris and, of course, had made Gaston famous beyond the world of French politics. Her dedication of the book 'To Gaston Palewski' did, however, cause difficulties, though as she observed, it was Gaston's love of publicity that created them. Nancy had anticipated that her politically controversial family might create problems, writing to Evelyn that Gaston was pleased with the dedication, though fearful that the Communists would fall upon it. Negotiations about the dedication went back and forth. 'I said shall I put To the Colonel, to G.P. and so on and he absolutely insisted on having his full name.' Nancy offered to remove it entirely from the French edition. Gaston was clearly unable to resist being portrayed as the greatest French seducer since the Vicomte de Valmont (indeed, in a letter to Princesse Bibesco, he declares himself very pleased with the dedication), but when the connection was made he became very anxious.

In February 1947 Nancy wrote to Diana that a left-wing paper was planning a splash with the headline 'Hitler's mistress's sister dedicates daring book to M. Palewski'. The general was apparently appalled, and Nancy could not resist adding chummily: 'You know how the one thing that can't be forgiven is getting in their way politically.' She mentions two more articles, though in fact nothing appeared, owing to a printers' strike which delayed publication. Nancy claimed that Gaston had not permitted her to see the pieces, which Diana Mosley found extremely odd: 'It is bizarre, Colonel *invented* it.'[2] At Gaston's request, Nancy returned to England for several months. This episode has been used as an example of how he manipulated her, with more than one writer suggesting he shunted her off for his own purposes, on the basis that, as he was by then out of office, such a scandal could not have hurt him. In fact, negative publicity would have been very damaging at what was a delicate time politically, since he was involved, as will be discussed, in the founding of a new Gaullist party, the RPF. And Nancy's letters to Gaston during her absence are packed with lively social news and confident jokes, in no way suggesting that she was in disgrace.

15

POLITICS 1944–6

'When we arrived in Paris,' Gaston recalled 'the great problem which posed itself, with the reordering of the country and the inauguration of an administration which contained a certain number of new elements . . . and the preparation of a new Constitution, was relations with the interior Resistance. Immense difficulties awaited us, on a material as well as a political level . . . we had to draw up political choices which were highly delicate to make.' De Gaulle had immediately confirmed Gaston in his position as Cabinet director, but though the general was now effectively the head of a real, rather than a nominal state, Gaston's initial tasks were domestic.

De Gaulle felt it was premature to install himself in the Elysée Palace, vacated by Albert Lebrun in 1940. Gaston suggested he take the Hôtel de Ville as his headquarters, but the general felt this was too revolutionary. He preferred to return to the Rue St Dominique, another gesture, like his refusal to proclaim the Republic, which emphasized the continuity of the legitimate French government. He took the traditional office of the war minister, with Gaston's *bureau* nearby. Since his flat in the Rue Bonaparte was at that time still under sequestration, Gaston had little choice other than to camp out in the ministry, sleeping in a bed which, it was claimed, had belonged to Napoleon's mother Laetitia. Nancy later admitted she had been fond of this arrangement, as she had always known where Gaston was, and they were both amused by the fact that the war ministry was housed in a former convent which had once hosted Mme du Deffand's famous salon. A favourite story was a conversation between the hostess and her lover, Pont-de-Veyle, with whom she had enjoyed fifty years of 'cloudless happiness'.[1] Discussing their relationship, which had never been troubled by the least disagreement, Mme du Deffand suggested: 'But perhaps it is really because we have been rather indifferent to each other?'

'Very possibly.'

A proper residence had also to be found for the De Gaulle family. Gaston located a suitable house on the Rue Champ d'Entraînement on the edge of the Bois de Boulogne, but De Gaulle was equally stubborn on the question of furniture, refusing to make use of the national collection. Gaston prevailed upon his friendships with the palace dealers to create a home of such prettiness that Mme de Gaulle, with her usual charm, confessed it was rather grander than she should have liked. As a stopgap country residence, Gaston appropriated a building in the grounds of Louis XIV's old pleasure house at Marly, which Tante Yvonne declared to be gloomy and insufficiently simple, so he was also obliged to find workmen to restore the De Gaulles' old home at Colombey-les-Deux-Eglises in the Haute Marne, which had been sacked by the Germans.

Despairing at Mme de Gaulle's insistence on provinciality *avant tous*, Gaston harried builders to complete the job as fast as possible which, given an almost complete lack of transport, raw materials and manpower, was a depressing task and one for which Mme de Gaulle never showed herself in the least bit grateful. Gaston himself was never less than charming about Yvonne, describing her 'perfect simplicity and modesty' and the 'great service she had rendered to her country' in discharging the general from all mundane concerns, permitting him complete freedom to concentrate on the 'immense duties' for which he was responsible. But the fact was that Mme de Gaulle never liked him. She was too plain for Gaston to bother to charm her, and she sensed and resented this lack of acknowledgement, though Gaston, who was well aware of her rancour, was not above making use of it when it suited him to keep Nancy at arm's length.

Rather more pressing than interior décor was the issue of maintaining order, with which the provisional government struggled in the face of the reprisals against collaborators known as the *épuration sauvage*. A legal framework for the purging of collaborators, the *épuration legale*, had been established by an ordinance passed in Algiers in 1943 and in March the following year five principal collaborationist offences were identified: participation in collaborationist organizations, co-operating in propaganda, denunciation or black-market activities and, rather vaguely, any form of 'zeal' towards the Germans. In August 1944, the offence of *indignité nationale*, 'national unworthiness', was added, covering any action considered harmful to the unity of France or to constitute neglect of national duty. Anyone found guilty of the latter could be sentenced to *dégradation nationale* in which civic, professional and particularly political rights were stripped away. Four categories of court, three civilian and one military, were set up to deal with the accused.

In total, 300,000 cases were investigated, 100,000 of those in Paris alone, as collaboration in the capital had been the most widespread and discernible. Nearly 7,000 death sentences, almost half in absentia, were passed, though only 791 executions actually took place. Almost 50,000 people, by contrast, lost their rights under *dégradation nationale*. While their dossiers were processed, accused *collabos* were interned in the camps and prisons where Vichy had held Jews and Resistants. Though the system had been rigorously formulated, its efficient implementation was almost impossible, not least due to an initial lack of magistrates, as only a single judge could be produced who had refused to swear allegiance to Pétain's regime. Bureaucratic inadequacy, which saw thousands of innocent people wait months for their cases to be called, was exacerbated by hideous overcrowding, disease and corruption in the prisons. Inexperienced administrators were often incapable of understanding the laws they were obliged to apply, while many local resistance committees, spurred on by the hysterical outpourings of hatred that immediately followed the liberation and subsequently the return of deportees, simply ignored government officials altogether.

Still, the *épuration legale* produced a few Mitfordesque jokes. In 1946, Nancy wrote to Gaston of a party for the reopening of the Tower of London. 'Violet [Trefusis] said, "When we got to the Traitor's Gate I heard two well-known voices and it was Emerald and Daisy."' Nancy's friend Daisy Fellowes, the daughter of an American heiress and a French duke, and married first to the Prince de Broglie, was distinguished in many ways, as a beauty, magazine editor, writer and mistress to Duff Cooper, among others (possibly including Gaston himself), but the war had not been her finest hour. Two of her daughters, Jacqueline and Emmeline, were punished for collaboration. Emmeline was incarcerated for five months at Fresnes prison, where she shared a cell with a group of prostitutes who spent their time shimmying their breasts at the men's wing opposite by way of diversion. Jacqueline had her head shaved in reprisal for the denunciation of Resistants by her Austrian husband Alfred Kraus. Daisy failed to rise to her daughter's defence in the manner of one mother of a seventeen-year-old girl who had been over-enthusiastic in consorting with the enemy. 'Why cut her hair off for it? She's just as willing to go to bed with Americans.'

Other members of the Parisian *beau monde* tried to keep up to the mark of chic even in the unpromising confines of the Conciergerie. Comte Jean de Castellane, the brother of the famous socialite Boni de Castellane, was informed that he had to surrender his shoelaces and braces to a guard. 'If you remove my braces,' he announced, 'I shall leave immediately.'[2] Sacha Guitry departed for the camp at Drancy in flowered pyjamas accessorized with a panama hat. Inside, he met his ex-wife, prompting him to remark that 'one's mishaps never come singly'.[3] The most famous *collabo* riposte, attributed to everyone from the film star Arletty to Coco Chanel, was the proud declaration of a woman accused of sleeping with Germans: 'My ass is inter-national, but my heart is French!'

The *épuration sauvage* left no room for even gallows gaiety. It seemed as though the French were so appalled by their collective guilt that they turned on themselves in a grisly penance which produced outrages similar to those perpetrated by the Nazis. One commentator in 1947 suggested that 'it was as though we were afraid of the very amplitude of the crime'.[4] Neighbours denounced one another, none more zealously than those who had turned their coats at the last minute to escape retribution, and hastily convened courts of Resistants bayed for *collabo* blood. Across twenty-two *départements*, over a hundred summary exe-cutions were carried out, while the total figure (confirmed by a Gendarmerie survey in 1952 and then by the French Committee for the History of the Second World War) was approximately 10,000, of which 8,867 were discovered to have been the direct responsibility of the Resistance.

Malcolm Muggeridge, who was serving with the British forces in Paris, described the 'horrifying callousness, arrogance and brutality' of the self-appointed 'purge' gangs. Women were often a particular focus for atrocities. Jean Cocteau recalled seeing a woman being paraded entirely naked down the Avenue de la Grande Armée, one of the wide boulevards leading off the Arc de Triomphe. 'They tore at her, they pushed her, they spat in her face … She was covered in bruises and carried around her neck a placard "I had my husband shot".'[5] At the Drancy internment camp, many women were raped, while shaven heads proclaimed their owners' shame long after the liberation. Allied Forces were reluctant to intervene, seeing the *épuration* as a peculiarly French issue. It therefore represented a direct challenge to the authority of the provisional government. As De Gaulle observed, 'nothing is more wounding than weakness,' and the 'purification' demonstrated not only the lack of control the provisional government was able to exercise but precisely the kind of disunity that would impede the general's aim of establishing France once more as a living and dignified nation.

The 'chronic weakness'[6] of France immediately after the liberation was manifest at a profound material level. Some 460,000 buildings had been destroyed, 1,900,000 damaged and over a million families found themselves homeless. The industrial infrastructure was in an appalling condition, with half the railway lines out of use, fuel supplies scarce and machinery, where it was not destroyed altogether, dilapidated and out of date. Agriculture, too, lacked machinery, and fertilizer and serviceable land (93 million cultivated hectares had been lost). Poor productivity in both spheres sent the public debt soaring to almost 2,000 billion francs by 1946. Correspondingly, the cost of living tripled, and gross prices increased by three and a half times.

The most severe problem was the shortage of food. The actress Arletty, who was sent to Fresnes for collaboration, had incensed the public not merely by cohabiting with her German lover at the Ritz, but by enjoying gourmet blow-outs there while the rest of the country starved. The government had only a tiny margin for manoeuvre, as the satisfaction of 'basic alimentary needs' was the touchstone by which it needed to conjure a durable popularity.[7] According to the rhetoric of the dying Vichy regime, the wicked Germans had been absconding with the fruits of the sacred Gallic soil, hence when they were defeated, abundance would return. Neither the provisional government, the Resistance, nor the British were prepared to contradict this fallacy too precisely, yet the agricultural crisis had to be solved before the country lost patience.

Nancy Mitford, wearing her self-declared rose-coloured spectacles, refused to acknowledge the fact that for most French people, the size of the ration had become an obsession. In a letter to Lady Redesdale she gaily announced that bread was no longer rationed, an absolute fabrication. The bitter winter of 1944–5, followed by heavy spring frosts, left a deficit of one third below requirements for bread, meat, butter and milk. Bread shortages were acute, as production had fallen from 63 million *quintaux* (a measure of 100 kilogrammes) to 42 million. From December

1945 to May 1947, the ration was 250 grammes per person per day, the equivalent of roughly four and a half pieces of modern sliced bread. Between September 1947 and May 1948 this was reduced to 200 grammes, then rose again to 250 until bread was eventually taken off the ration (despite Nancy's absurdly premature rejoicing) in 1949. The government introduced price controls and requisition of urgent supplies such as milk and attempted to repress the flourishing black market, but it was galling for law-abiding families to keep their children on little more than bread and the weekly ration of 60 grammes of meat when black-market goods were ubiquitous and the wealthy and unscrupulous still dined in opulent restaurants. Nancy's strict adherence to wartime regulations in London appeared to have been quite forgotten, and she revelled in black-market goodies, even as Gaston was attempting to deal with the repercussions of the many protests in French towns, where angry women assembled waving signs reading: '*Nos gosses ont faim*' ('our kids are hungry'). The battle France now faced, government publicity claimed, was production, but slogans like 'Off with our jackets and up with our hearts' did little to relieve the anguish of mothers serving out pathetic rations to weak and malnourished children.

The challenges confronting the provisional government were overwhelming, but nothing could be effectively achieved without concord at ministerial level. On 21 October 1945, France went to the polls. In her last novel, *Don't Tell Alfred*, Nancy has fun with the absurdly volatile and bathetic fluctuations of fortune of the French government. 'M. Moch, M. Pleven and M. Bidault all tried to form governments and all duly failed. Then Bouche-Bontemps tried again and was accepted by the Chambre the very day before our dinner party.' For now, though, it was Gaston's career that was at stake and Nancy wrote of her 'mule-like' struggle to remain in the Rue Bonaparte until the elections were over. She described the question of the elections to Randolph Churchill in a passage that might have come from the novel: 'Everywhere you come across groups of people saying "Moi

Oui-Non" "et moi Oui-Oui" and on all the walls is chalked up the Oui-Non of the Communists. Only real old Faubourg fogies will vote Non-Oui.'

The nation had to decide whether the Constituent Assembly (the legislative arm of the government) should be given supreme or limited power. The '*Oui*' of the Communists represented their determination that party power should be more democratically reflected, while the '*Non*' of the moderates and Gaullists corresponded to a wish for greater executive authority and a more limited role for the assembly, founded on the conviction that it was the limitation of such authority that had led to the collapse of 1940. The Communist plan to empower the assembly was based on their position as the strongest political force in the country. Membership of the party had increased from 400,000 to 900,000 in the previous two years. Revolutionary rhetoric was still much in evidence, directed especially at the 'Fascist fifth column of Vichy', but since it presently seemed possible that power might be obtained by constitutional means, the party leader, Maurice Thorez, had proved himself a firm supporter of De Gaulle. Much to the disgust of some members, who had joined in the belief that a French victory would inaugurate a socialist Utopia, Thorez had maintained a Gaullist line, emphasizing the need to bring the *épuration sauvage* to an end and concentrate on production. With the goal of building parliamentary muscle, the Communists proposed an amalgamation with Leon Blum's Socialist party in the summer of 1945, though this was rejected in August, with the Socialists maintaining that coalition was more in accordance with the spirit of the Conseil National de la Résistance. Nevertheless, the Communists had good reason to hope that their 'Oui-Non' would achieve a mandate, for De Gaulle's popularity was severely on the wane.

The wretched condition of most of the French population was understandably laid at De Gaulle's door, and though, as Duff Cooper observed, the general's *politique de panache* was rather popular, there was also a feeling that his high-handed refusal to engage in party politics and his emphasis on foreign affairs was causing him to neglect the real sufferings of the people, especially with regard to the economy. 'De Gaulle has his head in the clouds and his feet in the shit' ran one Parisian graffito. Rather than blame the sainted general, however, many chose instead to vilify the sinister *éminence grise* of the Rue St Dominique, Gaston Palewski. The newspapers, Nancy reported, never criticized De Gaulle directly. Instead 'all the attacks, and they are many and venomous, are directed against Palewski who is presented as . . . an enemy of the people'. The initials on ministers' official cars, GPRF (Gouvernement Provisoire de la République Française) were popularly deemed to stand for 'Gaston Palewski Regent de France'. De Gaulle was well aware of the tendency to blame the entourage rather than the leader, but he hardly leaped to Gaston's defence.

It was true that in the vertical hierarchy of De Gaulle's office, where Gaston assembled the service chiefs each morning in his own room to discuss the day's programme and give instructions, 'everything passed through him'. One colleague estimated that it was difficult to imagine the unique place Gaston occupied in French politics in 1944–5. 'He was the only one who at any moment could push open the door of [De Gaulle's] office, the only one to find himself constantly by his side . . . he transmitted requests and delivered instructions, directed projects and pro-posed nominations, smoothed over corners and interpreted silences.'[8] The harmony between the two men, the confidence, trust and unity of reasoning, seems to have been extraordinary, which makes it all the more surprising that so many Anglophone accounts of De Gaulle's career barely acknowledge Palewski's presence. Contemporaries agreed that Gaston was the man who had best understood De Gaulle's 'profound aspirations', and while the significance of their relationship may not have been appreciated by the majority of French people, and has been neglected by a number of historians, there were many who understood its importance at the time.

Arguably, Gaston's relationship with De Gaulle was the most

significant of his life, but he was never pompous about it. Just before the elections, he accompanied the general on a three-day visit to Belgium for what was effectively a public-relations exercise. The Belgian government needed to consolidate public support for the reign of the new regent, Prince Charles, and had planned a series of processions, receptions and visits. In turn, Gaston believed it would be a good opportunity to confirm De Gaulle's popularity abroad. Jacques Dumaine, chief of protocol at the Quai d'Orsay, called on Gaston before a dinner at the Embassy to find him struggling with a sock suspender, balancing a letter on his knee, his boiled shirt hanging up ready. 'His smile showed obvious delectation' as he explained that the letter was from a Belgian friend, declaring that what ex-King Leopold had lacked was a Palewski at his side. 'Delicious,' was Gaston's verdict on this dubious compliment.

As the vote drew nearer, Gaston fell ill. Rose Palewski had been concerned about his health earlier in the year – he was driving himself too hard, she thought – and on 15 October Nancy wrote to her sister Diana that he was in agony from an abscess on his spine. A dose of penicillin had him back at his desk within twelve hours, but the tension created by the enormity of France's difficulties and the increasing scepticism towards the provisional government produced a strained and despondent atmosphere at the Rue St Dominique. There were rumours that De Gaulle was heading for a crippling defeat. Gaston, however, kept up a serene façade, reiterating his perfect faith in the general's authority.

Yvonne de Gaulle tactfully chose a black ensemble to cast her vote in the sixteenth arrondissement. This was the first time women were represented among the 25.7 million French citizens who voted on 21 October. The Communists won 26 per cent of the vote, the MRP 24.9 per cent, the Socialists 23.8 and the 'Moderates' 13.3. Of the 586 available seats in the assembly, the Communists would thus take 161 and the MRP and the Socialists 150 apiece. On 6 November, Gaston delivered the letter from the president of the provisional government remitting his powers to the assembly. It was on 13 November that the assembly was to vote on the re-election of the general as the leader of the government. Rather ominously, Winston Churchill, fresh from his own defeat at the hands of the Labour party, decided to pay a call in Paris en route for a holiday in the south of France. Gaston attended a lunch with Churchill and his daughter, De Gaulle, and his aide Captain Guy and Duff and Diana Cooper. At this crisis of his leadership, De Gaulle showed himself at his best. 'He was smiling, courteous, almost charming,' wrote Duff, 'and on this day and almost at the hour when his whole future was at stake, not only was he perfectly calm but one might have thought he was a country gentleman living far from Paris. There were no interruptions, no telephone calls or messages, no secretaries hurrying in and out.' Churchill *would* remain at table reminiscing bibulously until half-past three, but even though the assembly had convened at three, De Gaulle remained implacably courteous. Duff declared that he had never liked or admired him so much.

With the exception of the son of former prime minister Georges Clemenceau, who abstained, the assembly voted unanimously to retain De Gaulle as prime minister. A second motion ruled that '*Charles de Gaulle a bien merité de la patrie*'. This was an extraordinary honour, and the confirmation ought to have been a moment of triumph, the political vindication for which De Gaulle had waited so long. Yet the party politics he so disliked and distrusted allowed no space for satisfaction. Reasonably, the Communists demanded major ministerial posts for their candidates, posts with which De Gaulle was determined not to invest them. By 16 November he had threatened to resign, and staff at the Rue St Dominique were instructed to clear their desks. The next day, in a radio broadcast, the general asserted that he had no intention of giving the Communists power in security matters, foreign policy or the military.

The new journal *Bref* (appropriately named – it didn't last long) was in no doubt as to who was really in charge. The first issue featured a colour portrait of Gaston with the headline 'Is the man who governs France Gaston Palewski?'. Stanley Karnow, the correspondent for *Time* magazine, nicknamed him 'Monsieur Lavande', a reference to his rather enthusiastic use of cologne, but also to his role of 'sweetening' De Gaulle's policies. It caught on – Nancy cut out a cartoon of a towering general striding through a field of mud with a portly Palewski spraying perfume in his wake.

On 19 November, Gaston received an officer's rank in the order of the Légion d'Honneur, which had him literally dancing for joy in his office, but while he celebrated with a few neatly executed *entrechats*, the diplomatic choreography was taking a tortuously modern turn. As Gaullist supporters marched down the Boulevard Raspail calling for Thorez to resign, the Palais Bourbon was surrounded by police. Jacques Duclos, the parliamentary leader of the Communists, denounced De Gaulle for his betrayal of his party and the '75,000' martyrs it had offered to France. (Gaston's friend, the diarist Galtier-Boissière noted drily that of the 29,000 people executed by the Germans, 75,000 of them were Communists.) Although the Socialists banded with the MRP to support De Gaulle, it was clear that the general's autocratic methods would not be tolerated and he was forced to accept an eventual compromise which, on 21 November, saw Thorez made vice-president of the Conseil des Ministres and Communists appointed to Labour, National Economy and Industrial Production. De Gaulle fudged his claim that he would not entrust a Communist with defence by giving Armaments to Charles Tillon, while classifying the post as economic and retaining overall responsibility for the armed forces. Four ministers were chosen from the Socialists and MRP, one radical, and René Pleven, Jacques Soustelle and André Malraux from among De Gaulle's supporters.

The general's government barely lasted a month. By January, Gaston's efforts to reconcile the argumentative ministers were becoming ever more frantic. De Gaulle was belligerent, even crude where he needed to be conciliatory, while Gaston's 'tenacious humility in the face of this wall of pride' was described by one witness of the ministerial meetings as quite beautiful.[9] On 17 January, the general summoned Gaston and explained that he intended to resign. 'To my last day,' Gaston wrote of this moment, 'I will reproach myself for not having insisted sufficiently that he did not follow through this plan.' De Gaulle knew that Gaston would be out of a job and said that he would find him an embassy or a position on the Conseil d'Etat, to which offer Gaston claimed he replied, with great nobility, 'There are many of our companions who have fought from the beginning and had nothing. It is right that your principal collaborator should leave with nothing.'

On 20 January 1946, Gaston personally carried the letter of demission of De Gaulle's government to the president of the Constituent Assembly. The general had retired to the villa at Neuilly and Gaston refused all requests to interview him. He was out of a job, and almost worse still, as he remarked that night at a dinner with the Duc de Brissac at the home of the art collector Jean Groult on the Avenue Foch, out of a car. How to romance his 'pretty ladies' if he was unable to offer them a ride home? 'Now you will have a holiday and be able to devote more time to the pursuit of love,' wrote Nancy from Blomfield Road. 'Oh dear.'

At the beginning of the year, Gaston spent a good deal of time at an office on the Quai Branly used by former members of De Gaulle's Cabinet. Elisabeth de Miribel, the first woman to join the Free French in London and now part of the general's staff, remembered it as an exciting but exhausting time. Weekends and evenings were devoted to planning a 'restoration', and Gaston keenly kept up his diplomatic contacts, though not always diplomatically. At two Gaullist rallies, in June and September, he denounced a regime in which party mercantilism took priority over the interests of the nation. Discussing the Marshall Plan with Jefferson Caffery, he claimed that the United States was supporting weak regimes in liberated countries to further its own ends.

'Would you have me recommend to my government that

France should not benefit from the Marshall Plan?' retorted Caffery.

As a Frenchman, Gaston replied, he could hardly want to deprive his own country, he merely wished to point out the results of US intervention, which would be to mask from the French people the real extent of the political challenges ahead. As much from necessity as from taking advantage of the opportunity to express such views, Gaston now accepted journalism commissions from the *New York Free World* (and later *Paris-Presse*), but his main professional preoccupation between 1946 and 1947 was the establishment of a new political party that would work to sustain the Gaullist vision. Gaston told De Gaulle of an encouraging conversation with Caffery, who had explained that the United States was resolved to do nothing for France as long as the government involved or was influenced by Communists. A French political landscape liberated from Marxist thinking, a debate that could demonstrate its coherence, was needed in order to attain American help. In Caffery's view, therefore, there was no better way of achieving this than putting in train the measures advocated by De Gaulle. Along with Malraux, Soustelle, Jacques Baumel and Colonel Rémy, Gaston set about drafting a fresh manifesto.

The statutes of the RPF (Rassemblement du Peuple Français) were entered at the Prefecture on 29 May 1947. Gaston Palewski was one of the seven signatories. Offices were established at 5 Rue de Solferino, the site of the present Institut Charles de Gaulle. De Gaulle wished the RPF to be a movement, rather than a conventional party, and 'double membership' was thus available to those who already belonged to other parties, with the exception of Communists. The aims of the RPF were drawn from an analysis Gaston had prepared for the general, expressing the contradictory aspirations that characterized the public. The French, Gaston wrote, were attracted by the idea of a strong state, controlled by a firm leader; conversely, they were obsessed with the idea of liberty to the point where it created the divisions presently tearing the nation apart. The RPF would combat the party regime insofar as it empowered 'anonymous societies' (effectively nationalizations on party lines) at the expense of the individual, promote constitutional reform which enlarged executive power and oppose the advance of Communism. The 'long, difficult, joyful fight' was on.

16

THE EMBASSY

In *Don't Tell Alfred*, Nancy's narrator, Fanny, describes her unforgettable first impression of the British Embassy in Paris.

The large, beautiful honey-coloured house, in its quiet courtyard, seemed a haven of delight. It has more the atmosphere of a country than a town house ... no town noises can be heard, only the rustle of leaves, the twittering of birds, an occasional mowing machine, an owl. The French windows in the garden side fill the rooms with sunshine and air in amazing quantities. They open to a vista of trees; the only solid edifice in sight is the dome of the Invalides, a purple shadow on the horizon, hardly visible through summer leaves. Except for that and the Eiffel Tower, there is nothing to show that the house is situated in the centre of the most prosperous and busy capital on the continent of Europe.

While the cobbled streets Nancy knew are gone, and although the Faubourg St Honoré is now thick with traffic fumes, little has altered within the Hôtel Charost since she wrote this description. The Embassy remains one of the city's loveliest buildings, its garden still a surprising green lake of calm in the centre of a hectic metropolis. Nancy knew the house from her visits to her friend Middy O'Neill in 1927. Middy's grandfather, the Marquess of Crewe, was ambassador to Paris from 1922 to 1928 and Nancy had spent a thrillingly sophisticated evening there with a dinner at the Embassy followed by a trip to the Florida nightclub. From the moment she arrived in Paris after the war, Nancy's friendship with the Coopers placed her at the heart of the city's diplomatic life. Their son, Lord Norwich, recalls that she was 'always popping in and out'. The Embassy was vital to Nancy in providing the basis for her social network in Paris in the otherwise disorienting atmosphere after the liberation. It was also the source of more practical comforts. Unlike nearly everyone else in the city, the lucky inhabitants of the Embassy had large supplies of food and fuel. Diana Cooper was initially criticized for apparently dispensing with protocol and receiving all comers, but in the terrible winter of 1945 this was a kind gesture, and one that fostered an essential atmosphere of security and camaraderie, a respite from the harsh and often threateningly anarchic conditions of the streets.

Diana had known she would eventually become ambassadress since Duff had accepted the post of British representative to the French Committee of Liberation in 1943. Her first reaction was 'flustered, hysterical, funky and giggly'. Her French was limited and Frenchwomen were terrifying – 'they make me feel at any time a smelly, untended, untaught, uncouth, dense bumpkin'.[1] The Coopers had an exciting, happy year in Algiers to accustom themselves to the idea of diplomatic grandeur, but it was still with feelings of deep apprehension that Diana had left for Paris in September 1944. She need not have worried. Her unconventional brilliance, her great beauty, her conversation and her own peculiar brand of chic made the Coopers a lighthouse of glamour for the short duration of their tenure. She was delighted all the same to encounter her 'Laughing Cavalier', Gaston Palewski – whom the Duffs had of course known in London and during the weighty hilarity of negotiations in Algiers – at a dinner party given by Jean and Marie-Blanche de Polignac in October. Duff, whose liking for Gaston ebbed and flowed according to how impossible De Gaulle was being at that moment, never entirely took to him, but for Diana he swiftly became her 'pilot fish', a sort of unofficial chief of protocol, helping her navigate the potentially disastrous social waters of collaboration.

Gaston found himself enjoying the greatest social success of his life. Just as exiled aristocrats returning in 1799 paid court to Josephine Bonaparte in order to ingratiate themselves with her husband, so those members of the *gratin* whose war record was less than patriotic cultivated Gaston for those coveted invitations from the Embassy which would relaunch them in post-liberation society. 'On pense que vous êtes l'entourage,' Jean Cocteau explained. Gaston was not so naïve as to have thought anything else, but he was aware that his social connections had a significant function in the legitimization of the provisional government. His colleague Pierre de Brissac emphasized the importance of his supple ease in Parisian society to the Gaullist project: 'He had the *pied Parisien* ... he could explain the complexity of the capital, this nervous and insurrectionary city, so sensitive, sceptical and versatile.'² At times, De Gaulle did not appear so much to consult Gaston as to leaf through him like a guide book.

Gaston's own attitude towards *collabos* was balanced between principle and pragmatism. At times he could be severe. In Algeria, Duff Cooper had noted that his attitude to Pierre Pucheu, former Vichy minister of the interior, transcended diplomatic exigence. Duff's view was that Pucheu's execution would be a disaster for French relations with Britain and America, but Gaston remained cynical and 'obviously would like to have him shot'.

Conciliation was more of a priority in 1944. Gaston was aware that some *collabos* were useful, whether for their connections, like the disgraced former minister and newspaper publisher Patenôtre, whose presence at dinner at the Embassy so infuriated François Mauriac that he left immediately, or Maurice Chevalier whose charm and popularity appeared to outweigh his dubious activities in the war. Vicomtesse Marie-Laure de Noailles was a difficult proposition. Gaston had known her for many years, she was a friend of Cocteau, who was very much persona grata, and her salon was one of the most important in Paris. But the De

Noailles' family home 'smelled of the black market, of corruption, of the greatcoats of the German Wehrmacht, who, we later learned, had been honoured guests during the occupation of France'. Marie-Laure herself had been severely compromised after an accident during the war in which she had been caught in a car with a German officer (since her husband preferred boys she was perhaps particularly vulnerable to Aryan charms), and Gaston made the error of allowing her to be seated next to a staunch Gaullist, M. Oberle, who showed his disapproval by refusing to speak a word to her during the entire dinner.

Even when it came to *collabos*, Gaston could never resist a duchess. In September 1944, during the first phase of the *épuration*, the apartment of the writer Alfred Fabre-Luce was raided early one morning. Fabre-Luce had supported Pétain, but had already been thrown into prison once for a book he had written criticizing the Nazis. He had managed to slip away, but in his place his butler and an overnight guest were arrested. His wife, Charlotte, telephoned her brother, Jean-Louis de Faucigny-Lucinge, who went immediately to the Fabre-Luce flat in the Rue Bassano. There he found the Duchesse de Brissac, wearing a fur coat over her underclothes (what *can* she have been doing there?), being interrogated about her friendship with Fabre-Luce as well as her acquaintance with certain German officers. When the duchess was escorted to the Conciergerie, 'like Marie-Antoinette', Faucigny-Lucinge telephoned her husband. Since the duchess had been foolish enough to get caught, the duke was disinclined to do anything about it, so Faucigny-Lucinge reported the incident to Gaston, a friend from before the war. Gaston affected to think the matter was unimportant, but the duchess spent only four weeks at Drancy. Several months later, she invited Faucigny-Lucinge to stay in the country. He was unsure how he could get there as there was so little available petrol. 'Oh, don't worry,' replied the grateful duchess. 'Gaston Palewski can give you a lift.'

Evelyn Waugh was sceptical of Gaston's anti-*collabo* views, seeing them more as a matter of convenience than principle. In

1946, Nancy accompanied Gaston to a ball given by the Princesse de Bourbon-Parme, 'duly binged up as one is before balls with champagne, black coffee and so on. We hadn't been there 2 minutes before the Col said we couldn't stay on account of the great cohorts of *collabos* by whom we were surrounded and firmly dumped me home.' Nancy was very embarrassed, fearful that she would offend both her hostess and her friend the Princess Radziwill, who had taken her to the party, and her feelings were not appeased when Evelyn scathingly pointed out: 'Collaborationists my foot. Does it not occur to you, poor innocent that the continental colonel went back to the aristocratic ball and that while you lay sleepless with your fountain pen he was in the arms of some well-born Gestapo moll?' Since Gaston was an extremely prominent politician at the time, he had to tread very delicately, and where the presence of *collabos* might be necessary (or, admittedly, desirable) in the discreet context of the Embassy, more public events required greater caution. In *The Blessing*, Nancy gives Charles-Edouard de Valhubert a wry take on this social nicety, the problem with *collabos* being that one had to endure two hours of maudlin self-justification before getting down to business.

Nancy and Gaston were frequently guests together at the Embassy, but there was no question of them being invited as a couple. The fiction would be politely maintained that they were friends who had perhaps given one another a lift, though everyone knew of the relationship. Gaston's extensive personal knowledge of the complexities of Paris's extramarital affairs was also useful to Diana Cooper in judging her guest list. Lord Norwich explains that while it was an accepted fact that men had mistresses, it was the wife, not the mistress, who was invited out. In the case of the ambassador himself, this dictum was naturally dispensed with.

Louise de Vilmorin was the divorced fifth wife of Count Paul Palffy ab Edod. She was among the guests at the Polignacs' first dinner for the Coopers and a month later they and Gaston dined with her at her family home at Verrières, outside Paris. Both the

Coopers were enchanted by her fragile, etiolated beauty, her talent for music and poetry and her whimsical, dashing, often outrageous conversation, in many ways similar to Diana's own style. She was soon a fixture at the Embassy, often staying there for weeks at a time in the first stages of what was to become a longstanding affair with Duff. Diana was fully in the know, commenting that 'Duff is deeply in love with the spell-binding Lulu, which is nice for him and good for his prestige, as she is acknowledged to be the most remarkable and attractive woman in Paris'.

Diana especially worshipped 'Lulu', but her name appeared on a list of 'pederasts and collaborators' issued by the Sûreté. Though Duff dismissed this as gossip, the prefect sent Victor Rothschild to warn him that Lulu was causing rumours and bad feeling. French by birth, she was a Hungarian by marriage and had travelled frequently across Germany during the war. There were also whispers that she had cohabited with a German officer during the occupation (Diana's biographer observes that this may have been a matter of misspelling – she had once been engaged to Prince Esterhazy and the 'officer's' name was given as Stuazi). Duff flew into a tremendous rage and turned Rothschild out. Peter Rodd later reported that when Lulu's brother appeared at a shooting party at the Rothschilds' he was treated as a servant and given his luncheon in the kitchen. Gaston, meanwhile, backed her up by saying that even if she was prosecuted he would still associate with her.

The extent of this association was to cause difficulties between Duff and Gaston. In May 1945, Duff recorded in his diary that Gaston had invited Lulu to his office and suggested he could provide her with an 'easy life' if she was prepared to pass on information about Duff. 'She was very much upset,' Duff wrote in his diary, 'and meant not to tell me about it. But what a frightful fool the man must be – and how unfit for any respons-ible position.' Lulu, who adored any drama in which she was the star, told Duff in December that Gaston was very anti-English and 'very pugnacious with regard to the future and says that he and De Gaulle would be prepared to use force rather than give up their position'. This was not only entirely untrue, but disastrous for relations between the British and De Gaulle, which were at a contentious stage. Many contemporaries claimed Lulu was also having an affair with Gaston. Duff dismissed this, but his diary entries become distinctly spiteful. On 1 January 1946 he saw Gaston at the general's reception for the diplomatic corps. 'Gaston Palewski was looking more revolting than usual ... It occurred to me that De Gaulle may have selected him as being one of the few men uglier than himself.'[3]

Whether it was the affair, jealousy over Diana's attention or anger at the trouble she was stirring up, Nancy refused to worship at what Diana called Lulu's 'fountain of rainbow waterdrops'. Evelyn Waugh loathed her – 'an egocentric with the eyes of a witch' – and Nancy was made nervous by her spite. They had great fun bitching about the 'Filth Marine' and the 'seed merchant' (her family money came from plant seeds). The Coopers were convinced that Lulu, who wrote novels as well as poems and songs, was a genius, a view shared by the distinguished composer Poulenc, who credited her 'sensitive impertinence, libertinage',[4] but the two friends thought her the most tremendous fraud. 'Life was made hideous by the arrival of a Hungarian countess who pretended to be a French poet,' wrote Evelyn. Nancy gleefully recounted a story about her old rival Romie Hope-Vere, whom Hamish Erskine had taken to stay with the Palffys in Austria. After dinner, when the ladies went to do their hair in Louise's bedroom, Count Palffy arrived and proposed a threesome. Romie fled to Hamish, insisting they left at once, but he told her not to be so middle-class. Olga, the pretentious Russian aristocrat who tries to seduce Sophia's lover in *Pigeon Pie*, is a prescient prototype of Louise, with her heavy accent and claims to be a poet. Neither Nancy nor Evelyn could see the point of Lulu. Professional writers both, they were infuriated by her literary posturings and Nancy begged Evelyn to expose her, consoling herself for Diana's neglect with the remark of a French dinner companion who told her, '*All* Vilmorins are dull.'

Although the contribution of the Embassy to Nancy's work is most obvious in *Don't Tell Alfred,* but her encounters with Louise provided a rich seam of material for *The Blessing.* Not only does Sir Conrad Allingham's professional lady turn out to be an energetic Hungarian countess, but Louise supplied a model for Albertine, the mistress of Charles-Edouard, a portrait so accurate Nancy worried it might be libellous. Albertine is Lulu to the life, incongruously blue eyes goggling from Gothic features. Her portrayal, however, is far from negative. Albertine is entirely self-interested – she marries an American in the war for the central heating (Nancy had obviously heard the gossip about Officer Stuazi) – and *jolie-laide* rather than sexy, but she is extremely clever with men. She can transform herself into whatever her companion needs, her conversation is a gourmet foam of anecdote and flattery and she is never, ever, a bore. This was very much the source of Nancy's fascination for Gaston. She teased him about marrying a clever American girl who, when he asked, 'What are the news?' would tell him the news rather than the mixture of stories, improbable scandal and sharp observation he loved. Albertine, though, is controlled in a way Nancy could never manage to be. Her Frenchness gives her a discipline and subtlety that thoroughly outfoxes plain-speaking, easily wounded Grace de Valhubert. Louise herself was kind to Nancy, finding her translation work which helped her to acquire that holy grail of expat life, the *carte de séjour,* and Lulu's exploits continued to delight her for years. In the Sixties she wrote to the Colonel from Venice reporting a remark she had overheard about a film Louise had made. It was so pornographic, it had been said, that it would even shock Gaston Palewski.

Diana Cooper had resolved in Algiers that she must not swell the list of mad English ambassadresses, and her failure was the source of her social triumph. She entirely ignored the French obsession with *placement,* which meant that seriously *gratin* dinners could take weeks to organize and end up with all the women sitting together. She merely dumped down a collection of people whom she thought amusing and observed the result. At one dinner, Princess Radziwill lit a cigarette and blew the smoke about before the fish to show that she thought she was *mal placée*. It was an uncomfortable indicator of the difference between the arriviste Gaston and the entirely entitled duke's daughter that he considered this proper form, while she viewed it as potty. Odette Massigli, the French ambassadress whom Nancy had admired in London, complained about the terrible set hanging round the Embassy, and even the supposedly bohemian Harold Nicolson called Diana's parties 'rather odd', but everyone came.

Cecil Beaton had introduced Diana to Cocteau; he also introduced Christian 'Bébé' Bérard, who looked and smelled like a tramp but designed the most exquisite and innovative stage sets in France. Lord Norwich remembers him as exuberant, unabashed by his 'septic' filthiness and a model of perfect manners. When one woman's nasty little Peke relieved itself in the *salon vert*, Bérard delicately picked up and removed the tiny turd without saying a word in case she should be embarrassed. Diana loved artists and felt that they had been singled out by the *épuration* while upper-class *collabos* remained unpersecuted. Edouard Bourdet, the director of the Comédie Française, Georges Auric, the composer and Jacques Février, the pianist, were guests, as well as Noël Coward and Laurence Olivier. Nancy and Noël recognized fellow blithe spirits. 'Bliss . . . he shakes like a jelly at one's jokes.'

If Diana's dinners were a cassoulet of unlikely elements, somehow they worked. 'Imagine,' wrote one guest, 'Evelyn Waugh, Lord Carlisle, the Bishop of Fulham, Harold Laski and Peter Quennell all under one roof and none of them loath to speak at table, and all outdone by Louise de Vilmorin.'[5] If Louise felt she was not sufficiently attended to, she would catapult her butter to the ceiling, where it would stick 'stronger than the planet Venus'. As the guests' eyes were drawn upwards, Louise used the silence to launch one of her Scheherazade fantasies.

A dinner which included Nancy, Harold Nicolson, Raymond Mortimer and Bob Boothby produced

> the best conversation I have ever known. The depth of erudition was never allowed to penetrate the surface, but without it could the talk have been so good ... Very fast English conversation between the Coopers and their friends was different, not better, but different from French conversation. This could be wonderfully amusing, stimulating, brilliant ... English women are wonderfully gifted, knowing just when to put in the aside or the question that brings out the best in men.[6]

Not all Diana's entertainments were a whiz, however. On one occasion she forced her French guests to sit through Coward's film *In Which We Serve*, which bewildered them, though they forced out a few polite and manly snuffles. At the height of tension between Britain and France over Syria in the summer of 1945, when diplomatic relations were practically broken off, she invited Gaston to lunch alone with her to tell him her plans for her summer party. She thought of turning the garden into a huge dance floor, hanging lanterns in the trees and opening the courtyard gates to any Parisian who cared to come, in the spirit of the opera balls under Louis XV. Gaston gently dissuaded her – on Bastille Day the Parisians were just as likely to torch the place.

17

THE PURSUIT OF CHIC

Before the war had even ended, the authorities in Paris were turning their attention to the vital matter of women's clothes. This was not quite such a trivial preoccupation as it might first seem. Since the seventeenth century, Paris had been synonymous with elegance and glamour, while the ingenuity of the Parisiennes during the occupation had not only boosted morale but made quite an impression on the arriving Allied troops. Stumping along in their wooden-soled shoes or bicycling in short A-line skirts stitched together from scarves (silk in the fashionable arrondissements, cotton in the bohemian sixth), with their sculpted hairdos and elaborately decorated hats reminiscent of Marie-Antoinette, they had, unlike the British, refused to surrender to utility. Paris fashion was the nexus of an economy that employed many, from the silk weavers of Lyon to the hundreds of specialist couture artisans in the capital; it was therefore economic necessity as much as national pride which required its reinvigoration.

In March 1944, the Chambre Syndicale staged an exhibition directed by Bébé Bérard featuring dolls costumed in the best the couture houses could produce. Jean Cocteau, Christian Dior and Jean Patou were among the team who produced the show, which was seen by over 100,000 people. The dolls – a traditional means of exhibiting French styles dating back to the days of Louis XIV, when they had enjoyed diplomatic status – wore satin and chiffon gowns accessorized with diamonds lent by Cartier and even tiny sets of silk lingerie. After the drabness of the war, they seemed like a cloud of exquisite butterflies to women who hadn't had a new dress for six years. The popularity of the exhibition reflected the need for colour, sensuality and luxury in the same manner that *The Pursuit of Love* sated the post-war hunger for charm and romance.

Like Linda Radlett's, Nancy's first priority when she established herself in Paris was to 'arrange' herself. She and her sisters loved clothes, which often feature in their letters, and Nancy was happy to declare that being well-dressed was a matter of health. She had deplored the dingy gowns and wooden suspender-belts of wartime austerity, and though she had always made efforts towards chic (her first biographer, Harold Acton, describes the elegance of her figure in a plain black skirt and velvet jacket when she worked at Heywood Hill) now, for the first time, she could indulge her passion.

Clothes had never been seen as frivolous in France. Like *quenelles de brochet* or a Watteau *boiseries*, the intricacy of their production and display was seen as part of the essential business of civilization, an idea Nancy thoroughly endorsed. Pierre Balmain recalled showing his 1945 collection, with those two unlikely fashion plates Gertrude Stein and her moustachioed companion Alice B. Toklas in the audience, 'sitting on the seats of honour watching the pretty striped numbers go by, noting them on their cards with the same intensity of interest as they had noted the Picassos and Matisses which had passed through their lives'. Nancy had no truck with the idea that clever women ought to be scruffy, and relished the whole complex ritual of fittings and pinnings, the discussion of the *toile*, the selection of hats. In *The Blessing* she enumerates with evident pleasure the complex process of assembling a Parisian *tenu*: 'the *elegance*, the manicurists, the *vendeuses*, the *modistes*, the *bottiers* and the *lingères*'.

Englishwomen's clothes had always been a source of derision to the French, rendering 'the British female abroad an object of terror and avoidance to all beholders'[1] and Nancy, who had so minded her serviceable frocks and shiny face on her first heavily chaperoned visit to Paris, was prepared to put in the hours it would take to transform herself into a Frenchwoman. Her 1951 essay 'Chic – English, French and American' compares 'chubby little red-faced Queen Victoria' with the effortless beauty of Empress Eugénie. In England, smartness has nothing to do with clothes. If one is a duchess, like the two she reports being turned away from Dior, one can afford to dress like a gardener. 'Ladylike' is the best the Englishwoman, with her stiff, porridge-coloured tweeds and her skirt dividing 'rather horribly' over her calves, can aspire to. Compare those few 'rich, ruthless and savagely energetic' Frenchwomen who, if they can't afford to dress well, don't bother at all. Admittedly, not all duchesses were dowdy. Nancy wrote to Gaston with glee to describe Deborah taking her daughter Emma to Notre-Dame: 'You've seen the outside, darling, you can *guess* the inside. Now let's go to Christian Dior.'

Nancy's first couture clothes came from Grès, from whom she ordered a black velvet ball dress with a chiffon waistband which showed off her adolescent slimness. (Cynthia Gladwyn was scandalized by both the price – £200 – and the fifty yards of fabric in the skirt.) The dress sailed through a dinner party, a rendezvous with Gaston, a gallery opening and cocktails at the Embassy, where the conversation next day was devoted to the miracle of Nancy's waist. Nancy's great love, though, was Dior. The impact of Dior's first show on the Avenue Montaigne on 12 February 1947 was such that even the dukes of the Jockey Club spoke of nothing else. The New Look, as christened by Carmel Snow of *Harper's Bazaar*, was Nancy's idea of perfection. 'You pad your hips and squeeze your waist and skirts are to the ankle, it is bliss.'

Nancy's tall, thin figure set off the New Look perfectly, though interestingly, she was always troubled by her slimness, which could turn into unattractive skinniness when she was anxious or overworked. Hard to imagine a modern woman writing with pleasure to her mother from the country: 'I am getting quite fat, you won't know me.' Nancy loved (well-disciplined) femininity. Grace de Valhubert is asked why she has ruined a Dior frock by having it made up to the neck, covering her beautiful breasts, while in *Christmas Pudding* Philadelphia Bobbin is misguidedly troubled by her 'beautiful, rounded body' which she squeezes into over-laced stays. In her essay on chic, Nancy describes American women as looking pretty in both youth and old age, but characterizes their taste as adolescent: 'Where are the grown up women in the prime of life dressed as adults?' In *Love in a Cold Climate*, Polly Hampton's beauty is dismissed by the callow debs' delights of the London Season who find her too statuesque, too large, preferring the thin, bird-like women who were the ideal of the Twenties. The fact that Nancy herself perfectly conformed to this ideal does not stop her criticizing it. The worship of the juvenile, which she saw as particularly representative of an immature American culture, tapped into all her beliefs about the threat to European values from a society that prized youth above all else. She agreed with Stendhal that while Americans might have the gaiety of youth, they were devoid of sensibility, of the capacity for pleasurable passion. To Nancy, a beautiful woman was very much a woman, breasts and hips proudly on display, and the New Look confirmed her prejudice that only the French truly understood this.

Not everyone agreed. The conspicuous consumption embodied in Dior's extravagant use of yards of cloth at a time when many French people didn't have enough to eat provoked violence. A publicity shoot in Montmartre was disrupted by angry housewives who attacked the model, pulling her hair and trying to rip off her dress. Nancy playfully feared that her own fate would be that of '*l'élégante de la Rue Lepique*' as 'people shout *ordures* at you from vans because for some reason it creates class feelings in a way no sables could'. The French might worship clothes, but they did not forget that it was the Austrian Queen's bill at Rose Bertin that contributed to her downfall.

Nancy was rich, she had her pretty flat and her pretty clothes and for the moment Gaston was not governing France. Although they remained discreet, they could now enjoy some sort of a life together, and within their circle they were perceived as a couple. Nancy was flattered when Violet Trefusis referred to her as 'La

Palewska' (it was never a sad little nickname she invented for herself), and her letters from England, where she still returned frequently, tease 'Colonel Mitford' with the confidence of a woman who was, at least for the present, secure in her relationship. Gaston introduced her to many of the friends he had known before the war, while her luncheon parties at Rue Monsieur became a regular event for both the English community in Paris and visitors passing through. There were never more than five guests, Marie would produce simple, delicious food – snails, roast chicken, salad and cheese, with a special English-style pudding if Gaston was asked – the Colonel adored nursery puddings, though Marie never thought much of them. Nancy never drank very much, but there was always plenty of champagne, wine and brandy for her friends, so much so that the less experienced ones occasionally over-indulged: 'Hugh, if you drink as much brandy as that you'll be dead before you're thirty!' Arthur Ross told Lord Thomas.

Lord Thomas met Nancy at the Cambridge Union and subsequently went often to the flat. He recalls that the conversation would be mainly in English, though it would switch to French for particular descriptions and phrases. It often touched on politics, though Nancy was discreet about her hotline to De Gaulle. '*How* did you know that?' asked Momo Marriott once. 'Oh, I listened to the news on the wireless before you came.' Nancy seemed 'very attractive, very happy, full of beans' and often spoke of the Colonel, though always as a dear friend. Paul Johnson, whom Lord Thomas introduced to Nancy, speaks of her as 'very correct, even for the 1950s'. The colonel was certainly a fixture, and always lunched at Rue Monsieur on Sundays when he was in Paris, but Nancy was careful about who saw them together. Guests had to be mindful of their manners, says Johnson, but 'laughter was the very essence of life to her' and her flat appeared to the young man as the acme of elegant living. Gaston himself was 'always popping in'. Another friend describes him arriving very late for a luncheon party and launching into a long anecdote about trying to book a burial plot at the Père

Lachaise cemetery. It was outrageous, he laughed, that a man in his position should not even have been offered a view.

Beyond the Rue Monsieur and the Embassy (whence the Coopers departed in 1947 – 'a richly lachrymose occasion, Diana was in tears, Duff was in tears, Gaston Palewski was in tears'[2]) a taste of post-war Parisian social life is given in the diaries of Jacques Dumaine. Within the span of a few months, he lists a concert by Francis Poulenc, a Vuillard exhibition, a recital of Prokofiev's violin concerto at the Beaumonts', with Picassos hung on the eighteenth-century woodwork. Or events like Marivaux's *Fourberies de Scapin*, featuring Bébé Bérard's last stage set, the final exquisite testament of this 'tender tramp'. Nancy saw her colonel at dinner at Maxim's, at the theatre, at innumerable parties and at receptions such as that described by the MP and socialite Chips Channon: 'Today was a day of fantastic elegance. Arturo Lopez gave a luncheon party for me at ... his small Versailles, with every object in it beyond price; it is, I suppose, the most elegant "set-up" in the world ... I was between the Duchess de Fesanzac and Nancy Mitford.'

Nancy herself didn't really get worked up about duchesses: she found *gratin* life too pompous and dull. She did sulk when Gaston went to Carlos de Bestegui's ball at the Palazzo Labia in Venice in 1951, described in her *Sunday Times* column as a frantic free-for-all as the *beau monde* scrambled for invitations. 'A certain lady ... intending to go as a Spanish Infanta, advertised for a dwarf to accompany her. She arrived home next day to find her hall filled with rich dwarves of her acquaintance who had not been invited.' She teased Gaston sourly about his careful pre-servation of his own precious *carton*. She often lamented Gaston's unavailability, and the comedy that ensued when she tried to steal a few moments with him, stuffed into the *escalier de service* and discovered by the concierge. In a letter of 1947 she scripted one such attempt, employing nonsensical timings for comic effect.

28h La Marquise de Bairn arrives Rue Bonaparte. Leaving,

she declares 'M. Palewski is a man who knows what's best for him.'

28h36 The Duchesse de la Rochefoucauld is introduced to the Director's office. 'This visit produced nothing,' she observes.

28h42 Mme Rodd leaves by the *escalier de service*. 'It's cold,' she remarks.

28h43 The Princess of Lichtenstein has an interview with the Director, she leaves after an hour and declares 'I have the impression than M. Palewski was in a hurry.'

29h43 Renewed visit of Mrs Rodd, who leaves five minutes later without making a declaration.

29h48 The Duchesse de Montesquiou comes to pay a visit to the Director. On leaving, she declares 'It's a good beginning.'

30h48 Lady Liz von Hoff left the office one hour later. 'I have just had the most encouraging conversation with M. Palewski.'

Conversations will begin again at 17h this evening.

Nancy never concealed her longing to be with Gaston, and she was unashamed to make herself available, waiting in the flat for a call or a snatched quarter of an hour's conversation, cancelling other plans at the last minute if he happened to be free. Does this make her pathetic, or the realistic lover of an extremely busy man? Marcel Schneider, who knew Nancy well, described her and Gaston rushing into one another's arms at every opportunity, and as the tempo of Gaston's political career increased along with his commitments to the RPF, those opportunities were scarcer. It is not necessarily true, as one of Nancy's biographers would have it, that the thrill of their meetings 'concealed a great emptiness'.[3] Her letters to Gaston are full of her need to be with him and her frustration when they are separated, but these are, after all, love letters. Lovers do not generally write to inform the beloved he or she is not much missed. Nancy also describes her many visits to friends, the fun she has in London or on the Riviera, jokes, 'shrieks', books, outings and, very often, work.

In an interview recorded in Versailles in 1970, Nancy explained that after the success of *The Pursuit of Love* she had simply 'meekly carried on' with her writing. Yet she took it extremely seriously and worked immensely hard. Between 1946 and 1960 she produced three novels, two scholarly biographies, a great many newspaper and magazine articles and reviews and translated both Mme de Lafayette's novel *La Princesse de Clèves* and André Roussin's play *The Little Hut*, with which she toured in England. Of her books of this period, the best known is perhaps her second bestseller, *Love in a Cold Climate*, in some senses a 'prequel' to *The Pursuit of Love*, featuring Fabrice de Sauveterre in a cameo which gives even sensible Fanny the chance to fall in love with him. In a much-quoted passage, Fabrice advises Fanny on the French method of keeping one's lover – that is, to give way to him in everything: 'Now you see, these English *femmes du monde*... They are proud and distant, out when the telephone bell rings, not free to dine unless you ask them a week before – in short, *elles cherchent à se faire valoir*, and it never never succeeds.'

This is not quite the dismal advice it might first appear to be. Nancy was able to laugh at her often comic attempts to snatch a few minutes with Gaston, and Fabrice's lecture is as much an in-joke at the expense of colonial pomposity as a prototype of *The Rules*. If one considers the sheer scale of the output Nancy achieved during her first decades in France, let alone its quality, it becomes clear that her work was neither a compensation for Gaston's absences, nor a hobby that she could pick up and put down at the shrill of the telephone. Her letters to him constantly discuss her work, describing her progress, asking his opinion. The tone is not quite the same as that used in her correspondence with her *cher maître* Evelyn Waugh, but nonetheless she addresses herself to someone she expects to be interested, who takes her as seriously as a professional writer as she does herself. She did structure her life around Gaston, but when she decamped to write, at the country home at Fontaines-les-Nonnes of her friend

Mme Costa, or the Coopers' château at Chantilly, it was not *pour se faire valoir*, but because she had work to do.

(*Love in a Cold Climate* contains another interesting little instance of a writing habit Nancy shared with Evelyn Waugh. Just as Waugh employs certain names for characters he dislikes (Cruttwell being the most frequent), in the novel she called 'Cedric' Nancy introduces the name Borley for a family of huntin' and shootin' Oxfordshire squires, notable for their physical hideousness and indifference to aesthetics. Caroline Dexter, in *The Blessing*, turns out to be a Borley. The name can only have its origins in the horrible landlord who turned Nancy's friend Cecil Beaton out of his beloved country house at Ashcombe.)

Waugh was always Nancy's lodestar as far as her writing was concerned and though she often disagreed with his recommendations they were united in their views six years after publication of *Love in a Cold Climate* on what they both referred to as 'the book of shame'. Nancy's essay on U and non-U, which began as a response to a serious philological inquiry, became a joke between friends and then a national *cause célèbre* that dogged her reputation for the rest of her life, has produced so much nonsense that it scarcely seems worth discussing yet again. Perhaps the best comment is Evelyn's, in his open letter in *Encounter* to Mrs Rodd on a 'VERY SERIOUS SUBJECT': 'Of the ramifications of the social order which have obsessed some of the acutest minds of the last 150 years, they know less than of the castes of India. Was it kind, dear Nancy, to pull their legs?'

Of Nancy's less-known works, her translation of *The Little Hut* might be read as a tantalizing hint as to the author's own situation. Explorers and adventurers had always fascinated her – she had a positive obsession with Scott of the Antarctic and remembered being disappointed as a child when her parents failed to take up their reserved cabins on the *Titanic*. The play maroons a triangle of lover, husband and wife on an island in nothing but their evening clothes (Susan is in Balmain), where they come across a shipwrecked cook. The three men take turns to spend the night with the wife in her hut. Husband and lover discuss adultery with cool detachment: bachelors are polygamists really, it's natural, but equally so for women. Philip, Susan's husband, proves very happy with the three-way open arrangement, less so her lover Henry, who insists that they go back to deceiving him when they are eventually rescued.

Nancy's theatrical tour brought plenty of journalistic opportunities for her newly acquired hobby of Brit-baiting, as did her visit to Russia in 1954. She did not attempt to write to Gaston from the USSR, but they would have had the chance to compare notes as he had spent time in Moscow in early 1945 to negotiate, among other things, the personally touchy subject of Poland. Gaston was appalled by the coarseness of Stalin's language and humour and had a disquieting taste of the realities of Soviet life, which he compared to the court of an Asiatic satrap. Irritated by the stringency of De Gaulle's position, Stalin turned to Gaston and remarked: 'I am as Polish as you are, but I want a democratic Poland.' Gaston countered: 'You are certainly Polish, but are you a democrat?' The interpreter translated only the first half of his response, and when Gaston asked why, the interpreter whispered that had he spoken it all, he would have spent the night in Siberia. Nancy herself rejoices in provocative approval for Uncle Joe in her article about her visit – 'the dear old soul did save our bacon' – and makes plenty of teasing comparisons between Russia and America. She also spends some time discussing her love of silver, a passion of Gaston's in which she herself acquired considerable knowledge. On her return he was, of course, the guest of honour at the caviare feast she threw for her friends.

Nancy was proud of her relationship with one of France's most influential men, though she was always sure to be offhand about it. Gaston, in turn, was proud of his connection with 'the French lady writer'. Anatole Muhlstein a Polish diplomat Gaston had met in the Thirties when he was en poste at the Polish Embassy, renewed his acquaintance with the Frenchman when he returned from the US after the war. Gaston would often come to lunch, formally dressed '*en Saint Denis*'. Muhlstein's daughters, who adored *The Pursuit of Love*, were astonished when their father's friend was revealed as the real Fabrice de Sauveterre, and begged Gaston to introduce them to Nancy. Anka Muhlstein recalls her coming to lunch, very elegant, though rather quiet, allowing the men to talk rather than putting herself forward. Perhaps if lunch at the Muhlsteins' found Nancy in a reflective mode, it was because one of the favourite jokes in the family was that Gaston always declared he would marry a *gratin* name. Did Nancy still hope, in the early Fifties, that it might be hers?

18

LES FEMMES DU MONDE

For there was, of course, the perennial question of the 'pretty ladies'. Gaston's proclivities were never a secret between them, nor did Nancy make one of them to others. In 1946, she wrote to Diana: 'Daphne was here – oh what a bitch she is. She made a terrific pass at the Col and her tactics were absolutely all in, for getting me out of the way. However, the Col roared with laughter and (I believe) resisted.' This does not seem very likely, as Lord Norwich recalls him sitting next to Daphne on a sofa at the British Embassy, bouncing up and down with excitement and murmuring 'j'ai envie de toi, j'ai envie de toi'. Was the rhythm of these words an aural inspiration to the lady who claimed that being made love to by Gaston was like 'being run over by an express train'? Not necessarily unpleasant. Despite his physical appearance – Louise de Vilmorin described 'wisps of smoke' puffing from the spots on his face, but then she would – he was considered far from unattractive. He could talk away that face in a demonstration of what Kingsley Amis called 'hypergamy', whereby unfortunate-looking but clever men are able to seduce their physical and social superiors. And, according to the memories of the ladies of the Flore, Gaston had hidden talents. He was also remarkably and, it must be said, more than creepily, persistent.

Virginia Forbes-Adam met Gaston at the Embassy, where she was dining without her husband. He invited her to lunch the next day, and the Coopers assembled in the courtyard to wave off the lamb to the slaughter. The lunch, including the time it took to drive to and from the Rue Bonaparte across the river, lasted from 12.45 to 1.15. Gaston had opened his own front door, stark naked and 'in a state of considerable excitement'. The doughty Mrs Forbes-Adam roared with laughter and ran back to her car.

Unlike Prod, Nancy's cousin Ed Stanley and even, on occasion, Duff Cooper, Gaston was not the type to go off on a 'bat' round the brothels. (Even Général de Gaulle had been known to indulge before his marriage, introduced to the pleasures of the *maisons closes* by none other than Maréchal Pétain.) Gaston's preference was for married society women, *les femmes du monde*. This may have been partly due to a fear of scandal: married women knew the rules, were in the main uninterested in jeopardizing their marriages and partings were civil and friendly. Oswald Mosley, in his early political career, boasted that he stuck to the maxim 'Vote Labour, sleep Tory'. By one contemporary, Gaston's seductions were attributed to Rastignac-like social climbing:

> ... a long career as a Don Juan of snobbery ... they were never below a certain title. Countesses, marquises, duchesses, princesses, miladies, succeeded one after the other without him ever marrying them. Nothing would have seen him courting a baronne, even were she a Rothschild. His success was to the credit of his hidden virtues, because they were nothing to do with his appearance or sensibility. The craters on his face seemed to be the imprint of the coronets embroidered on the pillows where he had slept.[1]

Even when not, as in Daphne Weymouth's case, her own friends, many of Gaston's *innamorate* were well known to Nancy. Marguerite, called Margot, de Gramont was the twenty-five-year-old daughter of Count Louis-René de Gramont, a distinguished veteran of the First War and (practically the ultimate prize apart from a Rochefoucauld) Antoinette *née* Rochechouart-Mortemart. Margot had had her portrait painted by Laszlo at the age of eight, was a Resistance heroine and had a huge crush

on Gaston. She was blonde and fat, 'handsome and distinguished' by virtue of her particule; irresistible. Nancy caught
Gaston dining with her in the most unfortunate of circumstances. She had taken Peter and his two nephews to a restaurant
and there at a nearby table were Margot and Nancy's colonel.
She then invited her guests to see the Louvre by night, surely
one of the loveliest sights in the world. As if they were all players
in a hideous farce, there were Gaston and Margot, hand in hand.
Later, she explained to Diana that what she couldn't bear was
that he had looked happy, 'so dreadful to prefer the loved one to
be unhappy . . . Oh the *horror* of love.'

The scene makes its way into *The Blessing*, where Charles-
Edouard de Valhubert plans to seduce a beautiful young woman
by taking her to see the statues lit up at night. By then, Nancy
had rationalized her feelings into comedy, but her immediate
reaction was nothing like the cool, assured response she gave to
Sophia Garfield when she catches Rudolph with her friend Olga
at the Ritz. In view of the setting, she convinced herself that
what she had seen was a proposal and, for the second time in
her life, she thought of suicide, planning to take some 'poison
pills' that Prod had left lying around. Luckily, she brought herself
to telephone Gaston first. He was sweetness itself. 'The rights of
passion have been proclaimed by the Revolution,' he declared (a
line she gave to Charles-Edouard de Valhubert), adding that,
contrary to appearances, it was he who was unhappy, having
seen her dining with her husband.

Violet Trefusis was a long term 'frenemy'. Gaston had known
her before the war, when, aged forty, she had tried to seduce
Paul Reynaud's thirty-year-old *chef de cabinet*. He had not been
attracted to her, despite her stories of being the daughter of
Edward VII (her mother, Mrs Keppel, had been the King's last
mistress). She was flabby and rather drunken, definitely not
'arranged'. This didn't stop Violet claiming that she and Gaston
had had an affair. He was altogether inclined to be tolerant of
the only woman in Paris he had never tried to seduce, and they
were friends for many years. Nancy and Violet knew one another

well in London, where Violet was perhaps most famous for her lesbian affair with Harold Nicolson's wife, Vita Sackville-West. Both women adored France. Rebecca West called them 'Les Françaises Imaginaires', though each claimed, quite untruthfully, that the other spoke the language badly. Nancy was quite fascinated by Violet, entertained and irritated in equal measure by what Gaston called her 'mythomania' and her literary pretensions. He couldn't resist a Proust connection any more than he could a duchess, and loved to visit Violet at her home at Saint-Loup-en-Naud, a former abbey, to which Proust had taken Antoine Bibesco in his pursuit of Gothic perfection. When Violet died, she left him a piece of Augsburg enamel. But Nancy never really forgave her for putting about the rumour that Gaston had succumbed to her Turandot charms so long ago. When Violet wrote her autobiography, *Don't Look Round*, in 1953, Nancy suggested that a more appropriate title would be *Here Lies Mrs Trefusis*.

Ethel de Croisset, another London acquaintance of Nancy's, became her neighbour in Rue Monsieur. An American heiress, she had married Philippe de Croisset, a veteran of Dunkirk, whose father, the playwright François de Croisset was (yet another) friend of Proust, and her salon brought together American café society and the French intelligentsia. She was a great patron of Stuart Preston, known as the 'Sergeant' and the model for Lieutenant Padfield in Evelyn Waugh's *Sword of Honour* trilogy. The famously good-looking Preston, who had had affairs with Nancy's friend James Lees-Milne and her social crony Chips Channon, was often invited by Nancy to her flat, where he and Gaston enjoyed talking about pictures (Preston was particularly interested in Vuillard and for a long time was an art critic for *The New York Times*).

Gaston was having an affair with Ethel, along with Nancy and at least one other married woman, in 1955, when Ethel's brother, William Woodward, was killed in a scandalous society murder. He had married (possibly bigamously) a former showgirl, Ann Crowell, to the horror of his rich Wasp family. After a dinner party for the Duchess of Windsor, Ann and William had returned home to the news that a prowler had been spotted on their property. They both went to bed with loaded shotguns, heard a noise in the night and met in the dark on the landing, where Ann shot William, apparently by accident, at point-blank range. The story was retold in Truman Capote's *Answered Prayers* and Dominick Dunne's book *The Two Mrs Grenvilles*. Until the late 1950s, Paris gossips believed that Gaston might be planning to marry Ethel. Nancy took a low view of Ethel, though her real ire was reserved for another American mistress, whom Gaston possibly shared with Duff Cooper. In all likelihood, she was not the only one.

Susan Mary Patten, later Alsop, arrived in Paris in 1945 to join her first husband, Bill Patten, an economic analyst in the American Foreign Service. Nancy always called him 'the World Banker'. Her family, the Jays, had an honourable connection with the city: her great-great-great-grandfather, the first chief justice of the American Supreme Court, had travelled to Paris with Benjamin Franklin and John Adams in 1782 to draw up the Treaty of Paris, the settlement of the American Revolutionary War. The Jays were as aristocratic as Americans could be, generations of marriages to Dutch heiresses had made them rich and service in the diplomatic and legal professions had made them grand and superlatively well connected. They had links with the Parisian *gratin*, Susan Mary's grandparents having lived in Paris in the nineteenth century while her grandfather, Augustus, served at the American Embassy. Boni de Castellane and the De Noailles were friends.

Her father, Peter, was a diplomat, serving in Rome, where Susan Mary was born in 1918, then San Salvador, Romania and Argentina. From 1927 they lived at a family property in Bar Harbour, Maine, where Susan Mary passed through the conventional boarding school and country club adolescence of the American upper class. Having developed an early interest in politics, she disliked Bar Harbour for its parochial smugness. If Wasp codes meant that she could never have much of a career in her own right, she would have the next best thing: proximity to powerful men. She was very pretty, well-dressed, extremely slender and an excellent conversationalist. In her portrait of Susan Mary as Mrs Jungfleisch in *Don't Tell Alfred*, which is not unaffectionate, Nancy conceded that 'one saw why she was such an asset in society; she could produce the right line of talk in its correct jargon for any occasion'.

Susan Mary's affair with Duff Cooper began in autumn 1945 when, according to Diana Cooper's biographer, the English ambassadress chose her as a suitable mistress, 'a refuge between the emotional storms of Louise and the Whore of Babylon [Daisy Fellowes]'.[2] At the time, Duff was having an affair with Gloria Rubio y Alatorre, universally considered to be the 'it girl' of Paris that year. Diana, with her usual disregard for precedence, seated Susan Mary next to Duff at an Embassy dinner. They became close, but did not begin sleeping together until 1947, after the glamorous Gloria had married Prince Ahmed Fakhri. In February 1948, Susan Mary told Duff that she was expecting a child.

Her son, William Patten, did not discover his true paternity until long after it was well known in Paris. He discusses it candidly in his book *My Three Fathers*, but does not mention the rumour that, for some time, *les gens du monde* believed Susan Mary's child was Gaston's. In her collection of letters and memoirs *To Marietta from Paris*, his mother alludes discreetly to the Frenchman Nancy was in love with, and Gaston is mentioned as a guest of the Pattens, or dining out with them with the Rothschilds and Momo Marriott. Two hints are dropped as to the nature of her relationship with Gaston – the gift of a ticket to a De Gaulle press conference and the rather odd statement: 'Frenchmen may be wonderful lovers. I wouldn't know. Certainly they are very good thwarted lovers, bearing no rancour.'[3] Is it possible that there was no affair with Gaston? That he made a pass and genuinely received a rejection? Or, given that Susan Mary carefully conceals her relationship with Duff, is her protestation of ignorance a red herring?

Nancy got on with Susan Mary, though she cannot have failed

to hear the gossip. She often asked her to her flat, where Susan Mary recalled the theatrical and literary conversation, and they shared a love of Parisian history, exchanging discoveries that would help them to pin down the dates of buildings in the ancient palimpsests of Parisian architecture. The story in *The Blessing*, where Grace de Valhubert discovers her husband in flagrante while taking a tour of a *hôtel particulier*, is, according to Susan Mary, quite true. It was Nancy's anti-Americanism, she suggests, that soured their relationship. Nancy had many American friends, including the journalist Art Buchwald, and liked Americans very much as individuals, though when this was pointed out she would remark archly, 'Yes, but they live *here*, and they have *chosen freedom*.' Susan Mary was distressed and annoyed by what she saw as the ridiculous prejudice of someone who had never even visited her country – Nancy once went so far as to claim she had been a Communist before the war to avoid going there – yet her assessment of Nancy was humble and generous. 'She caricatured me as the idiot American senti-mentalist that I probably was and am ... but I miss my clever, witty friend.'[4]

It must be said that Nancy was not very nice to Susan Mary, though, if the rumours were true, it wasn't very nice of Susan Mary to go to bed with Gaston. Nancy read her the manuscript of *Don't Tell Alfred*, which is fairly merciless about Susan Mary/Mrs Jungfleisch's passion for 'top English policy makers', and was quite open about the fact that Hector Dexter was an amal-gamation of Americans she had met as Susan Mary's guest. A more elaborate tease was plotted with Evelyn Waugh for the coronation of Elizabeth II in 1953. Evelyn knew Susan Mary from the Embassy, and invited her to stay in Gloucestershire after her trip to London for the coronation celebrations. She was met in a large Rolls-Royce, evidently hired for the occasion, and driven to the Waughs' home at Piers Court, which was decorated with a huge floral arch emblazoned 'God Save the Queen' (this was not actually for Susan Mary's benefit – it was left over from Evelyn's reception for the Dursley Amateur Dramatic Society, of which Evelyn had contrived to remain president for fifteen years without ever meeting a member). Susan Mary changed into a simple dress for dinner, to be received by Evelyn in white tie and decorations and his wife Laura in ball gown and tiara, eccentrically accessorized with crutches.

Evelyn gave a long speech about Queen and country, then announced to his bewildered children, who had not been permitted to watch the coronation on the television, that Mrs Patten had been present in Westminster Abbey and would now describe the rituals. Poor Susan Mary, who had been nowhere near the abbey, did her best with what she had seen on TV, but she felt like an 'underdressed fool'. The excursion concluded with Evelyn, got up now in full tweeded squire mode, driving her around the countryside in the embarrassing Rolls and treating her to a morning-long monologue on farming. 'Your torturing of Susan Mary is all over Paris,' wrote Nancy delightedly. 'Poor little thing looks more like a Nazi victim than ever.' If Susan Mary really had succumbed in the Rue Bonaparte, then time whirled in its revenges. William Patten's book, in which he solemnly and priggishly tries to persuade his mother that she is a dangerous alcoholic, might have been written by Hector Dexter.

Nancy's 1951 novel *The Blessing*, as well as being an encomium on the superiority of all things French, is effectively a guide to how to deal with adulterous husbands. Adultery was not unknown in the Mitford family tree, and the word had brought forth many suppressed shrieks from the Mitford children when it appeared in the lessons at Swinbrook church. Nancy's grandfather, 'Tap', was the illegitimate son of a Liberal MP and a servant, Susan Bowles; her 'Aunt Natty' (actually a great-aunt on her grandmother's side, Lady Blanche Hozier) was known to have had at least nine lovers, including her own brother-in-law Bertie Mitford. Both the Churchill and Mitford families agreed that Bertie was the natural father of Clementine, who married Winston Churchill. Aunt Natty's daughter Nellie was supposed to have carried on the family tradition by having an affair with

Winston, who, it was said, was the natural father of Jessica's husband Esmond Romilly, a rumour Esmond alluded to on several occasions. Incestuous love affairs appear in Nancy's books, most famously, of course, in *Love in a Cold Climate*, but there is also a set piece about uncles and nieces marrying in *Christmas Pudding*, just a hint of family lore. 'Your family,' Evelyn remarked darkly in 1963, 'were peculiarly tolerant of incest.' Whatever the truth, Lady Redesdale never approved of Nellie Romilly.

Nancy Mitford was much better equipped to deal with infidelity than many women today. Within her social class, adultery was regarded as entirely routine and had been for ever. So long as there was no scandal, both sexes were more or less free to do as they chose once a couple of legitimate children had been produced (hence the shibboleth of never remarking on paternal resemblance in an upper-class child). The burglary scene in *Love in a Cold Climate* is staged to little other narrative purpose than to demonstrate Nancy's familiarity with the mores of house-party corridor-creeping. The husbands all assume the burglar sneaking through their rooms is Fabrice de Sauveterre and mutter, 'Better try next door old chap,' before going back to sleep, while the wives 'breathlessly murmur what words of encouragement' they know in French. Nancy might also have observed the examples of two women to whom she was extremely close, Dianas Cooper and Mosley, whose husbands were the 'Olympic class adulterers of the pre-war period'.[5]

Duff and Diana Cooper's marriage was superlatively happy, as was that of Oswald and Diana Mosley, yet neither man made any secret of the fact that monogamy wasn't really up their boulevard. Diana Cooper positively encouraged many of Duff's liasions. One evening at Emerald Cunard's, Duff was clearly making a play for his dinner companion, so the hostess hinted that Diana might like to take him home. 'Why, he's not bored yet, is he?' asked Diana.

'Don't you mind?'

'I only mind when Duff has a cold.'

On another occasion, where Ann Charteris, the wife of

Viscount Rothermere and later Ian Fleming, was staying in the guest cottage of the Coopers' house at Bognor, Duff insisted on walking her down the garden path after dinner. Anticipating a lunge, Ann suggested that another guest might care to come along. 'Oh, don't spoil it!' whispered Diana. Her attitude, she explained to her son, Lord Norwich, was that other women might be the flowers, but she would always be the tree. She was not always entirely equanimous, however. When Daisy Fellowes turned up in Paris after the war and resumed her affair with Duff she was jealous, but not nearly so much so as Louise de Vilmorin, who made tremendous scenes. Diana comforted her husband's mistress so thoroughly that the Duchess of Windsor remarked she would never have an affair with Duff because it would mean having Diana hanging around the whole time being nice to her.

Diana Mosley also claimed that she always knew her husband would return to her, yet conceded that sexual jealousy was the worst possible kind, and that she had on occasion suffered a good deal. When they met, Mosley already had a reputation as a great philanderer. He had confessed his past relationships to his wife Cynthia Curzon when they became engaged ('well, all except her sister and her stepmother') but continued to cut a swathe through the most beautiful women of the London Season, an occupation process he referred to as 'flushing the coverts'. In twelve years of marriage to Cimmie, he had at least thirty-six affairs, an average of three lovers a year, following an efficient strategy of lunch at a smart restaurant like Boulestin's or the Ritz, then a hop back to his bachelor pad in Ebury Street. Harold Nicolson claimed that Mosley and his first wife were extremely fond of one another, despite their quarrels over his infidelities, but when he met Diana Guinness Cynthia knew that for the first time she had a serious rival. Diana's biographer suggests that she 'rationalized' her own affair with Mosley in the belief that if he had only one mistress then his wife would suffer less. Certainly Cimmie behaved outwardly with perfect restraint. It was quite common for adulterous couples to socialize together, as the

Rodds had done with the Sewells, and Cimmie permitted 'the Guinness' to be invited as a guest to Savehay, the Mosleys' family home in Buckinghamshire. Georgia Sitwell, another Mosley mistress ('of course I went to bed with Tom. We all did and then felt bad about it afterwards') recorded the 'irritating' behaviour of Diana and Mosley one such weekend. The Sitwells went to Antibes with the Mosleys, the Guinnesses met them in Venice and if Diana expected Mosley to change his ways when she had given up everything for him and his wife was gone, she was wrong.

Diana had left a husband who had only ever treated her with love and generosity and made herself a virtual pariah in doing so, yet Mosley began his affair with his second sister-in-law, Baba Metcalfe, practically as soon as Cimmie was buried. Diana was extraordinarily calm. Holidays were split between them. At Toulon in 1933 Diana stayed for the first two weeks, Baba the second, while the next year, when Mosley took the Rodds' villa at Posillipo, Diana arrived to be shown to the bedroom Baba had just vacated. 'It's not Auntie Baba in there, it's Mrs Guinness,' the housekeeper was obliged to explain to Mosley's son. At the time of Nancy's marriage, Diana went so far as to abort Mosley's child (a process which, aside from the emotional stress it caused, was at the time illegal and brutally unpleasant) to avoid a scandal, yet even after her own marriage to him in 1936, Mosley continued to see Baba and to claim to his sisters-in-law that he only saw Diana occasionally. 'All through the Thirties it was as if I had two wives,' he admitted. He took his business partners in the failed radio station project to Parisian brothels, and long after he married Diana and they had moved to Orsay he continued having affairs with younger women, sending them flowers and extravagant presents.

Diana's tolerance of Mosley's frankly appalling behaviour has often been presented as a model of dignity and restraint, but then what else was she to do? She had sacrificed her life twice over for Mosley, missed out on her sons' infancy, endured prison and virulent enmity. It was not her style to make scenes. 'If she disagreed with him she would simply close her enormous blue eyes and both she and Mosley would laugh. When she opened her eyes again the conversation would have changed and whatever was disagreeable would have disappeared.'[6]

Nancy's continuing love for a faithless man has, over and over, been seen as pathetic, deluded, humiliating; Diana's, by contrast, noble and intelligent. Paul Johnson suggests that Gaston ('a shit – a stereotypical Frenchman with a dash of Polish shit') exploited Nancy, Lord Weidenfeld that she was 'unsuccessful as a woman', Lord Norwich that she was 'making a fool of herself'. Yet in a world where monogamy was not seen as a prerequisite for happiness, why should Nancy be singled out as the patsy? 'We all pitied her,' adds Lord Norwich. 'Barking up a perfectly hopeless tree.' Had Gaston married Nancy, then no one would have pitied her at all.

Nancy decided, as her friend and her sister had done, that to elevate fidelity at the expense of everything else in her relationship was simply childish. Unlike many modern women who insist on sexual continence as 'non-negotiable' and make themselves extremely miserable in the process, Nancy, like others of her time and class, rejected this. She did suffer, she did feel jealous and vengeful, but she was prepared, as she had not been in 1941, to negotiate the inevitable 'falling off of physical love' in terms of a wider and ultimately more fulfilling idea of what love could be. *The Blessing* which, she wrote to Gaston, 'of course, all husbands love', is her articulation of this process, whereby the profoundly English Grace undergoes an unsentimental education in *l'amour à la Française*.

Early in the novel, Grace is warned by Mme de Valhubert that a woman who puts her husband first seldom loses him.

'Well, I daresay,' said Grace with some indignation, 'that a woman who lets her husband do exactly as he likes, who shuts her eyes to every infidelity and lets him walk over her, in fact, would never lose him.'

'Just so,' said Mme de Valhubert placidly.

And this is what Grace learns to do. She comes to believe that her husband's relationships with other women have no meaningful impact on her own, that they are merely a distraction which fills his time away from her, 'like hunting or racing, a pursuit that takes him from you of an afternoon sometimes and does you no harm'. In the days of celebrity love cheats, when disappointed wives are rallied by the press to leave their ratty husbands, this is tantamount to blasphemy, but Nancy's refusal to put sexual fidelity at the centre of her life with Gaston worked very well. 'In those pre-Freudian days the act of love was not yet regarded with an almost mystical awe,' she wrote in her biography of Mme de Pompadour. She was quite reconciled to the modern notion of friends with benefits.

And her reward, she perhaps thought, would be that one day her errant man would love her best as Charles-Edouard does Grace. It's there already, in *The Pursuit of Love*, in the eccentric episode of the Alconleigh mineral collection, Uncle Matthew's prize, which Uncle Davey cheerfully pronounces to be stone dead. The passage is often read as an example of Uncle Matthew's unpredictability, his odd liking for those who ought to offend him, but it makes much more sense when read in the context of Gaston's favourite English poet, Lovelace. The italics are this author's.

> Why should you swear I am forsworn
> Since thine I vowed to be?
> Lady, 'tis already morn,
> And 'twas last night I swore to thee
> That fond impossibility . . .
>
> Not but all joy in thy brown hair
> By others may be found
> But I must search the black and fair
> *Like skilful mineralists that sound*
> *For treasure in unplowed-up ground.*

Then, if when I have loved my round,
Thou prov'st the pleasant she,
With spoils of meaner beauties crowned
I laden will return to thee,
Ev'n sated with variety.

At Louisa's ball, Linda Radlett, whose pursuit of love will eventually end in the arms of Fabrice, 'did get as far as taking one of her partners to see the diseased stones'. The mention of the minerals hardly makes sense in the novel as anything other than a private and poignant joke for the colonel. Considered in this fresh way, it is revelatory. Before she even left for Paris, Nancy was letting him know she would be prepared to wait.

19

GOVERNMENT

Until 1951, Gaston was frequently on the move. As national radio was hostile to the idea of De Gaulle broadcasting, and those organs that did support him – *L'Etincelle, Le Rassemblement* and the *Liberté d'Esprit* – had only limited circulation, the general undertook a long series of tours in the regions to promote the RPF. The party gained 35 per cent of the vote in the municipal elections of October 1947 and within a year membership had risen to half a million, second to that of the Communists. As they traversed the 'hexagon' from Marseilles to Nancy, Rennes to Grenoble, Gaston, so often dismissed as a '*salonnard*', proved himself a powerful orator.

Meetings were often disorderly, interrupted by Communists who accused the RPF of Fascism, but Gaston reiterated: 'You will not prevent us from speaking ... we will come back, and earlier than you think. And you will be obliged to listen to us.' (Though stirring, Gaston found this speech rather a bore as he was sometimes obliged to give it three times a month.) His anger at what he believed to be the blindness of Communism was evident in his addresses, and he was prepared to take considerable risks to express his views. During a tour of the Midi Pyrenees in 1949, the Communists adopted the tactic of filling the halls where he was due to speak with gangs of heavies. A colleague, talking of the intimidation of RPF speakers in both Paris and the provinces, called Gaston the bravest of them all. While the Communists believed they were working for freedom and revolution, Gaston insisted, they were merely the drones of an imperialist military machine which was exploiting them. To their rage, he was actually speaking from experience, his visit to the Kremlin with De Gaulle having provided him with a first-hand perspective on Stalinism. In Perpignan, agitators threatened to throw him into a canal, at Albi they stormed the platform, knocking him over and kicking him, while at a small village in Ariège the attacks were so fierce that he ended up in hospital.

Despite a professed hatred of electioneering and party politics, Gaston was beginning to think about formalizing his political role, not least as his financial position was extremely precarious. The appointment of Georges Pompidou to his former position of *chef de cabinet*, on his own recommendation, released him, not without some relief, from his direct obligations to the general. 'Like me,' he wrote to the future president of the Republic, 'you know to what point it is necessary to be near him, how much he deserves, and, more than anything else, how much he needs disinterested advice.' It was 'an immense comfort', he added rather patronizingly, to know that he would have Pompidou in the rearguard of the RPF advance.

In the 1951 elections, Gaston won a seat as RPF member for the Seine and returned to the Palais Bourbon for the first time since 1940, taking his place on the first rank of benches of the Right. Officially, the RPF was still in Coventry so far as other parties were concerned, but despite the general's proscriptions against any steps towards compromise, Gaston began discreetly to establish links with them. He was particularly interested in education reform, and took up one of the many cultural posts which were to distinguish his later career, the presidency of the committee for the preservation of the cathedral of Saint Denis.

De Gaulle was also pushing for the RPF to present proposals for a European confederation. Such proposals had already been voiced in May 1950, when the foreign minister Robert Schuman outlined his ideas for a supranational European community. Gaston had initially spoken out against these, as although a European community with clearly defined aims was advocated by the Gaullists (and indeed Winston Churchill in 1946), the

RPF felt that Schuman's plan gave too much power to Germany, especially German industry, at the expense of France. A European community, the RPF believed, could never succeed without a European army. Nevertheless, Schuman's first initiative, the ECSC (European Coal and Steel Community) was passed in April 1951 with the signing of the Treaty of Paris. Six member countries signed, marking, in Schuman's words, 'the true foundation of Europe'. Sour grapes from the Gaullists who, in their August propositions, reiterated the generalities of Schuman's scheme: 'A European confederation ... of the cultural order, the development of intellectual, artistic and technical values ... and notably the sharing in common of scientific research and peaceful applications of atomic energy.' Much of Gaston's time over the following years would be devoted to these issues.

De Gaulle's complete incapacity to accept the realities of the system of the Fourth Republic was now creating fissures in the RPF. In January 1952, Jacques Soustelle arrived at headquarters in the Rue Solferino with the news that he had been asked to form a government. De Gaulle raged: 'You are all the same! All it takes is a red carpet rolled out under your feet for you to walk on it, whatever its direction!' Forty-five RPF deputies broke with De Gaulle that summer. The remainder capitulated the following year, supporting René Mayer's government. De Gaulle's response was to closet himself ever more closely at Colombey. Gaston's own career, however, was progressing well. From November 1952 to February 1955 he served as vice-president of the assembly, where his *acuité allègre* in conducting the debates was once again in evidence. He was also a member of the Commission for Foreign Affairs, with a special interest in the Soviet satellite states and East and West Germany, campaigning against German rearmament without French control. This post was followed by a place on the Commission for Work and Social Security, then, a year later, the Commission of Law.

The collapse of the RPF permitted him to present himself as a social republican in the 1955 elections for the presidency of the council, where he obtained only seventy votes, but a month later the Mendès-France government fell and Edgar Faure called on Gaston for the post of minister to the presidency of the council in February. He was attached to the Ministry of Defence, covering the Secretariat of National Defence and the Institute of Higher Studies for National Defence in addition to atomic energy. No one was happier than Pauline, his housekeeper at Rue Bonaparte, whose conception of a minister's position owed more to the seventeenth century than the twentieth. She congratulated him: 'Ah, Monsieur, finally the good times have arrived! No more money worries!'

'Are you suggesting I take bribes?' replied Gaston.

'No Monsieur, just perquisites.'

Gaston now found himself working alongside Schuman (at the Ministry for Justice) on plans for European economic union, to be proposed by France at the conference of Messina. He was also one of the signatories of the Franco–Israeli accord on atomic energy which was kept secret until 1958, when France officially declared she had ceased working with Israeli scientists. Although one of Nancy's favourite Colonel jokes was his response to a lugubrious official, when asked his views on nuclear energy, 'Comme amateur de porcelaine,' Gaston was fascinated by nuclear power and keen that France should follow Russia, the United States and Britain into exploring its potential for domestic energy. In the face of much scepticism in the assembly, he refined a plan initially drafted by Felix Gaillard for national investment in and development of nuclear power as well as an investigation of the potential of nuclear weapons. The 'Plan Palewski', which consisted of a nuclear power station at Marcoule, research into a nuclear submarine and a huge investment programme, was nonetheless adopted. He was concerned that Europe should agree a cohesive nuclear strategy, writing to his colleague Antoine Pinay in advance of a conference in Brussels with precise details of communal production aims for the isotopic separation of uranium, and its sourcing in Africa. To promote his views, Gaston published a book of research, ideas and strategies gloriously entitled *The Atom, Our Destiny*.

In another echo of his past, Gaston had also been charged with overseeing the Sahara, and co-signed the law of 3 April 1955 that declared a state of emergency in Algeria.

In November 1954, the National Liberation Front of Algeria (FLN) had begun a campaign against the country's colonial rulers. The ensuing war, which led to a debate at the United Nations, provoked a general election in December 1955, in which the Gaullists took just 4.4 per cent of the vote. The diplomatic catastrophe of the Suez Crisis in 1956 exacerbated the Algerian situation, and the FLN attacks became ever more frequent and deadly. The continuing troubles made it impossible for any government to remain in power for a significant time and by 1957 posters all over France were demanding the return of De Gaulle. In what can only be summarized as a superlative combination of bravado and political genius, after the 'crisis of May', on 1 June 1958, the General found himself back in power as president of France. But De Gaulle's emergence from the wilderness came too late for Gaston. In the elections of June 1956 he had obtained only 5.6 per cent of the vote in the sixth district of the Seine. Although he accepted his defeat calmly and humbly and claimed to be glad to have more time to devote to writing and the push for restoring De Gaulle, his situation was rather difficult. Without his ministerial post he found himself, at the age of fifty-two, with limited means and no real job. 'I know how you hate inaction,' wrote Nancy, and her letters of the summer of that year are deliberately light, chatty and touristy, as though she is trying to spare him her consciousness of what, despite his brave face, was a real humiliation.

20

DESPAIR

For Gaston Palewski, De Gaulle was prepared to do something he had denied Churchill, Roosevelt and a generation of French politicians: compromise a principle. De Gaulle had always adamantly refused to engage his personal influence with public office, but when Gaston heard of the possibility of a post of ambassador to the EU, the general contacted Louis Joxe, the secretary general to the Ministry of Foreign Affairs, on his behalf. It was the only personal favour De Gaulle ever asked of the government in his entire career. The EU appointment was blocked by the socialist Christian Pineau, but in August 1957 Gaston received something far better: Rome. Nancy cabled from Venice: 'O DESESPOIR. O RAGE. O FELICITATIONS.'

'Gaston has got his post in Rome,' Evelyn Waugh wrote to Diana Cooper. 'Is Nancy desolate? Does one congratulate or condole?' In a letter to Violet Hammersley, Nancy did her best to appear lighthearted: 'The Colonel is off to the Palais Farnese in the form of Ambassador to Rome. He is very much pleased and I think he'll love it, really made for him. He goes in October after which I shall be as free as air.' But her friend Victor Cunard reported from Venice that her gaiety was painfully forced.

> She goes on saying that everything is going swimmingly with the Colonel, but one goes on hearing rumours that the whole thing is breaking up, which, from loyalty, one always denies. But my theory is it really is all over bar the shouting, that all her good spirits (or at least most of them), are a bluff

and that her almost savage teasing of friends is a sort of safety valve operation. If I am right it is rather pathetic, because if she would only tell one she is unhappy then one would do what one could to comfort her.[1]

Nancy's teases grew so acerbic that she and Victor had a tremendous row, which left them both deeply disturbed and distressed. From Venice Nancy took refuge at Fontaines-les-Nonnes. Her letters from there show that the shop-front was firmly back in place. She describes a conversation about stigmata – '*After* dinner, M. l'Abbe!' and Mme Costa's suspicion that her kitchen had been infiltrated by Soviet spies. Nancy had returned to Paris briefly to say goodbye before Gaston left for Rome in the middle of October. By early November she wrote to him from London that the thought of going home and finding Paris without him was too much to bear. Still, she added, she longed to hear all about Rome, and had heard from Diana that the Colonel's new house was huge. ('Well, we knew *that*.')

The Palazzo Farnese had been commissioned in 1517 by Alessandro Farnese, the 'petticoat cardinal', whose appointment was owed to his sister Giulia being the mistress of the Borgia Pope, Alexander VI, a detail that cannot but have charmed Gaston. Work on the house was interrupted by the sack of Rome, but when Farnese himself eventually became pontiff as Paul III he commissioned Michelangelo to finish the third storey of the 150-foot façade of this 'most monumental of Roman palaces'. How could the boy from the Faubourg-Poissonière fail to be enchanted? In the grandeur of its austere simplicity, it was everything that Gaston loved, including a frescoed staircase, courtesy of Salviati and Zuccaro, a great spiralling swoop of white marble all of his very own. Gaston's scalophilia was clearly known to the Mitfords: the Duchess of Devonshire suggested mischievously in an interview that 'one must *note* the staircase'. The new ambassador wrote to De Gaulle that his heart rejoiced at the appointment to what he and Nancy soon referred to as the '*palais-exquis*'.

It was, nevertheless, controversial. The Italian authorities were suspicious of the name Palewski, which they associated with the annexation to France at the end of the war of Tende and La Brigue as well as Aosta. Rome had signed the Common Market treaty in March that year, and Gaston's brief, when it was eventually passed by the Quirinale, was to celebrate the historic links between Italy and France, to sustain co-operation between the two countries and to refine their relations in terms of their participation in Europe. Gaston spoke little Italian and had scant knowledge of contemporary Italian politics, so it was reassuring, when he arrived at the station, to be greeted by his counterpart at the Holy See, Roland de Margérie, who had been *chef de cabinet diplomatique* in the Reynaud administration of 1940. Another old Paris connection was Gaston's friend Alary, who had married a daughter of Aman Jan, and was in Rome as a correspondent to the Havas agency. Gaston had visited him there before the war, in the office which would later become his own. Indeed, Rome was full of ghosts. 'At the Farnese palace there was one room which I never crossed without an impression of unease: the little white salon which gave onto the terrace, decorated earlier by Mme Henri de Jouvenal, with armchairs and a deep sofa, perfect for summer parties.' This was the sofa on which Pierre Laval had discussed with Mussolini the dictator's plans for Ethiopia.

The French community in Rome was surprised to find such an unconventional, indeed entirely inexperienced ambassador in their midst, but according to André Malraux Gaston was 'an ambassador born'. A critic claimed that he had no idea of the niceties of Embassy etiquette, which could hardly have been the case, given the time he had spent at the British Embassy in Paris and his role as unofficial chief of protocol there. Most of the objections stemmed from the alacrity with which Gaston flung himself on a fresh crop of pretty ladies, quickly earning himself the title 'l'Embrassadeur'.

Gaston's first duties involved the protocol visits decried by Fanny in *Don't Tell Alfred*.

'You have to polish off the colleagues, visit them you know, and there are eighty embassies here so it takes a bit of doing.'

'Are there so many countries in the world?'

'Of course not – the whole thing is a great nonsense – but we have to keep up the fiction to please the Americans. There's nothing millionaires like so much as being ambassadors.'

Got up in a marvellous costume of gold-embroidered blue coat, bicorn hat with white feathers and a cape, Gaston first proceeded in a motorcade to present his letters of appointment to the Italian president, Giovanni Gronchi. Gronchi may have looked like 'a cross between a fig and a raisin', but he was sharp, greeting Gaston: 'Monsieur l'Ambassadeur, you are most welcome in Italy, everywhere in Italy. Even the Val d'Aosta.' They never became friends. He got on better at the Palazzo Chigi, the Ministry of Foreign Affairs, where he reassured the Italians of his personal commitment to the European Community. After the solemn honour of meeting the Pope, Pius XIII, was concluded, the new ambassador felt himself established.

The following spring though, the crisis the Gaullists had been expecting for so long finally broke over France.

'I long for your voice so passionately I can't imagine today without you being there . . . Yesterday, I stayed shut in the house all day, expecting you to telephone. Oh, Colonel, you see I'm in one of my states . . . Don't abandon me. Perhaps you've changed too. Are you too rich or too happy? Bourgeois perhaps, however that isn't a word one associates with you.' Nancy felt she was living the past all over again, the longing, the excitement, De Gaulle and Gaston in Algiers. Then she received word to go and meet him at Orly. 'After so long it seems unbelievable . . . we cried with happiness.' If Nancy chose to believe that Gaston's tears were for her, rather than the general, she could, for a few moments on a dusty airfield, believe herself Linda in the arms of her Fabrice.

Nancy accepted that she could hardly expect to see much of

Gaston during the crisis, but his refusal of a role at the heart of the new government was an incomprehensible blow. Gaston later explained: 'My mission in Rome had too particular a character for me to abandon it . . . It seemed that my duty was, for a time at least, to remain in Italy.' But Nancy knew him too well. She couldn't reproach him – after the years of effort, endless work and the exhausting grind of a hostile political culture, Gaston deserved all the beauties Rome had to offer, and which he was so perfectly equipped to appreciate, but she had to confront the reality of her place in his life. She had clearly forgotten Elizabeth Bowen's dictum that as soon as one is sad, one is ordinary. The dynamic of their relationship, that it was she who loved and Gaston *qui se laissait aimer*, had been something she could handle, and often joked about.

'Oh, Colonel, I love you.'

'That's awfully kind of you.'

Yet she now had to accept that Rome was worth a discarded mistress. Gaston had never lied to her. He had promised her nothing and that was what she had got. 'Why would you want to deprive me of all that I love for one thing?' he asked her. For years, Nancy had convinced herself that she was the most significant woman in his life, the Pompadour to the pretty ladies in the Parc aux Cerfs, and Gaston had exposed the illusion. She felt foolish and angry.

A letter in June was clear-sighted and reproachful. 'I'm no longer any use to you. When things go badly, you need me. When they go well you turn to other, prettier women. So, I no longer have a role, *le portefeuille est vide*.' (The metaphor is a glance at Gaston's new 'portfolio', but also a sharp reminder that Nancy may not have always felt as serene as she appeared to about their different financial status – '*portefeuille*' also means wallet. It's a horrid image, Nancy figuring herself as used up, turned inside out and cast aside.)

But there was still love there. Gaston could easily have used his position to keep his distance from Nancy. The guards of the Palazzo Farnese would have proved more effective Cerberuses than the bewildered aides-de-camp at the Rue St Dominique in 1945. Nancy could have nourished her bitterness into a final quarrel, as Victor Cunard had anticipated. Their relationship could have dwindled into correspondence, with dignity maintained on both sides, but it did not. The next summer she was Gaston's guest at the palazzo and returned there every year of his mission.

Her first visit took place in August 1958, 'in dead secret'. Gaston was sensitive about his unusual status as an unmarried ambassador (he had taken Pauline with him from the Rue Bonaparte, a move which made him unpopular with the staff. 'Pauline is a traitor' was scrawled on the walls of the palazzo). Her visit was timed to coincide with the flight of the *beau monde* to the coast. As hardly ever, Nancy had her lover to herself, and sightseeing with the Colonel was an altogether delightful matter, quite different from trailing round dusty ruins with Prod. Gaston showed Nancy his favourite walk, to the church of San Agostino to see the Caravaggio Virgin, they visited the galleries and the antique shops. Nancy adored the heat and after a morning in the city happily sunbathed away the afternoons. 'What the Colonel calls exposing my limbs to the Spanish Embassy,' she giggled. Paris seemed gloomy without him. 'I sigh for the land of cypress and myrtle, I loathe the oak and ash. After 101 degrees in Rome I find it freezing here and pitch dark.'

Why would Gaston have bothered to dedicate time to Nancy had he not genuinely wished to see her when he might have been at Portofino with the Agnellis? Guilt, possibly, but *every* year? And in 1961, propriety was clearly no longer of consequence to the '*seul ambassadeur celibataire*', as Nancy and Deborah visited in March, at the height of the Roman Season. The Duchess of Devonshire remembers it as a 'real outing', a week of non-stop parties at which she knew no one. Luckily, most conversation was in English. Italian ice cream was a joy, the smart Italian woman both a pleasure and a challenge. The duchess conjectured that by then there was little physical relationship between Nancy and Gaston, but recalls vividly after a week in their company their intense pleasure in one another, talking about art, food, dissecting the social life, chatting and laughing endlessly. Nancy's visits were not a duty to Gaston, they were a joy, and if she had had the strength to lock up the pain and resentment of early 1958 and allow herself to be happy again, does that make her a fool or suggest that finally she had become one of the women she had always written about, those who know how to handle their lovers?

Or, one might add, their husbands. At the end of 1957, Peter finally consented to a divorce. Prod had spite in his character, and while he had never cut up rough about Gaston it does seem rather pointed that he should have agreed to give Nancy her freedom at precisely the moment when her lover appeared to have slipped from her clutches. Since the early Fifties, Prod had been living on a boat at Golfe Juan, not far from Cannes on the French Riviera. 'He looks exactly like some ancient pirate,' Nancy wrote to Evelyn, 'bone thin, pitch black, white hair and beard and dressed in literal rags.' Peter claimed that he had found someone he wanted to marry, though the identity of the lucky lady is uncertain and, as with most of his projects, it never came off. Nancy was obliged to appear in court to give evidence that her marriage had broken down, with predictable 'peer's daughter' publicity from the papers. Given the Rodds' lengthy and well-known estrangement, it was difficult to find a judge who was prepared to hear the case and four in fact refused. 'Old dancers, I suppose,' Nancy remarked. 'I had no idea I knew four judges!'

Lord Redesdale's death in 1958 also came just as Nancy was learning to live with Gaston's absence. Even a decade before, Nancy had described her father, then almost seventy, as 'looking like ninety', and James Lees-Milne, encountering him in Heywood Hill during the war, had been unable to recognize the terror of his youth and the handsomest man of his generation in the wizened, patient creature Nancy presented to him. Lord Redesdale's life had ended with the war, and though she grieved, Nancy acknowledged this. 'It is sad,' she wrote to Evelyn Waugh, 'but the odd, violent attractive man he used to be had already gone except for an occasional flash. He was so very weak and so very deaf.' Uncle Matthew was to have a last hurrah in the novel Nancy began writing in August 1959, *Don't Tell Alfred.* Evelyn told Nancy he thought this her best novel, though it is generally considered the worst.

21

THEORY OF THE LEISURE CLASS

In an *Encounter* essay of 1955, Edward Shilson identifies a crucial shift in the attitudes of British intellectuals towards their own nation in the post-war period. In the 1920s and 1930s, he argues, the 'whole notion' of Britain or England was considered 'repellent'. This was the view of 'nearly everyone [who] was considered worthy of mention'. In contrast, after the war, a new spirit of patriotism was nurtured by anti-Americanism.

> From a harmless, amiable, good natured, powerful, ridiculous, loyal ally – a sort of loutish and helpful nephew, America suddenly seemed to develop into a huge challenging empire, wilful, disregarding Britain, criticizing Britain, lording it over Britain and claiming to lord it over everyone everywhere. Loyal British backs were arched at this peril and the terrible economic crises of the second half of the 1940s accentuated impatience with America.

In 1942, George Orwell had written a piece rehabilitating Kipling, with T.S. Eliot joining him to praise the poet formerly dismissed as a vulgar apologist for imperialism. Shilson correlates this shift with his suggestion that intellectuals were reconsidering their attitude to the culture of British gentry, returning to the security of reverence for establishment institutions: 'a process of submission to the moral and cultural – but not the political or economic – ascendancy of the aristocracy and gentry'. In such a climate of endorsement of values which Nancy's own generation had professed to despise, before the war robbed them of their sense of confidence and autonomy, *Don't Tell Alfred*, in other respects a slight little book, is bang on message.

The novel is once again narrated by Fanny, who finds herself after her husband's promotion to ambassador to France in the curious position of châtelaine of the Hôtel Charost. The book has very little plot, being more a collection of observations tied together by a (frankly cringeworthy) story about Fanny's youngest boy's obsession with an American pop star, Yanky Fonzy, a flattering portrait of Diana Cooper as Lady Leone, 'the most beautiful woman in the world', the reluctantly outgoing incumbent, and a charming but incompetent secretary, Northey, who may have been drawn on the French girl of good family who had been recommended to Gaston at the Palazzo Farnese and promptly packed off after the Embrassadeur learned she couldn't type. Presumably she wasn't pretty, either. Yet together, *The Blessing* and *Alfred* are in many ways a distillation of what Nancy had absorbed from her fifteen years' engagement with Gaston's politics and a gently melancholic elegy for the country she so loved.

Nancy always discussed her reading with those to whom she was closest – her brother Tom in the Twenties and Evelyn and Gaston after the war. In 1928, she was particularly struck by Clive Bell's *Civilization*: 'You must read it. He says that most people today are uncivilized (which I've always felt) ... that the only three real civilizations that we know of were the Greeks, the Italians and the French eighteenth century. It is a most charming book and expresses things I have always felt and sometimes tried to say.' Bell's book had been started before the First War, as a discussion of the 'manifestations of civility' in art and social mores, but the experience of 1914–18 led him to turn his rather bland assumptions into a questioning of what civilization actually was, or rather what kind of civilization could justify such destruction in its defence. In 1918, Leonard Woolf had concluded that 'hatred, fear and self-preservation' were the dominant traits of social psychology; in the decades between the wars these manifested themselves in two distinct generational reactions. In the Twenties, distress and disillusion about the future were demonstrated in frivolity; in the Thirties, the decade of political extremes on both left and right, in a challenging of values which led to a mass conversion to ideology. In both decades, the fear that civilization was under threat was so ubiquitous that 'there were few areas of intellectual endeavour, artistic, literary, scientific, philosophical, that were not affected in some form or other by the prevailing paradigms of impending decline and collapse'.[1] Bell had little to offer by way of conclusion than Matthew Arnold's nineteenth-century formula of 'sweetness and light', which he attempted to sum up as

> A taste for truth and beauty, tolerance, intellectual honesty, fastidiousness, a sense of humour, good manners, curiosity, a dislike of vulgarity, brutality and over-emphasis, freedom from superstition and prudery, a fearless acceptance of the good things of life, a desire for complete self expression and a liberal education, a contempt for utilitarianism and philistinism.

From her Parisian perspective on the transatlantic culture of the 1940s and 1950s, Nancy saw America as representative of precisely the opposite of this cherished list of values. She greatly enjoyed herself in the role of heretic. Sixty years after *The Blessing*'s publication, it is more true than ever that 'it is considered nowadays perfectly all right to throw any amount of aspersions at poor old France and England, but one tiny word reflecting anything but exaggerated love for new rich America is thought to be in the worst of taste'. Unlike many of Nancy's declared passions, including her devotion to France, which she exaggerated to tease friends like Evelyn, her loathing for America was entirely serious. In 1957 she told the *Herald Tribune*: 'I hate everything that has to do with American civilization, your plastics, your skyscrapers, refrigerators, psychoanalysis and Coca-Cola.' One really is not allowed to say things like that any more. People whom Americans term 'liberals' can get away with criticizing particular political policies, the injustice of big business, violence or racism perhaps, but to declare that one loathes everything about America is blasphemous. To be declaredly anti-American is to be instantly dismissed, as Nancy was by Rhoda Koenig in *The Sunday Times*: 'Mitford's anti-Americanism was merely the more obvious expression of her unpleasant personality.' Only nasty people, after all, dislike America.

At the ghastly Dexter dinner party in *The Blessing*, Hector D, who has taken over from Prod as the official most boring man in the world, delivers a speech on the 'malaise in this country, a spirit of discontent, of nausea, of defatigation, of successlessness around us here in this very city of Paris'. What Europe needs is 'some precognition of and practice of our American way of living. I should like to see a bottle of Coca Cola on every table in England, on every table in France.'

'But isn't it terribly nasty?' asks Grace, whose Valhubert millions, lest we miss the point, derive from wine.

In both novels, the Dexters and their acolyte Mrs Jungfleisch, Nancy's portrait of Susan Mary Alsop, embody everything Nancy thought she hated about Americans, from their inability to appreciate food to their terrifying earnestness. They are completely divorced from their bodies: they require drugs to sleep, eat and go to the lavatory, they rely on artificial sources of heat and coolness, they have no capacity for pleasure. So far, so obvious. Yet this dissociation of the *sensible* and the sensual has its roots in what Nancy perceives as a dereliction of duty on the part of the European governing class.

In *The Pursuit of Love*, Nancy derides Tony Kroesig who, of course, adores America, when he dares to criticize the House of Lords. Men like Lord Alconleigh, she argues, understand the people who work for them, because they share their land with them, live alongside them: they exist in a symbiotic relationship of rights and responsibilities which money-worshippers like Tony can never understand. In *The Stanleys of Alderley*, Nancy devotes a long passage to developing this theme.

We still put our trust in men of ample means, and in lords, but doubts are beginning to arise in the minds of those who observe the modern trend ... These lords, divorced from the land which was the reason of their being, do they fly, shuddering with strange new fears hitherto unknown in this country, into the arms of alien creeds! And worse still, do they begin to hate and fear the people? The segregation of classes, which has resulted from the abandonment of the now impoverished land by its former owners, who prefer to seek their fortunes in the City to struggling for a livelihood on the acres of their ancestors, has been most harmful to the aristocracy, they are losing their hitherto immense knowledge of, and trust in, the people.

This is very immature writing, painful in its purpleness, not to mention disturbingly reminiscent of Eugenia Malmains at her most evangelical. Yet here, in the early Thirties, Nancy is trying to articulate a belief in what constitutes a mature civilization. She puts it very awkwardly: 'We are the only adult nation and until the others come of age we must be their governess.' In *Civilization*, Clive Bell argues for the necessity of a leisured elite to produce a culture which conforms to his definition of 'sweetness and light'. It was precisely this which Nancy saw as lacking in American culture.

Americans, she thought, were simply not adults. This is sent up wonderfully in their attitude to sex. 'In America, if you hold a woman's hand you are expected to go round next day with divorce papers,' says Mme Rocher, while Albertine laments the fact that she had to marry her American lover in order to get him to perform in bed. Fear and hatred of sex leads to brutal bigotry. Nancy hated the 'American' line on gay men (compared ingenuously by Grace to the Jews in Germany), whom Hector describes as 'sickly, morbose, healthless, chlorotic, unbraced, flagging, peccant, vitiated and contaminated'. For her, intolerance of homosexuality and insistence on monogamy were indicators of cultural immaturity, the evil genie hiding in the

Coca-Cola bottle. Summing up Bell's arguments in his diary, the critic A.L. Rowse wrote: 'The essence of civilization seems to consist in a self conscious cultural tradition, created by the dominant class.'

Philip Roth thinks much the same thing. In *I Married A Communist*, Roth identifies the fault with intolerant, McCarthyite America as stemming from the fact that it is a proletarian culture, one that has passed from poverty to plutocracy without ever supporting a dominant leisure class. It has never had the chance to grow up, thus its aesthetic philistinism is correlated with its political ignorance and prejudices. 'The working man will conquer us all – out of his mindlessness will flow the slop that is this philistine country's cultural destiny. We'll soon have something in this country far worse than the government of the peasants and workers – we will have the culture of the peasants and the workers.' When Roth makes the argument, impeccably qualified Great American Novelist as he is, it stands; when Nancy makes it, daughter of a lord, relaxed rather than anguished about sex and rather good at jokes, she is dismissed as a snob, or worse.

By the time of *Don't Tell Alfred*, Nancy is a much more accomplished writer than the gauche and simplistic author of *The Stanleys*. American immaturity is gestured at, in Hector's delight in teenagers (shades of the Lecherous Lecturer), in Mme Rocher's inability to believe that the young might require amusing, in M. Bouche Bontemps's contempt for the cult of health, in people who think cleverly about Karl Marx but are not adult, in an American school being 'a large light building with a swimming pool', in Mrs Jungfleisch's very name, pronounced 'Youngflesh'. Fanny acts as a moderator for these views, gently deflecting their conceit and questioning their assumptions. The crescendo of *Don't Tell Alfred* is Fanny's drive with Charles-Edouard de Valhubert across the battlefields of the Marne to visit Fabrice's mother, the Duchesse de Sauveterre. Charles-Edouard has moved on from the stubborn urbanity of *The Blessing* – 'Nature I hate' – and launches into an elegy for the passing countryside. 'I love this country so much, but now it makes me sad to come here. We must look at it with all our eyes because in ten years' time it will be utterly different. No more stooks of corn or heaps of manure to dot the stubble with light and shade, no more peasants in blue overalls, no more horses and carts, nothing but *mécaniciens* driving tractor and lorries.'

Here is Nancy's love for the atmosphere of Fontaines-les-Nonnes, here her gently mourning memories of the bleakly beautiful landscape of her adolescence. Charles-Edouard's Enlightenment insistence that towns are the only civilized place to live is softened by a more English Romanticism, a melding of a culture that celebrated artifice and one which valued its lost relationship with the land. He goes on to speak of Europe, of the world as it has been for a thousand years, each country with its own discrete architecture and cuisine, as compared to the uniformity seen everywhere. Venice survives, but Rome is engulfed in an 'American rind' of skyscrapers and tangles of wire. He concludes that since his children have never known this world, the gap created by unshared experience has produced the greatest divide between generations the world has ever seen. This is the statement made by Albert in *Highland Fling*, but Nancy now identifies America, not the First War, as the origin of fission. Fanny counters that if the next generation are happy and good, then a few apple trees don't really matter, but Charles-Edouard argues:

> Will they be happy? I think modern architecture is the greatest anti-happiness there has ever been. Nobody can live in those shelves, they can do no more than eat and sleep there; for their hours of leisure . . . they are driven onto the roads. That is why a young couple would rather have a motor car than anything else – it's not in order to go to special places but a means of getting away from the machine where they exist.

This idea of a communally rooted culture torn up by a soulless, impersonal, mechanized society is close to the German sociological idea of *Gemeinschaft*. Nancy's feeling, expressed from *The Pursuit of Love* onwards, is that there is a crucial connection between elite culture, the standards of elegance and taste set by the educated and cultivated, and the life of the land, of the people. American society is what happens when this connection is fractured. Charles-Edouard continues that this is how the Americans have lived for a generation, and the consequences are 'gloom, hysteria, suicide'. Fanny responds with the platitude that his preferred period to live in, any time between the Renaissance and the Second Empire, would only be viable if he were a privileged person. 'If I were not, I wouldn't be me.' True, Fanny concedes. Men of the type of Charles-Edouard and Uncle Matthew 'would not have been themselves if they had not always been kings in their own little castles. Their kind is vanishing as surely as the peasants, the horses and the avenues, to be replaced, like them, with something less picturesque, more utilitarian.'

Bell's argument, Nancy's argument, founders on this, the 'picturesque'. A political philosophy which is essentially aesthetic is no redoubt against evil – or money. De Gaulle's politics of grandeur had ceded their place to financial negotiations, confirming Roosevelt's view in the late Thirties of France as a decadent country even as American money restored the civilization Nancy revered. Sweetness and light is simply an inadequate response. This is the mournful theme of Evelyn Waugh's *Put Out More Flags*; his characters, he wrote in his dedicatory preface to Randolph Churchill, 'are no longer contemporary in sympathy, they were forgotten even before the war, but they lived on delightfully in holes and corners'. He and his kind, who had fought for what they professed to despise as Bright Young Things of the Twenties, were no more than 'a race of ghosts'. His profound depression towards the end of his life, compounded by Vatican II, had as its source this despair at a world he could not, nor wished to understand. Nancy's response was more robust. She deplored the submersion of all that she believed in by American values, but if civilization was to be wiped away by a cleansing tissue, she was determined to go down laughing.

22

A L'OMBRE DE
L'EMBRASSADEUR EN FLEUR

B ack in his Renaissance palace, Gaston found that politics
had taken a deliciously *quattrocento* turn. Pius XII had died,
and Gaston found himself in the position of an Ascanio Sforza
or Giuliano della Rovere, plotting to install a pro-French candidate on the papal throne. In the aftermath of the liberation,
when the provisional government was struggling to establish its
authority with the Communists, Gaston had contacted the papal
nuncio to Paris, Monseigneur Roncalli, in the hope that he could
influence the '*prêtres ouvriers*' who had contacts in the party to
work towards a degree of national concord. The Dominican
Marie-Dominique Chenu called these 'worker priests' 'the greatest religious event since the French Revolution'. Established in
1940, the '*ouvrier*' order were integrated into secular life, often
working in factories or trade, with the aim of reinforcing the
Catholic faith among a social group in which it was in marked
decline while contributing to the war effort. Many of them
joined the Communist party and took part in strikes and
demonstrations, which aroused the suspicions of Rome, and the
order was dissolved in 1954.

Gaston credited Roncalli with a great intelligence combined
with a blunt good sense drawn from his peasant roots (so they
had much in common) and was encouraged by the prelate's
interest, though Roncalli sighed that the worker priests *would*
carry on getting married. Roncalli was Gaston's type of priest, a
man of deep integrity who was at home in the salons of the
Faubourg, including that of Mme Abrami, where he and Gaston

had first been introduced. Gaston did what he could to promote Roncalli's candidature to the Holy See and was rewarded when his old acquaintance became Pope John XXIII. Protocol forbade the pontiff to make direct contact with foreign ambassadors, but the day after the election, Gaston found the Prince di Colonna, an assistant to the Vatican, in his office.

'What happy wind blows you here?'

'The wind of Saint Peter.'

The prince explained that although the pope might not telephone the palazzo, he had asked that his thanks and personal blessing be conveyed to the French ambassador.

The ambassador's thoughts remained in the sixteenth century when he wrote a paper on the historical causes of contemporary weakness in Italian democracy. Provincial absolutism, he argued, had created a lethargy which was only swept away by the French Revolution, but the legacy of this had left a social and intellectual gap between Italy and her European neighbours which it was still struggling to fill. This was not, it must be said, a particularly scintillating analysis – it reads as though cribbed from Guicciardini – but his conclusion was more provocative. Italy had not yet achieved democratic equality; the Italian people remained politically immature. A prescient point, given the present-day antics of Silvio Berlusconi.

Gaston the kingmaker was finally enjoying his day in the sun. The Italians, though, were disturbed by the restoration of De Gaulle, which to them, naturally, had disquieting overtones of Il Duce. Gaston called a meeting at the Embassy for prominent Romans, who listened to his explanation of Gaullist policy with a polite lack of conviction. The temptation to Fascism, they felt, would be too strong after what they perceived as a 'military coup d'état'. Gaston's efforts towards greater mutual understanding were also impeded by trade relations in the Maghreb. Paris was increasingly concerned by the engagement of the Italian government in North Africa. Following a commercial treaty of July 1957, Gaston learned that one of the main Moroccan industries, phosphates, was moving under Italian control, while

Enrico Mattei, the director of the ENI, was negotiating an interest in Algerian petrol. The French felt that this implied a dangerously pan-Arabic approach to trade in the region and Gaston warned Mattei in a meeting against any prioritization of Italian over French interests in the Maghreb. The Ministry of Foreign Affairs admitted that it was under American pressure to pursue Italian trade agreements, so the French were now anxious that Algerian rebels would be supplied with Italian arms. The matter dragged on, and Gaston continued to pay 'indignant' visits on the subject into the spring of 1959, when De Gaulle made a state visit to Italy.

Gaston had dreamed up a flattering wheeze whereby De Gaulle's visit would celebrate the tricentennial of the Franco–Sardinian alliance that defeated the Austrians at Magenta and Solferino. De Gaulle was thrilled with his reception, which included a speech on the 'Latin fraternity' in Milan and a personal audience with the new pope. He complimented Gaston: 'I wish to say how satisfied I was with the manner in which you prepared and set in motion my visit to Italy . . . Very clearly, you have achieved a personal position there which is in every way exceptional.'

Gaston had evidently learned a great deal from his tenure as 'pilot fish' to the Coopers at the Hôtel Charost. A contemporary recalled that the parties at the French Embassy soon became one of the main attractions of Roman life. 'His discretion, his taste for secrecy, the great interest he showed in the marvels of antiquity, the renaissance and the century of Tiepolo flowed over the Italian soil [as well as the] interest he brought to modern life, all, in a word, which could excite and serve the interests of our country demanded the recognition of the Italians.' Among luminaries such as Moravia and Silone, Gaston, of course, welcomed the 'pretty ladies'. He was delighted by the world he discovered, 'so shut off and enclosed in the prejudices of the past', which precisely suited his own temperament. In Rome he found a 'primacy of sentiment and passion which were the delight of the author of the Charterhouse of Parma . . . the absence of divorce assured relationships, as in Stendhal's time, with a conjugal stability'. The perfect hunting ground for 'M. Lavande'.

The pal-exquis was now ornamented with Gaston's own collection of pictures, and he intended during his tenure to restore the Farnese to the full lustre of its past. The project, he wrote to his friend, the antiquary Yvonne de Bremond, was the most agreeable he could imagine, 'far from the worries of diplomacy'. He received permission and funds to restore the Carracci gallery and placed Tournier's *La Mort des Sens* in the red drawing room. This 'strange' allegorical painting 'seemed happy to find itself once more in Rome'. Gaston rejoiced in his huge desk, set between eighteenth-century armchairs beneath Salviati's fresco *La Gloria di Rannuccio Farnese* and lit with two polished red marble lamps. Writing later of an exhibition of the French *caravagistes*, of whom he was an early champion, at the Villa Medici, he described the mysterious accord by which the enthusiast discovers those paintings and sculptures best fitted to please him and how, like women, 'objects of art arrange themselves to fall beneath the gaze of those to whom they wish to belong'.

Gaston's receptions at the Palazzo Farnese introduced him to the 'black aristocracy', those subjects of the Holy See who had shut up their palaces in 1870 in sympathy with the pope's self-imposed confinement in the Vatican. They included the Colonna and Orsini, the great Roman warlords whose feuds had directed papal policy throughout the Renaissance, the Pallavicini, Savelli, Borghese, Boncompagni-Ludovisi and the Caetani, dukes of Sermonetta. Gaston had a relationship with Cora Caetani, a widow five years older than himself whom he had encountered in Paris. Cora was passionate about interior décor, having directed the Jansen agency in Paris, and, like Nancy, loved to chat in both French and English. Gaston succeeded in obtaining the Légion d'Honneur for Marguerite Caetani, now in her eighties.

Since Gaston was unmarried, he would often ask women like Cora to act as his hostess, though as his nickname recalls, his seduction techniques were not always so subtle. Lord Weiden-feld, who dined at the Palazzo Farnese with the art collector Jayne Wrightsman, whom Nancy later came to know in Venice, commented on l'Embrassadeur's undoubted sex appeal, despite his 'repulsive' skin and teeth. Stories proliferated of Gaston bounding after girls through the palazzo's magnificent salons. Nancy was not the only Parisienne to make discreet trips to the Farnese. Gabrielle d'Arenberg came, as did Ethel de Croisset. Violette de Pourtales, with whom Gaston had been having a serious affair since at least 1951, also visited. Her husband refused to divorce her and, conscious of both their reputations, she spent her time closeted in the palazzo. One of the favourite anecdotes about l'Embrassadeur crops up in Rome, though like most apoc-ryphal stories, all the witnesses place it differently. Gaston offered an attractive girl a lift home in the ambassadorial car, to which she replied, 'No thank you, I'm much too tired this evening. I'd rather walk.'[1]

Gaston's snobbery was exalted beyond measure by his forays into the Roman *gratin*, but new money was also alluring. Nancy had always commented on the restlessness of his character, which had found satisfaction in the early days of the RPF in the marathon journeys across France, where he had appreciated the usefulness of personal contact in communicating his message. To further knowledge of and support for France, he undertook a series of trips described by his brother: 'One saw him opening exhibitions, commercial fairs, pausing before Greek and Roman temples, in the north for discussions with industrialists, in the south dreaming at once of the sweetness of the climate and the miseries of the people, which did not prevent him from showing beautiful Italians that Frenchmen, even ambassadors, had not forgotten the rules of gallantry.'[2] A gourmet fair in Bologna, the opening of La Scala in Milan, car factories in Turin, the French Cultural Institute in Genoa, the silk works at Caserta were all honoured with visits, though perhaps the hospitality of the Agnellis, Pirellis and the Fosca-Crispis added to their attractions.

In October 1958, Gaston made a pilgrimage to Florence to

visit Bernard Berenson, the ninety-three-year-old critic who was considered to be the greatest American expert on Italian Renaissance art. He stayed as a guest of Violet Trefusis along with his old companion from his Travellers' Club days Harold Nicolson and Harold's wife, Vita Sackville-West, whose affair with Violet had been one of the great scandals of the early 1920s. Gaston later wrote that the great storms of their passion had clearly passed, and that Vita, who looked like an 'old shepherd' and Violet, 'a Hanoverian grenadier' treated Harold with a degree of condescension as the four of them strolled along the banks of the Arno. Gaston's visit to Berenson's villa, I Tati, at Fiesole, was a joy. Many aspects of his life seemed to echo Berenson's. Born Bernhard Valvrojenski, Berenson was a Lithuanian Jew whose parents had emigrated to America when he was ten; like Gaston he had converted as a young man. His career as a critic had been as controversial as his love life, but through his brilliance and his network of equally brilliant friends he had transformed himself into the *grand seigneur* of Italian art. During Gaston's several short calls the two men discussed Lorenzo Lotto and relived memories of Paris in the Twenties. Gaston was always glad he had made time for these visits, as Berenson died the next year.

Despite the happiness of her visits to the pal-exquis, Rome was always something of a cursed city for Nancy. Shortly after her return from her trip with Deborah in 1961, she heard that one of the women with whom Gaston had been having an affair had borne him a son. There has been some biographical confusion about dates: Nancy learned the news that year, but the boy was already about nine. *Le tout Paris* was already in the know. Gaston wrote that his affection for her had in no way diminished, that this 'small and sweet new element' in his life should not affect their relationship. 'I *mind*' returned Nancy, and how could she not have done? The scab beneath which she had concealed her very private pain at being unable to have children of her own had been brutally torn away. Gaston tried to be sensitive, explaining that the situation was so natural there was no reason for her self-respect to be wounded. What might have been left of it suffered a further violent shock the next summer in Venice, when Nancy read in the *Daily American* that Gaston was to be married. She felt, she wrote, as though her whole life had collapsed. The story was merely gossip, Gaston reassured her; there was no question of marriage.

Maybe this was the point at which Nancy accepted that there was to be no happy ending. The colonel was never going to descend from the blue skies of Rome and carry her away. As ever, he had made her no promises, told her no lies, he had simply complacently expected that she would absorb the cruel blows with the dignity and reticence of a Princesse de Clèves. And Nancy did, and there was still love between them, proud, bruised, but enduring. It is utterly antithetical to modern sensibilities, such unconditional love, but it is not ugly, and Nancy refused ugliness all her life.

23

POLITICS 1962–9

As Gaston's tenure in Rome was drawing to a close, he received a call from his former protégé Georges Pompidou. After the referendum on the Evian agreement on 8 April 1962 and the resignation as prime minister of Michel Debré, De Gaulle had asked Pompidou to form a government. His choice of a man who had never held any political office was indicative of De Gaulle's needs and his perception of how France ought to be governed. Pompidou would be a manager, an administrator, rather than a leader. Gaston immediately accepted Pompidou's offer of a post as De Gaulle's minister for scientific research, atomic energy and space. His new offices overlooking the Place de la Concorde softened the wrench of leaving the pal-exquis. Gaston had never personally doubted De Gaulle's regard for him, and the Palazzo Farnese had more than compensated for the lack of a governmental position in the general's first administration. However, he had hoped for the Foreign Ministry when De Gaulle returned to power in 1958 and although both he and the general had been equable about its refusal, this had been interpreted by some of Gaston's political opponents as a slight. Gaston's reputation as a society butterfly still hampered him, and an enemy had been quick to suggest that on seeing him in Paris, De Gaulle had asked: 'Vous ici, Palewski? Pourquoi vous n'êtes pas à Rome?' The new job would be a chance to prove to his detractors that the general still respected both his political talents and the legacy of their shared experiences.

Gaston's administration was not, however, a resounding

success. The new minister's portfolio was everything an inquisitive schoolboy might wish for. Its four sections comprised civil and military nuclear power, new information technology, oceanography and space. Just two weeks after his appointment, Gaston found himself once more in Africa to oversee an underground nuclear test in the Sahara. Dressed in shorts and shirts, the dignitaries watched as the device, codenamed 'Beryl', shot a horizontal flame out of the side of a mountain directly at the command post. Luckily no one was killed, but one witness claimed that even the flight of 1940 had not been accomplished so quickly. The radioactive minister clearly felt that if he could stand it, so could the inhabitants of Polynesia, and January 1964 saw him at Mururoa supervising further tests, having overridden the security objections of the senate. *Tant pis* for the Polynesians, but Gaston did take a certain pleasure in selling a nuclear reactor to the Fascist government in Spain.

Gaston confronted another old enemy, Communism, in a bizarre meeting with Nikita Khrushchev at his dacha in October 1963. His purpose was to orchestrate a visit by De Gaulle which would inaugurate a Franco–Russian programme of space research. The Russian leader seemed quite taken by the idea of French-style colour televisions, but resisted the idea of co-operation in space. The CNRS (Centre National de la Recherche Scientifique) was a more congenial environment, but Gaston's attempts to refine its bureaucracy and encourage more effective relationships with the grands écoles were countered by researchers who had grown too attached to their state sinecures, and Gaston's idea of attracting foreign funding failed. Research into UFOs also formed part of his jurisdiction, but the French government was not particularly interested in mysterious objects flying over Madagascar. Interviewed by the editor of *Phénomènes Spatiaux*, Gaston was asked why no books had appeared in France on such a fascinating and important subject, as was the case in America. Gaston could not resist. Serious inquiries such as that had to be pursued by the gendarmes, but perhaps the president could take a trip to have a look?

In February 1965, Gaston resigned from the government. He had not, surprisingly, been sacked. To his immense delight, 'Monsieur Atom' was now president of the Constitutional Council. Proving the dictum that French politicians never die, they just move to a different arrondissement, his new workplace the Palais Royal, also housed his old companion André Malraux at the Ministry of Culture. He appreciated the intimacy of his rooms on the Aile Montpensier, designed by Fontaine for Louis-Philippe. Here, he could support De Gaulle in his campaign for a second mandate from the French people.

Gaston had been among the signatories of the controversial law of November 1962 which changed the Constitution to permit the election of the president of the Republic by direct vote. At the time, he had emphasized the collapse of the executive in 1940 as the justification for this reform, and in 1965 he was still as convinced as he had been so long ago that France needed De Gaulle. As the election approached, De Gaulle held a dinner for Gaston, André Malraux, Georges Pompidou and Michel Debré, at which he asked their opinion on standing for a further term. Gaston said firmly that he believed there remained too much to do for the seventy-five-year-old general to resign.

The presidential election was the first in France to be conducted with a direct universal suffrage. Gaston was asked to run the campaign. On 18 November, he appeared for the first time on television, reading the list of candidates; on the 19 December he appeared again, to announce a winning vote of 13 million for De Gaulle. Gaston's role now became in many ways similar to the one he had fulfilled during the first De Gaulle administration, that of communicator between the general and the outside world. His colleague François Luchaire confirmed the symbiotic relationship between the council and De Gaulle. 'Although we affirmed that the council exercised a juridical function, no one could believe it.' In Gaston's own words, 'So long as General de Gaulle was head of state, it seemed difficult to me to have a different conception of the council than of the author of the constitution himself.' Keeping the constitution on a Gaullist path was not desperately onerous: the committee took an average of eight decisions a year and made only four challenges. All the members had time for other activities, and Gaston continued his involvement with the Save Venice programme, in which both he and Nancy had been engaged since 1961.

The anti-Americanism of *Don't Tell Alfred* may also have been informed by the difficulties Gaston had as ambassador in reconciling Franco–Italian relations at a time when the Italians were pushing strongly for an 'atlanticized' Europe. The Americanisation of Europe seemed nowhere more obvious nor more threatening than in Venice. Nancy despaired at what was happening to her beloved city where she had spent so many happy summers, more so because the Venetians themselves appeared to be colluding in her depredation. She described their to her eyes pitiful attempts to convince visitors of their modernity, that Italy too could be as prosperous and impressive as the United States in its most brash and banal manifestations.

Nancy could be very funny about the naïveté of American visitors, who, 'tired of mass-produced, synthetic materials looking like the froth from detergents which choke up the 5th Avenue emporiums', were easy prey to the tourist cons of Torcello, where the old 'lace-makers' collected their work on sale or return from Burano and the priest rounded up holy processions to coincide with the arrival of the steamer. She was appalled, though, when she heard from Anna-Maria Cicogna of a proposal to build a monorail over the lagoon to the Piazza San Marco which would transport cars and tourists to the city. Nancy detested the idea of skyscrapers, described by Evelyn during a New York trip of 1947 as 'negligible in everything but bulk ... they bear the same sort of relation to architecture as distempering a ceiling does to painting. They are nothing nothing nothing at their best. At their worst, that is to say when they attempt any kind of ornament, they are actively wicked.

Now though, high-rise buildings were to be constructed at the Venice railway station to house cut-price visitors. Car ferries would take them from the Zattere to the Lido. The city in which time appeared to have stopped during Nancy and Gaston's revered eighteenth century was to be brutalized into the twentieth.

Gaston immediately wrote of this 'crime against aesthetics' to a journalist contact, Gerard Bauer, who launched a campaign in *Le Figaro*, in which he described Venice as the only remaining city in the world which preserved the grace of the eighteenth century, the only one time had not disfigured and which, intact, retained a unique power to renew the human soul.

In 1966, floods were as much of a threat as skyscrapers. That autumn, both Venice and Florence were underwater. Gaston was elected president of the France–Italy Association which, under his supervision, raised funds for the restoration of the Ca d'Oro, the Tiepolo frescos in the Palazzo Salzi and a room at the Bargello, among numerous other rescues. By the end of the year, thanks to Gaston's request to the UNESCO director general René Maheu, the Save Venice fund was launched, with Gaston as leader of the French committee. Initially there was very little money, so Gaston worked for three years at raising awareness and donations. Nancy reported on the situation on annual visits and organized publicity for a photographic exhibition mounted by Anna-Maria to illustrate why immediate action was necessary. She also persuaded Gaston to help Anna-Maria place articles in the newspapers. Gaston's efforts were rewarded with an honorary seat at the Venetian Institute of Arts, Sciences and Letters, a particularly flattering tribute as this had previously been accorded to Bernard Berenson. There was something more profound in his passion for Venice than snobbish distaste for budget holiday-makers. He believed it was only in the collective effort to preserve its cultural heritage that Europe could retain its place in the world. Faced with the superpowers on one side and what he called 'the famished and threatening crowds of the Third World' on the other, the world needed the enlightened humanism only Europe possessed as never before.

A cultural confederation of European states had been a key Gaullist goal since Gaston had presented their proposals to the assembly in 1951. He was convinced that France had a primary role in guiding such an institution because, as he saw it, she had always given primacy, in the modern world, to humanism. The continuing parlous position of European federation was dangerous not just economically, he feared, but at a profoundly spiritual level, that of the only recourse against 'the great misery of the individual delivered to the torrent of mass technology'. One could barely imagine even a French politician today making such an unashamedly elitist case for *l'exception Française*. However unacceptable such a view might have become, it is one of the keys to understanding Nancy and Gaston's relationship. Nancy's ardent Gaullism might well, as in the case of her sisters Unity and Diana, have had as much to do with the cause as the man, but it had been her cause since she wrote to Tom about Clive Bell's book in 1928. It is the message of her two last novels and the ideology which underpins her historical writing. This shared conviction appears again and again in her letters. It was something deeply felt between them and it connected them powerfully even at the lowest points in their affair.

Nancy did not, however, accompany Gaston when he visited La Serenissima with De Gaulle in May 1967. Since his return from Rome, their relationship had become calmer. Once she had recovered from the shock news of Gaston's son, Nancy was reassured by his insistence that he had no intention of marrying the mother, and she soon recovered herself sufficiently to make jokes about it. 'I might call my memoirs *The Real Sauveterre*. Bound in full morocco it would be a nice wedding present (Who for?).' She had been aware for some years of Gaston's relationship with the mother of his child and seemed capable of absorbing the fact into their relationship, as she had done with so many others. In 1966 she wrote from Venice that Anna-Maria had told her she had seen 'Gaston's offspring'. The boy was at this time about fourteen. Nancy panicked rather, but it turned out that Anna-Maria meant Marc de Beauvau-Craon, reviving the old tease about him being Gaston and Nancy's son and not, as Nancy referred to him in a private code, 'the Profile'.

The absence of the colonel in Venice that season was made up for by the presence of Marlon Brando, a guest at Peggy Guggenheim's, with whom Nancy went to the beach, and the continuing pleasure of Yank-teasing. Babe Paley, 'toothy, little upstairs' failed to live up to her reputation as the best-dressed woman in the world – she looked just like everyone else. At a dinner, the subject of Vietnam came up. With a sober face, Nancy said that she believed the only solution was to drop the bomb. 'But if the Chinese retaliate?' asked a horrified Mrs Paley. Nancy replied that since there were so many Americans, a few million or so fewer couldn't really make much difference, 'at which she began to scream'. Brando was a hit, but Nancy wrote to Deborah that her enjoyment of Venice in 1966 was patchy, as the Lido was becoming popular with film stars like Brigitte Bardot and Audrey Hepburn, who was deemed an idiot, albeit a pretty one. 'They are all quite without grey matter. *Actors*, and when you've said that you've said everything.'

So there were jokes, always jokes, and there was Venice and, as the Sixties drew on, there was also sadness shared between Nancy and Gaston. Comtesse Costa de Beauregard died that year, as, in April, did Evelyn Waugh. Nancy heard the news on the radio, and was very deeply upset. She wrote to Laura, Evelyn's widow:

> Oh Laura, I am so miserable. I loved Evelyn really the best of all my friends, and then such an old friend, such a part of my life. As for you, what *can* one say? If I feel like that about him what must his loss mean to you? ... For him, one can only say he did hate the modern world, which does not become more liveable every day. (It is always my consolation for the death of my brother Tom, how much he would have hated it.)

Gaston wrote a tribute to Evelyn, praising his extraordinary penetration and declaring *Brideshead*, '*un tableau douloureux de décadence et de désespoir*', one of the great novels of the era.

Like Nancy, he grasped that the essence of Evelyn was humour, that devouring and often brutal satire which permeated his writing, and which so many took for malice. 'What nobody ever remembers about Evelyn is everything with him was jokes. That's what none of the people who wrote about him seem to have taken into account at all,' commented Nancy in a television interview. But even Gaston could not fully grasp what Evelyn had meant to Nancy, how irreplaceable he was.

In November Dolly Radziwill died. She had been, Nancy said, her best friend apart from her sisters. Nancy did not go to the funeral – she was too afraid she would break down and make a spectacle of herself – but Gaston attended and afterwards talked to the priest, Rzewuski, a former artist turned monk who had painted Dolly in the Twenties. It turned out they had a lot of acquaintances in common, and Gaston reported a melancholy conversation about so many lost friends.

Dolly's death may have been one factor in Nancy's decision in 1966 to leave Paris for Versailles. Although they were still very close, she was seeing less and less of Gaston, and Dolly's absence made his unbearable. She also took a low view of the English in Paris. 'There are so few agreeable English people here now ... they are all true horrors and loathe the French as common English always have.' Conversations about French plumbing were one irritant, the noise of the increasing traffic and children in the courtyard at Rue Monsieur another. 'When I see *fillette dans le coma depuis 4 jours* I so wish it could be the children in this courtyard,' she grumbled. With her refuge at Fontaines-les-Nonnes gone, the longing for country life which had always run through her letters had now become a powerful call. She loved Versailles which, thanks to her biographical research, she now knew even better than Gaston, and she wanted a garden and a peaceful environment. There she could tramp about the park or even go riding in the fresh air. 'I can't always live in a town, not even Paris.' Gaston helped her through the bureaucracy, writing personally to the prefect to obtain the essential *carte de résidence*, and Nancy was able to move in January 1967.

Her new home was 4 Rue d'Artois, a low, white-painted eighteenth-century house in a side street. Harold Acton described it as very pretty; others were surprised to see the famously chic Miss Mitford in this rather bland suburban setting. What made the house for Nancy was its half-acre of walled garden. As she did everywhere she lived, she invested the house with glamour and drama. The garden, where she planted rose trees, wistaria and her '*champ fleuri*' of poppies, irises, orchids and buttercups became the backdrop for a creatures' soap opera. Her letters to Deborah suddenly become full of the doings of hedgehogs, tortoises and birds. If there was something wilfully childish about Nancy's insistence on her enchantment in her new home, Versailles was also a retreat from the crassness and ugliness of modernity. To Hugh Jackson, she wrote of the château: 'they've done up all the rooms ... and it's like a very expensive hotel ... Give me that great crumbling fairy palace I used to love so much. Anyway, they can't spoil the outside.'

The writings of both Nancy and Gaston at that time show their distress and bewilderment at the assaults on their shared conception of civilization. The Sixties had been happening for a while, and the students of France only just caught on in time. Nancy generally had a low view of the latest generation of rebels – compared with the talent for debauchery of the Bright Young Things, they seemed positively babyish. Worse still, they were earnest. The fatuity of the students' position is encapsulated in one of the most celebrated encounters of '*les Evénements*', of 1968, between the student leader Daniel Cohn-Bendit and the minister for youth and sport, François Missoffe. After listening to the minister open a new swimming pool at the university of Nanterre, Cohn-Bendit denounced the government for omitting any mention of the sexual problems of young people (still forbidden, in theory, to have sex outside marriage under the age of twenty-one) in a recent lengthy report. Swimming pools, he said, were a Fascist attempt to sublimate the students' sexual energies into sport. Sociology proved that sexual equilibrium was the only form of freestyle that mattered. Missoffe ill-advisedly attempted a joke, suggesting Cohn-Bendit should 'cool off' in the pool. 'Fascist,' Cohn-Bendit replied.

De Gaulle was unable to take the students seriously, even when sit-ins, strikes and demonstrations broke out at Strasbourg, Nanterre and Bordeaux. He had, he believed, given his life to the cause of French freedom, and it was simply beyond him to understand what these rebellious children wanted to do with it. In April, 2,000 students marched in Paris, where twenty-four years before the Parisians had torn up the tarmac to build barricades against the Germans. Even when Cohn-Bendit was arrested for sitting on a committee that put out a leaflet featuring a recipe for Molotov cocktails, the government remained both uncomprehending and condescending. It would be absurd, claimed Prime Minister Pompidou, to lock up a boy for a prank.

By 3 May, following a fractious reinauguration of the traditional May Day parade, it seemed that Paris was once more at war. The Sorbonne was closed and policemen were attacked by missiles from St Michel up to the Luxembourg Gardens. Rioting continued for another five days. On 11 May, the police were finally deployed against the barricades on the Boulevard St Michel, with significant numbers of arrests and casualties, though since officers had been instructed not to use guns there were, mercifully, no deaths. By 20 May the workers had joined the students and over six million people were said to be striking; within four days this had risen to ten million. France was in panic, housewives stockpiled food and the country was paralysed. The general election that year returned a vote that was more indicative of the panic of the bourgeoisie than faith in the Gaullist project. De Gaulle survived, and a new government headed by Maurice Couve de Murville took power on 11 July. Life gradually regained its regular rhythm. But *les Evénements* had fractured more than shop windows, they had exposed the gaping generational crevasse that yawned beneath the confident surface of consensus which had obtained in France for ten years.

At Versailles, Nancy had been less exposed than her Parisian friends to the immediate threat of this latterday terror. Cristiana

Brandolini telephoned her to share her fear at the 'furious animals' who surrounded her flat. Writing to Deborah, Nancy reported: 'Ann [Fleming] said they looked so beautiful and good. The ones I saw on *télé* looked beautiful and bad.' She was quick to nickname the student leaders: Geisemar, Sauvageot and Cohn-Bendit became 'Fat Boy', 'Savage' and 'Cohn-Bandit'. She wrote two columns for the *Spectator* detailing the events of May 1968 but, as had been the case with Fascism in the early Thirties, she was unable to accept that the students' grievances were anything more than regrettable 'showing off', based on the kind of modern quasi-philosophizing she had satirized in the character of David Wincham in *The Blessing*. To some extent, she could sympathize with their views. 'One can't help seeing the point of the poor little things – the dullness and ugliness of daily life. One of their cries is down with concrete,' she wrote to Deborah, but their essential lack of civilization recalled everything she had despised and poked fun at in *Wigs*. The screams of the students were 'simply lovely', but their strutting and speechifying was merely silly.

The *Spectator* columns give an insight into Nancy's life at Versailles quite contrary to her image as an aloof, upper-class tease, aiming her darts from the heights of her exquisite Parisian drawing room. Her direct knowledge of the strikes is drawn from 'a great friend', a workman with the Renault family, who has dined at Nancy's home with his wife. Other callers are the Saclays, whose daughter is training to be a chemist, and the Lebruns, modest, middle-class people who clearly like Nancy and are liked back. These Versailles friends, Catholic, Gaullist, agree with Nancy that much of the tension in French society is caused by the geographical separation of social classes, which breeds fear and mistrust, very much the point Nancy had made in *The Stanleys* and in an essay on life at Fontaines-les-Nonnes. Nancy's politics are old-fashioned, conservative, paternalistic, but her belief in the psychological trauma created by ugly, inhuman modern environments, that gutting and rebuilding of the countryside 'in the American manner', no longer seems quite so retrogressive. If Nancy was conservative, it was because she thought she perceived something worth conserving in French society, something that had already been lost in England, and which buyers of *A Year in Provence* or expats in the Dordogne have been seeking in their millions for the last twenty years.

As president of the Constitutional Council, Gaston had no choice but to get involved in *les Evénements*. On 27 May, when the council sat to decide on a referendum on social and economic reform with regard to the universities, he telephoned Pompidou to point out the implications for the government of engaging in the process. De Gaulle said to him mournfully, 'You will take me for Pétain.' The *Evénements* also made it painfully clear to Gaston that, in the words of the political commentator Pierre Viansson-Ponté, he was 'prehistoric'. The times they were a changin', but not in the Palais Royal. Gaston had hoped once again for the Ministry of Foreign Affairs in the post-May reshuffle, but the idea was not even considered. Nancy was better able to cope with the brave new world than he. When asked about the fashion for miniskirts (which Yvonne de Gaulle hoped her husband would ban), she cheerfully declared she would rather be dowdy than ridiculous, but otherwise she was content in the eighteenth-century world of her research, her garden and her friendships. Gaston, conversely, had to accept that in political terms, 'Monsieur Atom' was now as decorative and dated as one of his beloved antiques.

24

MARRIAGE

Gaston still called frequently at the Rue d'Artois, often coming for lunch. In spring 1969, he made two such visits, as he had something serious to tell Nancy, something that the great orator of the RPF, the seasoned speaker of the assembly, found almost impossible to articulate. Yet he had to tell Nancy, before the news broke in *Le Figaro*, that he was to be married.

Violette de Pourtales, born Talleyrand-Périgord, was among the *'femmes du monde'* with whom Gaston had been having relationships for years. She was technically a duchess, though she never used the title, which derived from Polish estates commandeered by the Soviets. Although she and Gaston had been involved with one another for at least eighteen years, Violette's husband, James-Robert de Pourtales, had only recently agreed to divorce her. Eleven years younger than Nancy, she had three children, Hélie, born in 1938, Anna in 1944 and Charles-Maurice, the youngest. Educated in America, she was elegant, perfectly dressed by Courrèges, from one of the most distinguished *gratin* families and possessed of Le Marais, one of the most wonderful chateaux in France, often compared with Vaux-le-Vicomte.

Gaston was to write several essays on the history of his new in-laws. One of the oldest families in France, they boasted one ancestor, Boson, who had elected Hugh Capet as king. When the king asked him, 'Who made you count?' he was said to have replied, 'Those same who made you king.' This established the Talleyrands' shared belief as to their place in the social hierarchy. Another ancestor was murdered by Richelieu and there were several cardinals, but the most famous Talleyrand was the greatest political chameleon of all time, minister to every French ruler from Louis XVI to Louis-Philippe. Duff Cooper had written his biography, though Nancy didn't think it very good. Once Gaston was definitively installed at Le Marais, he and Violette set up a Talleyrand museum, an echo of the long-ago games in the Palewski salon with Jean-Paul.

Gaston had known Violette's parents from his own personal Guermantes way. Her mother was Anna Gould, who first married Paris's greatest playboy, Boni de Castellane. Anna was short, ugly, with a spine covered in black hair, but she was possessed of fifteen million railway dollars, and Boni knew how to spend them. 'After all,' he said, '*elle est surtout belle vue du dot*'. (Since the French word for dowry, *dot*, is pronounced in the same way as *dos*, back, this could be interpreted as either 'She's especially beautiful for her money' or 'from behind'.) Boni's extravagance was legendary. He purchased Le Marais, an important eighteenth-century château, from the Noailles family, as well as constructing the Palais Rose in Paris, but when Anna Gould had had enough of this extravagance, she divorced him, married his cousin, Hélie de Talleyrand-Périgord, Prince de Sagan, and took her houses with her. Her second husband was not much more gallant than the first; the Prince de Sagan remarked that one might as well dispense with the 'u' in his new wife's maiden name. Boni was so outraged at the loss of the lovely millions that he attacked Hélie with his cane at a funeral. Undeterred, Hélie fathered two children with Anna, Howard, who killed himself, and Hélène-Violette, who thus became her mother's heiress.

Violette sold the Palais Rose in 1968, not, according to some, without a little help from the president of the Conseil Constitutionnel, as the council of Paris had initially opposed the sale. Throughout the Sixties, Gaston had been spending more and more time at Le Marais, just 36 kilometres from Paris, an enclosed world in its own 8,000 acres. He got to know Violette's friends, the Duc d'Harcourt, his wife Thyra and his sister Lydie de

Pommereu, and lunched with Violette's aunt, Florence Gould, who lived at the Meurice. During the war, Florence had been a collaborationist hostess, entertaining the German author Ernst Jünger and propaganda officer Gerhard Heller. Claude Mauriac described how the atmosphere of 'champagne and sympathy' led him to shake hands with officers whose company he would have shunned in the streets. A scathing piece appeared in Cyril Connolly's *Horizon*, depicting Florence's 'salon' as the dregs of literary Paris who had found only acclaim in the wake of Nazi tanks, though Cocteau was not above accepting her hospitality. Nor, many years later, was Gaston. A writhingly sycophantic passage in a novel of the period describes one of Florence's gatherings at the Meurice.

> The Talleyrand-Périgord-Palewskis were at the top of the guest list, Palewski presided opposite Florence ... Mme Palewski spoke of the Lido. 'What a sumptuous spectacle', she said, 'What an orgy of colours ... We have nothing to envy the Americans'. 'You could make M. Palewski Prince de Chalais', 'What? Is it possible? But did a misadventure not occur when Guillemette de Bauffremont published in the *Figaro* that she would make her husband, Mr I-don't-know-who Duc d'Atrisco?' 'With M. Palewski's friends in high places you could obtain him the right to remain covered before the King of Spain! He would only remove his hat for General de Gaulle!' Laughter.

Gaston ought to have choked on his *langoustes*.

Nancy knew Violette, and described her as a 'sort of non-person'. Like her famous ancestor and her mother's witty first husband, she was very distantly descended from the Rochechouart-Mortemarts, the family of Athénais de Montespan, Louis XIV's greatest mistress and a particular favourite of Nancy's. She and her siblings were famous for the '*esprit Mortemart*', the funniest people of their century, everyone said, but obviously the gene had died out. Nancy was not the only one who thought Violette had no apparent reason to exist: even her greatest flatterers concede that she was no intellectual. Cynthia Gladwyn said that she was 'nice, but very simple, not amusing or interesting or pretty'. Nancy's description of Lady Prague in her first novel sums up a particular type of aristocratic woman to whom those who did not know Violette well might believe she corresponded, 'a creature so overbred that there is no sex or brain left, only nerves and the herd instinct'. She was perfectly kind, and had kept her relationship with Gaston as discreet as possible, hating the gossip that her mother had attracted. 'She has a horror of people talking about her,' Gaston told a friend. The wedding, on 20 March 1969, was so discreet that Gaston did not even tell his brother Jean-Paul, who was offended to hear of it from Général De Gaulle. Nor was Violette's son Charles-Maurice informed until after the event.

As a wedding gift, Gaston received a little bit of Poland. His wife's Sagan title derived from Zagan, formerly in Lower Silesia on the German–Polish border, and had come into the family in 1843. Originally Prussian, it was authorized by imperial decree in France in 1862, so the men in the family were dukes of Talleyrand-Périgord and princes of Sagan. In 1945, Zagan had been repopulated by Poles, who enterprisingly rebuilt the picturesque red-roofed château, with its hundred rooms, which had been burned down in the war. The iron curtain prevented any honeymoon plans for a return to the Palewski roots, but *quand même*, it was a pretty irony. It was Le Marais that was truly made for Gaston. Receiving a guest from Rome just after his marriage, Gaston greeted her shrugging his shoulders and looking bashful. 'What do you want?' he said. 'I've always loved high ceilings.'

Nancy didn't stand a chance against Le Marais, and she knew it. A friend of Gaston's claims that 'yes, he did love Nancy Mitford. But he loved châteaux and duchesses more.' Another suggested that 'the darling old Colonel' was only in love with organizing the decoration of a wonderful château. Nancy had her shop-front firmly in place. In a letter to Gaston in 1962, Nancy had described a lunch where one of the women present announced that her lover was shortly to marry another woman. 'She said, "Why should I be jealous? She is ugly and stupid and frightfully rich. I don't mind a bit."' This was to be Nancy's line and she stuck to it. She must have been extremely convincing, as Diana wrote to Deborah:

> Just spoken to Naunce and Col has told her he's going to marry Violette and she (Naunce) really doesn't seem to mind in the least. As I knew this was looming (or thought I knew), it was one of the things I most dreaded, but it has come so late in the day (Col is almost seventy) that she has got over the annoyance years ago, evidently, and now just thinks it a bore for him and also (which is true) rather silly to give up one's freedom.

A letter from Nancy to Deborah dated the day after the wedding begins: 'I'm *felled* by disappointment.' She goes on to explain that she has been deceived by a tricky farthing, mistaking it for an enormously valuable 1933 penny, then discusses the activities of her tortoises. To both Deborah and Alvilde Lees-Milne she explained that she expected things to go on as usual, with Gaston spending most of his time in the Rue Bonaparte. Deborah wrote to Pamela: 'That wretched Colonel has chosen that week to get married to that person he has been more or less with for ages. One simply does not know how much she minds as she is a very private person and so desperately reserved one perhaps never will know.'

Airily, Nancy remarked to a friend that Le Marais was well worth seeing. Her true feelings can only be a matter of conjecture. Intimate conversations, she wrote, had never been in her line. In the Forties and Fifties, Peter's refusal to give her a divorce had kept marriage as a fantasy; after that, as a divorcée and a Protestant, she was out of the question because of Gaston's career. Madame de Gaulle might once have been said to faint at the sight of a divorced woman, but now that career was settling comfortably into a belaurelled and rather pompous twilight,

Gaston had married a Protestant divorcée. If she raged, called him a liar and a whore, vented her humiliation and frustration, she gave absolutely no sign of it. By the end of the year, she was writing a placid, affectionate note to remind him to send a Christmas card to her old housekeeper Marie. One tiny, poignant twist of the knife: 'Remember all the chickens she has cooked for you.'

Or perhaps Diana was right, and she truly wasn't angry at all. In her meditation on her marriage to Peter Rodd in 1941, she had written that 'love should never be allowed to interfere with the continuity of marriage'. Why should not the reverse be true? Twenty years before, when she had caught Gaston admiring the Louvre by night with Margot de Gramont, Nancy had told Diana in a letter that she couldn't live through Gaston marrying. He said then that she had a 'novelist's view of marriage', that he would only take a wife to have children and that it would make no difference at all to his feelings for her. Everything she had written about love since then had endorsed this calm, rational view, that love and marriage were quite different things, and only barbarians tangled themselves up into emotional and legal messes by conflating the two. But did she believe it?

Many people who have written about Nancy take the view that Gaston's engagement coincided with the cancer that was to kill her. 'Her family always felt that [it] was the result of years of repressed longings and jealousy, followed by the deathblow of Col's marriage.'[1] Diana Mosley contradicted this, pointing out that it was unfair, that Nancy was already ill before she knew of the engagement; indeed, her greeting to Gaston when he arrived to tell her the news was 'Hello, Colonel, I've got cancer'. Yet still the view persists that she died of a broken heart. True, Diana did write that Nancy had 'poisoned' herself with 'spitefulness', though it was not her fault, but this was years later, after she learned in 1983 of Nancy's wartime denunciation.

Tests showed a large tumour on Nancy's liver ('I wonder if it's my twin brother . . . little old Lord Redesdale shrieking away'). She was operated on, apparently successfully, though her illness

(Hodgkins' disease) was never properly diagnosed by the thirty-seven doctors she eventually saw. As pain took over her life, Nancy's sisters drew closer to her. Diana visited every day, Deborah and Pamela came frequently, Jessica twice made the journey from America. For a time, her last book before *Frederick the Great* acted as an analgesic. Her sisters, fearing she might die before it was completed, discreetly arranged for the publishers to pretend they needed it early. Nancy was very proud of this work. She said she loved it best and summoned all her strength to undertake the research, travelling to Potsdam, Berlin and Dresden with Pamela in 1970. She wrote to Gaston from a London clinic with a list of questions in French to be typed up and sent out to museums and libraries. Dedicated to Diana, the book is a celebration of the 'Europe Française' so beloved of Gaston and Nancy – 'When the princes began to desire a better way of life than that of robber baron it was to Paris they turned.' While Nancy's evocation of Frederick's military strategies impressed even those critics who still thought of her as a frivolous historian, the book is very much a celebration of the eighteenth century in all its superlative Frenchness.

Nancy managed one last trip to Venice in 1970. She was now very ill, her letters to Gaston increasingly dominated by suffering, but still took time to describe the restoration projects he had done so much to initiate. She saw the Wrightsmans and several other friends, though she was often unable to get up, staying in her room overlooking the Zattere, watching the rush of the boats. Gaston sent incense for her to 'inhale voluptuously', and arranged to have scans sent from the Hôpital Rothschild to her Italian doctor, but Nancy's gratitude – 'Colonel how powerful you are' – came with a twist. 'I am reading a life of Helen Ligne Potecki of whom you say you have got a picture. She was a very horrid person but lovely and RICH.' Her last letter from Venice ends: 'I can't go on, I've got such a dreadful pain.'

Meanwhile, Général de Gaulle retired definitively to Colombey in April 1969 after a referendum on reform of the senate, aimed at eradicating the memory of *les Evénements*, was rejected.

Gaston was involved in one last political controversy, concerning the interim mandate before a new president of the Republic was chosen. Since De Gaulle was the first president to have been elected by direct vote, there was no protocol in place to cover his resignation. Gaston suggested that the Constitutional Council write a letter to the president of the senate, Alain Poher, transferring interim powers to him, but did not feel he could deliver the message in person as he had done to De Gaulle in 1965. The council's letter was delivered to the Luxembourg on 29 April at 12.10pm, De Gaulle having officially resigned at 12.00pm, so for ten minutes France was without a president. Poher insisted on summoning Gaston to the Elysée as soon as he arrived there to make a point; he had nothing to say to him.

Psychosomatic illness was clearly in the air: Emmanuel d'Astier de la Vigerie, a resistance hero, dropped dead of a heart attack at the news of De Gaulle's departure. Gaston's position was assured – his tenure as president of the council was fixed until 1974 – and he now became involved in the election campaign for a new president. Anti-Semitism was still an unpleasant shadow over French politics: when the candidature of Pierre Sidos was quite properly rejected by the council on the basis that his recommendations failed to meet the minimum constitutional requirement, *Le Soleil* argued that this was due to the 'ascendance of foreign Jews' such as Gaston Palewski and René Cassin over the presiding body. Gaston was satisfied by the election of his friend and colleague Georges Pompidou. In a touching coincidence, Pompidou now worked from Dolly Radziwill's former apartment in the Boulevard de la Tour Maubourg and it was here, time regained, that Gaston went in his official capacity to convey the news.

Gaston wrote that as one aged, life became an Appian Way, a journey bordered by tombs. Dolly and Evelyn, Duff Cooper and Mark Ogilvie-Grant were gone, and at the end of 1969 Louise de Vilmorin died. She had taken up late in life with André Malraux, much to everyone's surprise, and remained irrepressible, though Violette disapproved of the raucous atmosphere the couple's drinking created at Le Marais. Gaston went to her funeral at Verrières. Her chosen epitaph was 'Help'. Charlie de Bestegui and Marie-Laure de Noailles died in early 1970, and in November Charles de Gaulle passed away at Colombey. Gaston grieved violently. It was as much as he could do to control himself as he stood in the guard of the Companions of the Liberation, silent beneath a soft autumn rain.

25

THE HORROR OF LOVE

'I t is not a very reassuring reflection,' Nancy wrote in *The Sun King* in 1966, 'that in another two hundred and fifty years present day doctors may seem to our descendants as barbarous as Fagon and his colleagues seem to us . . . In those days, terrifying in black robes and bonnets, they bled the patient; now, terrifying in white robes and masks they pump blood into him. The result is the same: the strong live; the weak, after much suffering and expense, both of spirit and money, die.' Nancy had joked for a long time with Evelyn about the English response to death, always said to be much the best thing; now she too began to pray for it. By the end of 1970, she weighed less than six stone. She was terribly humiliated by being increasingly unable to care for herself and even Gaston's longed-for visits became an agony of self-control. 'I used to think I wish he'd come,' said Diana, 'and then I'd almost wish he hadn't . . . He tired her quite, because she'd always try to think of things to amuse him. It was quite a drama, really.'[1]

Her husband could not have been more different from Gaston Palewski. Oswald Mosley's last attempt to win a British Parliamentary seat had come to nothing in 1960, while by any standards Gaston had enjoyed a brilliant political career. Now that Mosley's views had mellowed, Gaston, whose early belief in De Gaulle had been so triumphantly vindicated, could afford to be generous to a man whose intelligence and charisma were still remarked upon even by those who approached him with the most negative of preconceptions. 'Oh yes,' agrees the

Duchess of Devonshire, 'he liked Mosley.' Before Nancy became too ill, she and Gaston had often visited the Mosleys at their home, Le Temple de la Gloire, though Diana diplomatically declined invitations to Le Marais until after Nancy's death. Gaston was extremely fond of Diana, whose great beauty was still in evidence, slender and sculpted in the simple monochrome clothes she preferred. He was interested by her restoration of Le Temple, and recalled her there, seated on a low stool before the fire, laughing with her sister at the Mitford jokes he had always loved. In another instance of the manner in which their generation delicately ignored the inconveniences of love and focused on its essential truths (you ruined my sister's life!), Diana was able tactfully to comfort Gaston as Nancy declined.

When they were together, Nancy desperately kept up her 'shop-front'. She loved the story of the Windsors dining at Orsay, and Daisy Fellowes asking mischievously for Coca-Cola. Diana, of course, had no such thing in the house, so the Duke of Windsor rang up his butler to send some over, bellowing into the telephone '*Ich bin der Herzog!*' Her letters grow increasingly more desperate, thankful for the little gifts Gaston sends, but repeatedly dwelling on her agony and her wish to die.

Gaston had been asking for some years for Nancy to be awarded the Légion d'Honneur for the services her books had done to France. On 8 April 1972, he arrived at the Rue d'Artois with the cross and ribbon in a little box. Diana helped her down the stairs and he pinned the decoration to her breast. 'A little rouge looks well among the laurels.' Her last letter was written to him just over a year later. 'I think and hope to die, but the doctor thinks not, or not yet. It is too much, this torture. You don't know ... the pain is so strong that I can hardly write.'

On 30 June, Gaston was driving from Le Marais to Paris when he was struck by a premonition that he must see Nancy. He found Jessica and Diana at Versailles. He ran past them up the stairs to Nancy's bedroom. She was unconscious and immobile, but when he spoke to her and held her hand, she smiled. An hour after his return to Rue Bonaparte, Nancy died.

Gaston lived another eleven years. He was among the founders of the Institut Charles de Gaulle and received the highest order of the Légion d'Honneur. He was president of the *Revue des Deux Mondes*, for which he wrote many articles, of the Commission for Cultural Affairs to UNESCO, the Fondation Lyautey, the Society of Friends of Marcel Proust, and vice-president of the Council of National Museums, elected to the Académie des Beaux Arts. The archive devoted to Gaston Palewski at the Bibliothèque Nationale comprises seventy-two boxes stretching 24 metres. And yet, in his speech to the Académie, he talked of the peculiar sadness of satisfied ambition. 'All her life,' Nancy wrote of Amabelle Fortescue in *Christmas Pudding*, 'she had had before her one ambition, to be a success in the world of culture and fashion and to this end alone her considerable talents and energy had been directed ... If the fulfilment of this ambition brought with it the smallest degree of disappointment, she managed very successfully to conceal the fact from all but herself.'

As Gaston grew older, he confessed that memories of the war dominated his thoughts – of Ethiopia and Algiers, of De Gaulle of course – but also, why not? of Nancy. Had he, in the end, been true to his vows to honour? He had his château and his duchess, but his marriage was not ideal. His Palewski nephews, who came less and less often, remembered that he seemed 'constrained' by Violette's presence. Old friends distanced themselves because, though they dared not say so at the time, they were tired of the coldness between Gaston and his wife. When he became ill and wheelchair-bound, Violette said airily, 'Oh yes, I know, but there are doctors ...' Gaston was not comforted by a loving and supportive family as the end drew near. Some friends go so far as to claim Violette did not care for him in hospital, where he died on 3 September 1984. She was too 'bereft' to arrange his funeral, and the ceremony was planned by the members of the Institut Charles de Gaulle. After his death,

Violette commemorated him in a little museum she established at Le Marais; after her own, the bulk of Gaston's collections were auctioned at Sotheby's by her children.

Nancy had been cremated at Père Lachaise. Her grave is at Swinbrook, marked with the Mitford mole that she used latterly on her letterhead, the descendant of the '*charmante avalanche grise*' with which she had scattered Gaston in Algeria. Gaston's ashes are interred at Passy. Nancy loved the story of the Marquise de Sévigné complaining that the air of Paris was filled with clouds of the famous poisoner, Mme de Brinvilliers. So perhaps somewhere, in that Parisian sky, which Linda Radlett watches as it turns from bright blue to dark green to yellow to moleskin, that first summer of the war ...

Nancy always warned Gaston that marriage was not for him. She wrote a scenario of his future:

'So, did you go to the Palewskis last night?'

'Yes, poor people, I did feel sorry for them – all ruined by the thunderstorm. Gaston had spent the whole afternoon hanging up Japanese lanterns, you can't think how sad and sopping they looked. Then we were packed into those downstairs rooms like sardines, you know how hot it was, with the band on the staircase, you couldn't hear yourself speak. Goodness, she has got a lot of relations, hasn't she?'

'I know, whenever one goes there, all those deadly in-laws. Poor Gaston, he's really very patient but one can see what he feels. What happened to all those nice pictures he used to have in the Rue Bonaparte?'

'*She* doesn't like old things, except of course Antoine Bibesco.'

'I rather like their glass furniture you know. Did you see the little girl last night?'

'Oh yes. Gaston kept telling her to go to bed, but she only said "oh, fa la" and took no notice.'

'Goodbye, Colonel, *à samedi*.'

Better this way?

'"*Racontez*," said the Regent, and fell dead at the feet of a little gossip just as she was opening her pretty little mouth to recount some piece of scandal.'

Fin

NOTES

General Notes

Citations from Nancy Mitford's letters are collated from three volumes:

Love from Nancy: The Letters of Nancy Mitford, ed. Mosley, Charlotte (Hodder & Stoughton, London, 1993).
The Letters of Nancy Mitford and Evelyn Waugh, ed. Mosley, Charlotte (Hodder & Stoughton, London, 1996).
The Mitfords: Letters Between Six Sisters, ed. Mosley, Charlotte (Fourth Estate, London, 2007).

Letters from Nancy to Gaston Palewski, where not duplicated in these volumes, are cited from Nancy's unpublished correspondence, which was very kindly made available to the author by Charlotte Mosley.

Except where otherwise stated, citations from Gaston Palewski are from *Mémoires d'action 1924–1974* (Plon, Paris, 1988) and *Hier et aujourd'hui: Des hommes, des idées et des faits* (Plon, Paris, 1975).

Quotations from Lord Weidenfeld, Lord Thomas, Viscount Norwich and Mr Paul Johnson, the Dowager Duchess of Devonshire and Mrs Louis Begley (Anka Muhlstein) are drawn from interviews with the author. Further interviewees are credited in the Acknowledgements.

Further sources

PROLOGUE

1. This description is Laura Thompson's in *Life in a Cold Climate: A Portrait of a Contradictory Woman* (Review, London, 2003).
2. Edith Cresson is quoted in *The New York Times*, 20 June 1991, from an earlier interview with the *Observer.*

PART ONE: 1901–39

1: GASTON

1. This section of Jean-Paul Palewski's memoir is available online in French and Polish at http://palevsky.myrelatives.net/trees/pa.html A full family tree is usefully provided here.
2. Ibid.
3. Palewski, Dominique: 'Oncle Gaston' in *Gaston Palewski* (Publications de l'Institut Charles de Gaulle), p.58.
4. Bernot, Jacques: *Gaston Palewski: Premier Baron du Gaullisme* (François-Xavier de Guibert, Paris, 2010), p.19.
5. Larose, Yvon: 'La Guerre des Mondes' in *Le Dernier Fil*, 20 February 2003.
6. Palewski, Jean-Paul: *Mémoires* (five volumes, unpublished), Vol. I, p.75.
7. Druon, Maurice: 'Du Côté de Chez Gaston' (Publications de l'Institut Charles de Gaulle), p.62.
8. Palewski, Jean-Paul, op cit., Vol. II, p.14.

2: NANCY

1. Mitford, Nancy: 'Blor', *The Sunday Times*, 1962, reproduced in *A Talent to Annoy*, ed. Mosley, Charlotte (Hodder & Stoughton, London, 1996), p.137.
2. Ibid., p.144.

3. Palewski, Gaston: *Mémoires d'action*, ed. Roussel, Eric (Plon, Paris, 1988), p.52.
4. Waugh, Evelyn: *Brideshead Revisited*.

3: COMING OUT

1. The Dowager Duchess of Devonshire, in an interview with the author.
2. Quoted in Acton, Harold: *Nancy Mitford: A Memoir* (Hamish Hamilton, London, 1975).
3. Viscount Norwich, in an interview with the author.
4. James Lees-Milne, quoted in Thompson, Laura, op. cit.
5. Gerald, Lord Berners: *A Distant Prospect* (Condatre, London, 1945), p.27.
6. Taylor, D.J.: *Bright Young People* (Vintage, London, 2008), p.203.
7. Quoted in an interview with Laura Thompson, op. cit.

4: FAUX PAS

1. Palewski, Jean-Paul, op. cit., Vol. II, p.14.
2. The quotation is from Shelley's notes on Shakespeare's tragedies, with reference to *Troilus and Cressida*, though the attribution is more correctly Samuel Johnson's: he gives it as a replacement for 'joy's soul lies in the doing'.
3. Palewski, Dominique, op. cit., p.60.

5: THE FASCISTERS

1. Thompson, Laura, op. cit., p.104.
2. Mitford, Jessica: *Hons and Rebels* (Indigo, London, 1996), p.27.
3. Taylor, D.J., op. cit., p.42.
4. Jessica Mitford, in an interview with the *Chicago Tribune*, 23 October 1977.
5. De Courcy, Anne: *Diana Mosley* (Vintage, London, 2004), p.114.

6. Mosley, Charlotte: Introduction to *Wigs on the Green* (Penguin, London, 2010).
7. Taylor, D.J., op. cit., p.236.
8. De Courcy, Anne, op. cit., p.138.
9. Thompson, Laura, op. cit., p.120.

6: THE PURSUIT OF HONOUR

1. Painter, George D.: *Marcel Proust: A Biography* (Chatto & Windus, London, 1989), p.285.
2. Lacouture, Jean: *De Gaulle: The Rebel 1890–1944* (Norton, New York, 1993), p.104.
3. Ibid., p.107.
4. Ibid., p.212.
5. Ibid.
6. Palewski, Gaston, op. cit., p.93.

7: LOSING

1. Romilly, Esmond: *Boadilla* (Hamish Hamilton, London, 1937), p.196.
2. Pryce-Jones, David: *Unity Mitford: A Quest* (Weidenfeld & Nicolson, London, 1976), p.235.

8: WAR

1. Taylor, D.J., op. cit., p.269.
2. Nancy's principal biographers, Selina Hastings and Laura Thompson.
3. De Courcy, Anne, op. cit., p.213.
4. Details of Mosley's speech and notes on the question of Fascist versus British loyalty are in Home Office 144/21429/18 and 45 2374/860502.
5. Lord Moyne's letter of 26 June 1940 was sent to Sir Alexander Maxwell at the Home Office.

9: LE PREMIER DES GAULLISTES

1. Lacouture, Jean, op. cit., p.193.
2. Ibid., p.195.
3. Ousby, Ian: *Occupation: The Ordeal of France 1940–44* (John Murray, London, 1997), p.48.
4. Roussel, Eric: introduction to *Mémoires d'action*, p.10.
5. Quoted by Gaston Palewski in *Mémoires d'action*, p.69.
6. Lacouture, Jean, op. cit., p.211.
7. Spears, Edward: *Assignment to Catastrophe*, Vol. II: *The Fall of France* (Heinemann, London, 1954), p.32.

10: FLIGHT

1. Churchill, Winston: *The Gathering Storm* Vol. I (Cassell, London, 1948).

11: POOR FROGS

1. Atkin, Nicholas: *The Forgotten French: Exiles in the British Isles 1940–44* (Manchester University Press, Manchester, 2003), p.106.
2. Tombs, Isabelle and Robert: *That Sweet Enemy: Britain and France, the History of a Love-Hate Relationship* (Pimlico, London, 2007), p.536.
3. Cited in Fenby, Jonathan: *The General: Charles de Gaulle and the France He Saved* (Simon & Schuster, London, 2010), p.133.
4. Cremieux-Brilhac, J-L.: *Georges Boris, trente ans d'influence* (Gallimard, Paris, 2010), p.179.
5. Lacouture, Jean, op. cit., p.226.

12: LOVE

1. Lacouture, op. cit.
2. James Lees-Milnes quoted in Acton, Harold, op. cit.

3. Mahoney, Daniel J.: *De Gaulle: Statesmanship, Grandeur and Modern Democracy* (Transaction, New Jersey, 2000), p.33.
4. Cooper, Diana: *Trumpets from the Steep* (Hart-Davis, London, 1960), p.194.
5. Cooper, Duff: *The Duff Cooper Diaries*, ed. Norwich, John Julius (Weidenfeld & Nicolson, London, 2005), p.292.

PART TWO: 1944–73

13: LIBERATION

1. Cadogan, Alexander: *The Diaries of Sir Alexander Cadogan*, ed. Dilkes, David (Cassell, London, 1971), p.634.
2. Lacouture, Jean, op. cit., p.527.
3. Galtier-Boissière, Jean: *Mon journal pendant l'Occupation* (La Jeune Parque, Paris, 1944), p. 25.
4. Beevor, Antony and Cooper, Artemis: *Paris After the Liberation: 1944–1949* (Hamish Hamilton, London, 1984), p.45.
5. Muggeridge, Malcolm: *Chronicles of Wasted Time* Vol. 2: *The Infernal Grove* (Collins, London, 1973) p.211.

14: THE ADVANCE ON PARIS

1. Cited in Thompson, Laura, op. cit., p.257.
2. Diana Mosley, in an interview with Mary S. Lovell quoted in *The Mitford Girls* (Little, Brown, London, 2001), p.409.

15: POLITICS 1944–6

1. From Nancy's essay 'Some Rooms for Improvement' in *The Water Beetle* (Hamish Hamilton, London, 1962).
2. Beevor, Anthony and Cooper, Artemis, op. cit., p.84.
3. Ibid., p.134.
4. Domenach, Jean-Marie: 'Y a t'il une justice en France?' in *Esprit*, August 1947.
5. Cocteau, Jean: *Journal 1942–1945* (Gallimard, Paris, 1989),

cited in Horne, Alistair: *The Seven Ages of Paris* (Macmillan, London, 1998), p.424.

6. Rioux, Jean-Pierre: *La France de la Quatrième République* (Seuil, Paris, 1980), p.191.

7. Ibid., p.175.

8. Lachaise, C.B.: 'L'Entourage de Charles de Gaulle président de GPRF à Paris' in *Histoire.Politique* No.8 (May–August 2009).

9. Mauriac, C.: *Un autre de Gaulle* (Hachette, Paris, 1970), p.150.

16: THE EMBASSY

1. Ziegler, Philip: *Diana Cooper* (Hamish Hamilton, London, 1981), p.217.

2. De Brissac, Pierre: *La Suite des Temps* (Grasset, Paris, 1974), p.141.

3. Cooper, Duff, op. cit., p.367.

4. Poulenc, François quoted in Ivry, Benjamin: *François Poulenc* (Phaidon, London, 1996).

5. Alsop, Susan Mary: *To Marietta from Paris 1945–1960* (Weidenfeld & Nicolson, London, 1974).

6. Ibid.

17: THE PURSUIT OF CHIC

1. Mullen, Richard and Munson, James: *The Smell of the Continent: The British Discover Europe 1814–1914* (Macmillan, London, 2009), p.218.

2. Ziegler, Philip, op. cit., p.258.

3. Hastings, Selina, op. cit., p.173.

18: LES FEMMES DU MONDE

1. Quoted from an interview given to the author by a contemporary source.

2. Ziegler, Philip, op. cit., p.239.

3. Alsop, Susan Mary, op. cit., p.330.
4. Ibid., p.151.
5. Pugh, Martin: *We Danced All Night: A Social History of Britain Between the Wars* (Random House, London, 2008), p.131.
6. De Courcy, Anne, op. cit., p.159.

20: DESPAIR

1. Victor Cunard to Billa Harrod, quoted in Thompson, Laura, op. cit., p.329.

21: THEORY OF THE LEISURE CLASS

1. Overy, Richard: *The Morbid Age: Britain Between the Wars* (Allen Lane, London, 2009), p.15.

22: A L'OMBRE DE L'EMBRASSADEUR EN FLEUR

1. Palewski, Jean-Paul, op. cit., Vol. IV, p.147.
2. Ibid., p.148.

24: MARRIAGE

1. Peyrefitte, R.: *Le mal français* (Fayard, Paris, 1976), p.177.

25: THE HORROR OF LOVE

1. Diana Mosley in an interview with Laura Thompson, op. cit., p.395.

SELECT BIBLIOGRAPHY

Nancy Mitford

A Talent to Annoy: Essays, Journalism and Reviews 1929–1968, ed.
   Mosley, Charlotte (Hodder & Stoughton, London, 1986)
Christmas Pudding (Thornton Butterworth, London, 1932)
Don't Tell Alfred (Hamish Hamilton, London, 1960)
Frederick the Great (Hamish Hamilton, London, 1970)
Highland Fling (Thornton Butterworth, London, 1931)
Love in a Cold Climate (Hamish Hamilton, London, 1949)
Madame de Pompadour (Hamish Hamilton: London, 1954)
Pigeon Pie (Hamish Hamilton, London, 1940)
The Blessing (Hamish Hamilton, London, 1951)
The Ladies of Alderley (ed.) (Chapman & Hall, London, 1938)
The Little Hut (trans.) (André Roussin, Paris, 1956)
The Princesse de Clèves (trans.) (Euphorion, London, 1950)
The Pursuit of Love (Hamish Hamilton, London, 1945)
The Stanleys of Alderley (ed.) (Chapman & Hall, London, 1939)
The Sun King (Hamish Hamilton, London, 1966)
The Water Beetle (Hamish Hamilton, London, 1962)
Voltaire in Love (Hamish Hamilton, London, 1957)
Wigs on the Green (Thornton Butterworth, London, 1935)
The Letters of Nancy Mitford and Evelyn Waugh, ed. Mosley,
   Charlotte (Penguin, London, 2010)

By the Mitford Family

Devonshire, Deborah: *Wait for Me* (John Murray, London, 2010)
Guinness, Jonathan: *The House of Mitford* (Hutchinson,
   London, 1984)

Mitford, Jessica: *Hons and Rebels* (Gollancz, London, 1960)

Mosley, Charlotte (ed.): *The Mitfords: Letters Between Six Sisters* (Fourth Estate, London, 2007)

Mosley, Diana: *A Life of Contrasts* (Hamish Hamilton, London, 1977); *The Pursuit of Laughter,* ed. Rynja, Martin (Gibson Square, London, 2008)

Volumes

Acton, Harold: *Nancy Mitford: A Memoir* (Hamish Hamilton, London, 1975)

Alsop, Susan Mary: *To Marietta from Paris 1945–1960* (Weidenfeld & Nicolson, London, 1974)

Atkin, Nicholas: *The Forgotten French: Exiles in the British Isles 1940–44* (Manchester University Press, Manchester, 2003)

Atkins, John: *Six Novelists Look at Society* (Calder, London, 1977)

Beaton, Cecil: *Self-Portrait with Friends: The Selected Diaries of Cecil Beaton 1922–1974,* ed. Buckle, Richard (Times Books, New York, 1979)

Beevor, Anthony and Cooper, Artemis: *Paris After the Liberation* (Hamish Hamilton, London, 1994)

Berners, Gerald: *A Distant Prospect* (Condatre, London, 1945)

Bernot, Jacques: *Gaston Palewski: Premier Baron du Gaullisme* (François-Xavier de Guibert, Paris, 2010)

Berstein, Serge, Birnbaum, Pierre, and Rioux, Jean-Pierre: *De Gaulle et les élites* (La Découverte, Paris, 2008)

Bothorel, Jean: *Louise ou la vie de Louise de Vilmorin* (Grasset, Paris, 1993)

Buisson, Patrick: *1940–1945 Années Erotiques: De la Grande Prostituée à la revanche des mâles* (Albin Michel, Paris, 2009)

Channon, Henry 'Chips': *The Diaries of Sir Henry Channon,* ed. Rhodes James, Robert (Weidenfeld & Nicolson, London, 1993)

Cooper, Artemis (ed.): *Mr Wu and Mrs Stitch: The Letters of Evelyn Waugh and Diana Cooper* (Hodder & Stoughton, London, 1991)

Cooper, Diana: *Trumpets from the Steep* (Hart-Davis, London, 1960)

Cooper, Duff: *Old Men Forget* (Hart-Davis, London, 1954); *The Duff Cooper Diaries*, ed. Norwich, John Julius (Weidenfeld & Nicolson, London, 2005)

Cooper, Diana and Duff: *A Durable Fire: The Letters of Duff and Diana Cooper 1913–1950*, ed. Cooper, Artemis (Collins, London, 1983)

De Courcy, Anne: *Diana Mosley* (Vintage, London, 2003)

De Faucigny-Lucinge, Jean-Louis: *Un gentilhomme cosmopolite* (Perrin, Paris, 1990)

De Gaulle, Charles: *Mémoires d'espoir*, 3 vols. (Plon, Paris, 1970); *Mémoires de guerre*, 3 vols. (Plon, Paris, 2007)

Delpla, François: *Churchill et les Français* (François-Xavier de Guibert, Paris, 2010)

Dumaine Jacques: *Quai d'Orsay* (Juillard, Paris, 1945)

Fenby, Jonathan: *The General: Charles de Gaulle and the France He Saved* (Simon & Schuster, London, 2010)

Fisher, Clive: *Cyril Connolly: The Life and Times of Britain's Most Controversial Literary Critic* (Macmillan, London, 1996)

Fouchet, Christian: *Au service du général de Gaulle* (Plon, Paris, 1971)

Galtier-Boissière, Jean: *Mémoires d'un Parisien*, 3 vols. (La Table Ronde, Paris, 1961)

Gardiner, Juliet: *The Thirties, an Intimate History* (HarperCollins, London, 2010)

Gladwyn, Cynthia: *The Diaries of Cynthia Gladwyn* ed. Jebb, Miles (Constable, London, 1995)

Glass, Charles: *Americans in Paris: Life and Death under the Nazi Occupation 1940–44* (HarperCollins, London, 2009)

Goncourt, Edmond and Jules: *French Eighteenth Century Painters* (Phaidon, London, 1948)

Hastings, Selina: *Nancy Mitford: A Biography* (Hamish Hamilton, London, 1986); *Evelyn Waugh: A Biography* (Sinclair-Stevenson, London, 1994)

Hitchcock, William I.: *Liberation: The Bitter Road to Freedom 1944–45* (Faber & Faber, London, 2009)

Horne, Alistair: *Seven Ages of Paris: Portrait of a City* (London, Macmillan, 1998)

James, Lawrence: *Aristocrats: Power, Grace and Decadence, Britain's Great Ruling Classes from 1066 to the Present* (Little, Brown, London, 2009)

Karnow, Stanley: *Paris in the Fifties* (Times Books, New York, 1997)

Kersaudy, François: *De Gaulle et Roosevelt: le Duel au Sommet* (Perrin, Paris, 2004)

Lacouture, Jean: *De Gaulle*, 3 vols. (Editions du Seuil, Paris, 1984)

Leigh-Fermor, Patrick and Devonshire, Deborah: *In Tearing Haste: Letters Between Deborah Devonshire and Patrick Leigh-Fermor*, ed Mosley, Charlotte (John Murray, London, 2008).

Lovell, Mary S.: *The Mitford Girls* (Weidenfeld & Nicolson, London, 2001)

Mauriac, C.: *Un autre de Gaulle* (Hachette, Paris, 1970)

Myers, William: *Evelyn Waugh and the Problem of Evil* (Faber & Faber, London, 1991)

Mullen, Richard and Munson, James: *The Smell of the Continent: The British Discover Europe 1814–1914* (Macmillan, London, 2009)

Muggeridge, Malcolm: *Chronicles of Wasted Time*, Vol. 2: *The Infernal Grove* (Collins, London, 1973)

Nicolson, Nigel: *Portrait of a Marriage* (Weidenfeld & Nicolson, London, 1973)

Nossiter, Adam: *The Algeria Hotel: France, Memory and the Second World War* (Methuen, London, 2001)

Osborne, Frances: *The Bolter* (Virago, London, 2008)

Ousby, Ian: *Occupation: The Ordeal of France 1940–44* (John Murray, London, 1997)

Overy, Richard: *Countdown to War* (Allen Lane, London, 2009); *The Morbid Age: Britain Between the Wars* (Allen Lane: London, 2009)

Painter, George D.: *Marcel Proust* (Random House, London, 1959)

Palewski, Gaston: *Mémoires d'Action 1924–1974*, ed. Roussel, Eric (Plon, Paris, 1988)

Patten, William S.: *My Three Fathers and the Elegant Deceptions of my Mother, Susan Mary Alsop* (Perseus, New York, 2008)

Ponty, Janine: *Les Polonais en France* (Du Rocher, Paris, 2008)

Pugh, Martin: *We Danced All Night: A Social History of Britain Between the Wars* (Random House, London, 2008)

Rioux, Jean-Pierre: *La France de la Quatrième République*, 2 vols. (Seuil, Paris, 1980)

Saumarez-Smith, John (ed.): *The Bookshop at 10 Curzon Street: Letters between Nancy Mitford and Heywood Hill 1952–73* (Frances Lincoln, London, 2004)

Smith, Colin: *England's Last War Against France: Fighting Vichy 1940–1942* (Weidenfeld & Nicolson, London, 2009)

Spears, Edward: *Assignment to Catastrophe*, 2 vols. (Heinemann, London, 1954)

Taylor, D.J.: *Bright Young People* (Vintage, London, 2008)

Thompson, Laura: *Life in a Cold Climate: Nancy Mitford* (Review, London, 2003)

Tombs, Isabelle and Robert: *That Sweet Enemy: Britain and France, the History of a Love-Hate Relationship* (Pimlico, London, 2007)

Ziegler, Philip: *Diana Cooper* (Hamish Hamilton, London, 1981)

Articles

Published by the Institut Charles de Gaulle, Paris:
André-Brunet, Adolphe: 'A la société des amis de Marcel Proust'

André-Gillois, Maurice: 'Enfance et adolescence'

Brouillet, René: 'Rue Saint-Dominique 25 août 1944–21 janvier 1946'

Burin des Rosiers, Etienne: 'Ambassadeur à Rome'

Burrus, Manuel: 'L'association France-Italie'

Charles-Roux, François: 'A Londres en 1942 et 1943'

Chatenet, Pierre: 'Président du Conseil constitutionnel (1964–1974)'

Curien, Gilles: 'Un grand ministre de la recherche'

Debré, Michel: 'Au cabinet de Paul Reynaud'

Decaris, Albert: 'A l'académie des Beaux-Arts'

De Courcel, Geoffrey: 'Gaston Palewski et le général de Gaulle'

Druon, Maurice: 'Du côté de chez Gaston'

Durosoy, Maurice: 'Avec Lyautey au Maroc en 1925'

Fornari, Giovanni: 'Le dernier des Stendhaliens'

Fouquer, R.P.: 'Mission en Ethiopie'

Frey, Roger: 'Un militant'

Gaussen, Gérard: 'Au comité français pour la sauvegarde de Venise'

Giron, Charles: 'A l'association des amis de René Capitant'

Guillaumat, Pierre: 'Une action décisive en matière nucleaire (1955)'

Horbette, Jean-Louis: 'Rue Royale 1962–1965'

King, Harold: 'Un homme d'une loyauté totale'

Lefranc, Pierre: 'La bataille des tribunes 1947–1951'

Lelong, Pierre: 'Ministre d'état, chargé de la recherche scientifique et des questions atomiques et spatiales'

Offroy, Raymond: 'A Alger 1943–44'

Palewski, Dominique: 'Oncle Gaston'

Polaillon-Kerven, Gisèle: 'Un proche de Eugène Delacroix'

Rosenberg, Pierre: 'Au conseil des musées de France'

Zimmer, Paul: 'A la Fondation Lyautey'

Viansson-Ponte, Pierre: 'Gaston Palewski ou le gaullisme prehistorique' in *Après de Gaulle, qui?*, ed. Le Seuil, 1968

Yverneau-Glaser, Elisabeth: 'Gaston Palewski, acteur et temoin
  d'un demi-siècle de vie politique française 1924–1974',
  unpublished doctoral thesis (supervisor: Maurice Vaisse),
  Centre d'histoire de Sciences Politiques
'Memoirs of the late Princesse Edmond de Polignac', *Horizon*
  No. 68 (August 1945)

INDEX